Pro SQL Azure

Scott Klein
Herve Roggero

Apress®

Pro SQL Azure

ISBN-13 (pbk): 978-1-4302-2961-2

ISBN-13 (electronic): 978-1-4302-2962-9

Printed and bound in the United States of America (POD)

President and Publisher: Paul Manning
Lead Editor: Jonathan Gennick
Technical Reviewer: Fabio Claudio Ferracchiati
Editorial Board: Steve Anglin, Mark Beckner, Ewan Buckingham, Gary Cornell,
     Jonathan Gennick, Jonathan Hassell, Michelle Lowman, Matthew Moodie, Duncan Parkes,
     Jeffrey Pepper, Frank Pohlmann, Douglas Pundick, Ben Renow-Clarke, Dominic Shakeshaft,
     Matt Wade, Tom Welsh
Coordinating Editor: Anita Castro
Copy Editor: Tiffany Taylor
Compositor: Bytheway Publishing Services
Indexer: BIM Indexing & Proofreading Services
Artist: April Milne
Cover Designer: Anna Ishchenko

Distributed to the book trade worldwide by Springer Science+Business Media, LLC., 233 Spring Street, 6th Floor, New York, NY 10013. Phone 1-800-SPRINGER, fax (201) 348-4505, e-mail orders-ny@springer-sbm.com, or visit www.springeronline.com.

For information on translations, please e-mail rights@apress.com, or visit www.apress.com.

Apress and friends of ED books may be purchased in bulk for academic, corporate, or promotional use. eBook versions and licenses are also available for most titles. For more information, reference our Special Bulk Sales–eBook Licensing web page at www.apress.com/info/bulksales.

To my parents, Richard and Carolyn. —*Scott*

To my dear wife, Frederique. —*Herve*

Contents at a Glance

Contents

v

About the Authors

Scott Klein is a Microsoft SQL Server MVP and co-founder of Blue Syntax Consulting, a company that specializes in Azure training and consulting. Scott has been working with SQL Server for nearly 20 years, working with companies large and small all over the United States, and working in a wide scope of fields such as medical, finance, and retail. Scott is also a veteran author, having written a number of books including Professional SQL Server XML, Professional LINQ, and Pro ADO.NET Entity Framework 4.0. Scott is president of the South Florida SQL Server Users Group and president of the newly formed Azure PASS Virtual Chapter. He speaks frequently at SQL Saturday events and user groups, and was lucky enough to speak at the 2008 European PASS conference in 2008.

Herve Roggero is the founder of Pyn Logic, a company focusing on advanced SQL Server security (`www.pynlogic.com`); and Blue Syntax Consulting, a company focusing on Azure consulting and training (`www.bluesyntax.net`). Herve's experience includes software development, architecture, database administration, and senior management with both global corporations and startup companies. Over the last 15 years, Herve has worked in the education, financial, health care, management consulting, and database security sectors. In his last full-time position, Herve was a director of software development at a health-care company in Florida. He has been freelancing as a .NET and SQL Server architect since 2007. Herve is a member of the ISSA. He holds multiple certifications, including MCDBA, MCSE, and MCSD. He also holds an MBA from Indiana University. Herve is heavily involved with the South Florida SQL Server community, speaks at multiple venues, and runs SQL Saturday events in south Florida. He also promotes the use of Azure in many ways including through the development of training materials and consulting engagements.

About the Technical Reviewer

■ **Fabio Claudio Ferracchiati** is a prolific writer on cutting-edge technologies. Fabio has contributed to more than a dozen books on .NET, C#, Visual Basic, and ASP.NET. He is a .NET Microsoft Certified Solution Developer (MCSD) and lives in Rome, Italy. You can read his blog at `www.ferracchiati.com`.

Acknowledgments

This book is here simply due to several individuals who never gave upon the idea and worked tirelessly to make it happen. First and foremost, we'd like to thank Jonathan Gennick, our editor at Apress for letting us run with this idea. Jonathan's patience and understanding made this process absolutely delightful. Also at Apress we'd like to thank Anita Castro, the Coordinating Editor, for keeping us on the ball. We'd probably still be working on Chapter 3 if it weren't for her.

A lot of the information in this book is due to the ever-friendly and extremely helpful people at Microsoft. Their passion and excitement for this technology is contagious, and that made it so much more enjoyable to work with them. We'd like to thank David Robinson, Liam Cavanagh, Cihan Biyikoglu, Mike Flasko, Michael, Pizzo, and Jack Greenfield for their wonderful support and tireless help with all our questions.

We'd also like to thank our friends and other community people who listened to us over the past year and provided valuable and much-needed feedback. Joe Healy is and always will be near and dear to us. Joe, you rock. Mark Scott was a guy we talk to frequently and let us bounce ideas of him. Thank you both. Jared Kirkpatrick, while not directly involved with this book, was an awesome sounding board. Jared's love for technology is delightfully infectious.

Nothing in this life is worthwhile without the love and support of family. As such, Scott would like to express deep thanks to his wife and children for their endless love, support, understanding, and patience (lots of it). Scott would also like to express profound appreciation to Herve for his friendship. Through life you meet people who have a deep impact on your life. Scott has been lucky enough to find a small handful of those, and Herve is one of them.

Herve would like to specially thank his family for support and understanding, and specifically to his amazing wife who always knows how to support him with a smile. Herve would also like to thank Jim Mullis, a long-time friend and partner who has an amazing ability to listen and breathes technology so much that his passion drives others to higher standards of perseverance.

Last but not least, Herve would like to thank Scott Klein for his amazing guidance through natural leadership skills, humility and friendship.

■ ■ ■

CHAPTER 1

Getting Started with SQL Azure

Born only a few years ago, cloud computing is capturing the imagination of startups and large corporations alike. In its simplest form, cloud computing is an evolution of traditional hosting models; as such, it isn't necessarily a new technology. Rather, it's a new concept that offers new opportunities and challenges not found in existing business models. Much as agile programming provided a new software development paradigm, cloud computing provides a new delivery model for Internet-based solutions.

Introduction to Cloud Computing

Let's begin with what cloud computing has to offer compared to traditional hosting services. The following capabilities are generally expected from large cloud-computing providers:

- **Automatic and unlimited scalability.** The promise that if your service needs more resources, more resources will be provisioned automatically or with limited effort. For example, if you deploy a web service, and you experience a sudden surge in processing needs, your services will automatically expand to additional servers to handle the temporary surge and contract to fewer servers during off-peak activity.

- **Unassisted deployment.** The promise that if you need to deploy additional services or databases, you don't have to call anyone or open a service ticket. The cloud service provider will give you the necessary tools to perform self-service.

- **Built-in failover**. The promise that if one of your servers fails, no one will ever notice. For example, if the server on which your service is installed crashes, a new server immediately takes over.

- **Grow as you need; pay for what you use.** The promise that you only pay for the resources you use. For example, if your service experiences a sudden surge in processing needs for a day, but it scales down to its usual usage for the rest of the month, you're only charged marginally more than usual for the temporary surge.

Who Is Doing What in the Cloud?

Smaller companies, including startups, are building services that can run in the cloud, whereas larger companies are investing in building cloud-enabled infrastructure. Some corporations are building consulting services and offering to assist customers implement cloud-enabled solutions; others, like Microsoft, are investing in the core infrastructure and services that make the cloud a reality.

Microsoft has traditionally been a software provider, but the company has slowly moved closer to hardware solutions over the years. In the late 1990s, Microsoft engaged with Unisys, HP, Dell, and other hardware manufacturers to provide highly available Windows-based platforms (Windows Data Center Edition). At the same time, Microsoft invested significant resources to build its Microsoft Systems Architecture (MSA). This program was designed to help corporations plan, deploy, and manage Microsoft-based IT architecture. These initiatives, along with many others, helped Microsoft develop strong knowledge capital around highly available and scalable architectures, which are a prerequisite for building cloud computing platforms.

Amazon entered the cloud computing space with its Elastic Compute Cloud (EC2) services in 2005. A few years later, Google and IBM joined forces to enter this market, and Microsoft announced many of its cloud computing plans during 2009, including the Azure platform. As part of its Azure platform, Microsoft delivered a very unique component in its cloud computing offering: a transactional database called SQL Azure.

Typical Cloud Services

Generally speaking, cloud computing comes in one of three flavors:

- **SaaS: software as a service.** This delivery platform is usually in the form of web applications that are made available on the Internet for a fee. This model has been around for a few years.

- **PaaS: platform as a service.** This service offers a computing platform that facilitates the use and deployment of other services and scales according to the general expectations of cloud computing, such as scalability and pay-as-you-go.

- **IaaS: infrastructure as a service.** This offering provides the necessary infrastructure that offers the scalability typically associated with cloud computing.

SaaS, PaaS, and IaaS are considered the fundamental building blocks of cloud computing. Other acronyms are being manufactured to depict new flavors of cloud computing, such as desktop as a service (DaaS), hardware as a service (HaaS), and even research as a service (RaaS). Pretty soon, the entire alphabet will be consumed in describing the many flavors of services that can be created in the cloud.

Discovering the Microsoft Azure Platform

Let's discover the three major components of the Microsoft Azure platform, also called the Azure services: Windows Azure, Windows Azure AppFabric, and SQL Azure. All three offer unique capabilities that provide a complete array of services needed to build highly scalable and secure solutions:

- **Windows Azure.** A collection of virtual Microsoft operating systems that can run your web applications and services in the cloud. For example, you can create a web service that converts US dollars to Euros; then, you can deploy the service on Windows Azure and allow it to scale as needed. Note that Windows Azure can run .NET applications and other platforms as well, including PHP.

- **Windows Azure AppFabric.** A set of services that provide core capabilities such as federated identity for access control, and a service bus for a messaging-based subscriber/publisher topology.

- **SQL Azure.** Microsoft's transactional database offering for cloud computing based on Microsoft SQL Server 2008. For example, you can store your customer database in the cloud using SQL Azure and consume customer data using services deployed in Windows Azure.

Figure 1-1 shows a simplified corporate environment connecting to the Microsoft Azure platform and consuming all three services. This diagram is overly simplified, but it conveys an important message: Microsoft Azure is designed to extend a corporate environment securely for web applications, services, messaging, and data stores.

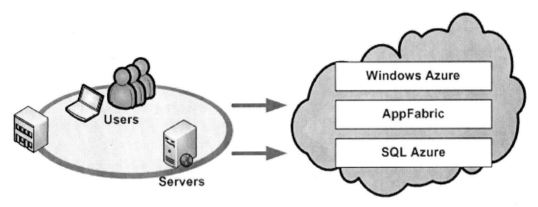

Figure 1-1. *Microsoft Azure platform overview*

Why Microsoft Azure?

One of the fundamental questions that's frequently asked is, "Why?" Who's interested in developing applications in Windows Azure in the first place? To answer this question, let's look at the evolution of web platforms.

About 15 years ago, when the public Internet was all about bulletin board systems (BBBs), Gopher services, and $500 9600-baud modems, the question was, "Will the Internet stick as a technology?" That question has been answered, but many new concepts have grown since then, including web sites, hosting centers, and SaaS.

This evolution relies on a common theme: *decoupling*. BBSs decoupled public information from libraries; web sites decoupled user interfaces from computers; hosting centers decoupled hardware from a company's own infrastructure; and SaaS decoupled complex applications from corporate computers.

Cloud computing on Microsoft Azure is a natural evolution of computing flexibility in which the actual physical storage and implementation details are decoupled from the software solution. For example, deploying services in Windows Azure doesn't require any knowledge of the machine running the service or any of the core services (IIS version, operating system patches, and so on). You may never know which machine is running your software. Connecting to a Windows Azure server is performed through logical names, just like connecting to SQL Azure.

The ability to disassociate machines from data and services is very powerful in itself. Although it's still an early-stage platform, Microsoft's Azure environment allows multiple business scenarios to flourish, including these:

- **Seasonal applications.** Developing web sites or services that have a tendency to grow and contract over time provides potential savings opportunities because cloud computing uses a pay-as-you-use model.

- **Short life span.** Development of prototypes or applications with short lifespans is also attractive, such as event-registration sites. You can also build development and test environments for remote teams.

- **Split storage.** Certain applications need to keep storage in a safe location but may not require frequent access, or may require high availability. Designing or modifying an application so that the data is stored locally and in SQL Azure (or other data-storage formats) may make sense.

- **Small companies and ISVs.** Smaller companies that can't afford large and complex infrastructure to start their business can take advantage of the financial and inherent infrastructure benefits of Microsoft Azure. Independent software vendors (ISVs) can also benefit from cloud computing. For example, an ISV can use SQL Azure to store application logs or centralize reporting features from multiple disconnected locations.

See Chapter 2 for more information about design patterns and application scenarios that use the Azure platform.

About Geographic Locations

In order to provide high availability, Microsoft established regional data-center operations that allow customers to select geographically dispersed services. When you create your Azure servers, you need to specify which geographic location the servers should be provisioned in. This feature is called *Windows Azure geolocation.*

Initially, it may be tempting to choose your company's geographic location for improved performance. However, if the availability of your Azure services is more important than response time, you may need to pick another location. When selecting a geographic location, make sure to consider the following:

- **Performance.** When your data is closer to your users, network latency may be noticeably lower, improving customer experience.

- **Disaster recovery.** If ensuring the availability of your cloud platform is important, you may want to disperse your services and data across multiple regions.

- **Legal factors.** Consider the type of information that will be stored in the cloud, and ensure that you aren't bound by specific regulations and mandates that may prevent you from selecting remote geographic locations.

At the time of this writing, you can select from one of the following geographic locations, each of which is supported by a regional data center:

- Anywhere Asia

- Anywhere Europe

- Anywhere US

- North Central US

- North Europe

- South Central US

- Southeast Asia

In addition, you can create an *affinity group* that lets you keep certain Azure services together. Such a group creates a geographic dependency between Windows and data services deployed in the Microsoft Azure platform. If Microsoft is obligated to move a service to another geolocation for regulatory reasons, the related services will likely move along. For example, if you develop an Azure service that depends on a SQL Azure database, you may want to ensure that they both reside in the same geolocation and that they belong to the same affinity group.

Additional locations will be added over time. As a result, you may need to reevaluate on a regular basis whether a service is deployed in the most appropriate geographic location.

Storing Data in Azure

As you can imagine, cloud computing is all about storing data in a simple yet scalable manner. The Microsoft Azure platform doesn't disappoint and offers a variety of storage models that you can choose from. This section summarizes the four ways you can store your data in Azure; three of these approaches are considered part of the Azure services.

Figure 1-2 provides an overview of the storage options and the available access methods. The set of storage options provided by Windows Azure is referred to as *Windows Azure storage*, which includes blobs, tables, and queues. Windows Azure storage can be accessed directly from a corporate environment using HTTP/S calls, providing a simple hook into the Microsoft Azure platform. In addition to using Windows Azure storage, consumers can make requests directly to a SQL Azure database using ADO.NET or ODBC, because SQL Azure supports the Tabular Data Stream (TDS) protocol that SQL Server uses. As a result, applications and services connecting to a SQL Server database can just as easily connect to a SQL Azure database.

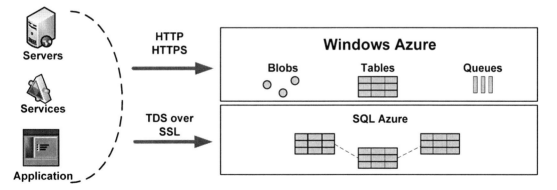

Figure 1-2. Microsoft Azure data storage access

Following are further details of the four storage types:

- Azure services storage. The Azure services offer three distinct storage models that are tailored to specific needs:

    - **Table.** A named value-pair storage that allows you to store very large amounts of data. This storage model includes automatic load balancing and fail-over. It's called a table because you can store multiple values in each row. However, this isn't a transactional storage mechanism; no indexing or table joins are possible. Also, the columns defined in a table have storage limitations. For example, a string data type is limited to 64KB.

    - **Blobs.** An interface to store files, with a maximum limit of 50GB of storage for each blob. You can easily access blobs using a straight HTTP request through a Representational State Transfer (REST)) call.

    - **Queue.** A highly available mechanism for storing messages for consumption by other applications or services. A typical usage of queues is to send XML messages. Certain limitations apply to queues, but you can access queues through REST as well.

- **SQL Azure.** SQL Azure is a transactional database that provides familiar data access through ADO.NET or other providers and gives you the ability to manipulate the data using standard T-SQL statements. Databases in SQL Azure are limited to either 1GB or 10GB, depending on the edition selected.

Table 1-1 summarizes the current characteristics of these data-storage options available in the Azure platform.

Table 1-1. *Storage summary in Azure*

Storage Mode	Maximum Size	Access	Format	Relational
Table	N/A	ADO.NET REST	Rows and columns	No
Blob	50GB	REST	File	No
Queue	8KB*	REST	String	No
SQL Azure	1GB 10GB	ADO.NET	Rows and columns	Yes

* Recommended limit

SQL Azure Primer

As you've seen, SQL Azure is a relational database engine based on SQL Server technology. It supports many of the features of SQL Server including tables, primary keys, stored procedures, views, and much more. This section gives a brief primer to get you started using SQL Azure. You see how to register for Azure, how to create a database and then an account, and how to log in.

Registering for Azure

To register for Windows Azure, visit the Pricing page on the Windows Azure web site:
`http://www.microsoft.com/windowsazure/offers/`. Figure 1-3 shows some of the available options.

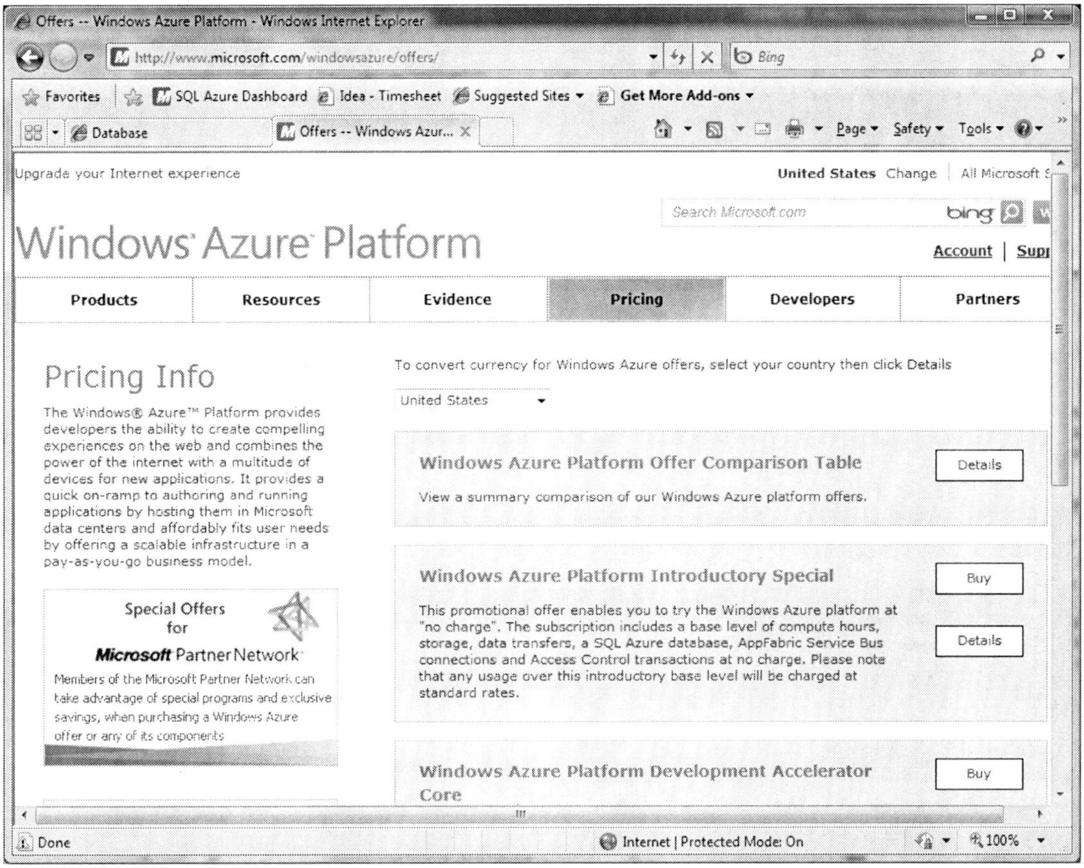

Figure 1-3. *Choosing a Windows Azure plan*

From this page, you have the ability to pick the offer that best fits your profile and needs. After you've chosen your preferred plan, click Buy, and follow the onscreen instructions. When this is complete, you receive an e-mail with instructions on how to configure your Windows Azure platform.

To access the Azure portal, you can use one of the following URLs. They all point to the same master portal:

- `http://sql.azure.com`

- `http://appfabric.azure.com`

- `http://windows.azure.com`

For step-by-step instructions on how to create your Azure account, see Chapter 3. When you create your Azure account, you're required to create an administrator account for SQL Azure. This account is used to create databases and other logins.

Creating a Database in SQL Azure

When the SQL Azure server is created, the master database is provisioned automatically. This database is read-only and contains configuration and security information for your databases. You can then create your user databases. You can either use the SQL Azure portal or issue a T-SQL statement against the master database.

Using the SQL Azure Portal

One way to create a database is to do so from the SQL Azure portal. From the Server Administration screen, click Create Database at the bottom of the screen, as shown in Figure 1-4.

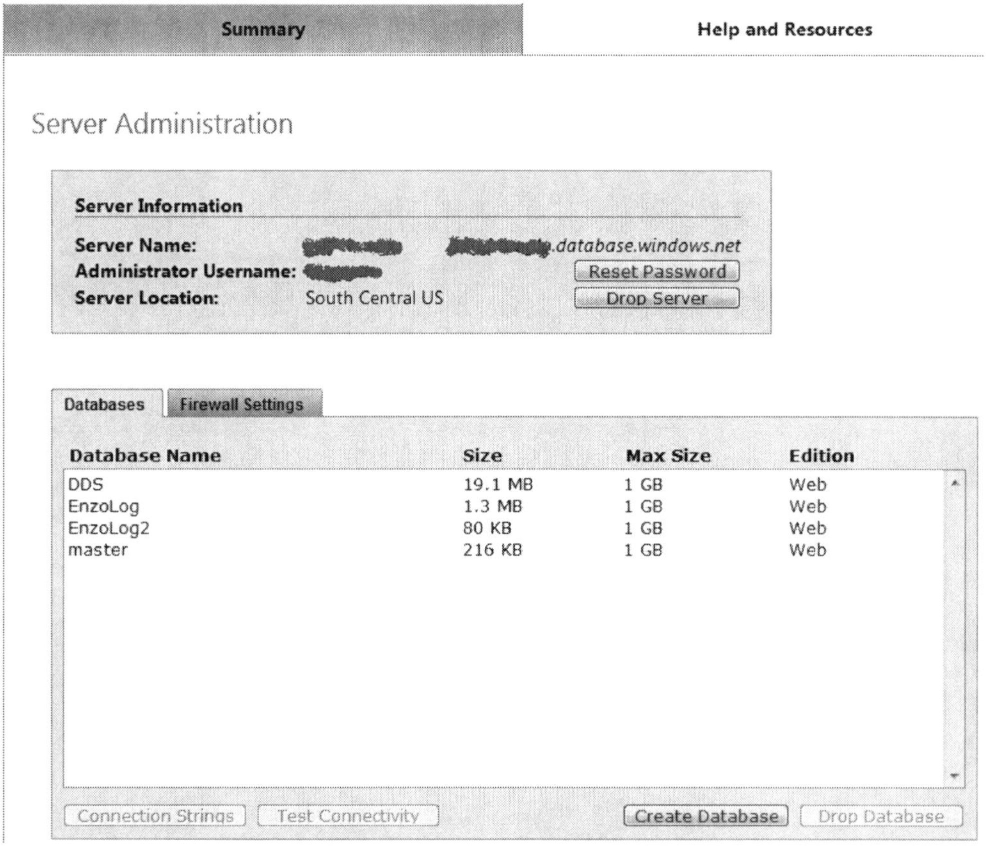

Summary		**Help and Resources**	

Server Administration

Server Information

Server Name:		.database.windows.net
Administrator Username:		Reset Password
Server Location:	South Central US	Drop Server

Databases | Firewall Settings

Database Name	Size	Max Size	Edition
DDS	19.1 MB	1 GB	Web
EnzoLog	1.3 MB	1 GB	Web
EnzoLog2	80 KB	1 GB	Web
master	216 KB	1 GB	Web

Connection Strings | Test Connectivity | Create Database | Drop Database

Figure 1-4. SQL Azure databases

A small window opens, as shown in Figure 1-5. Enter a database name, select a database edition (Web or Business), specify the size of your database, and click Create. You can choose the Web edition if 1GB or a 5GB is sufficient for you. If you need to create larger databases, choose the Business edition, which lets you select a size between 10GB and 50GB, in 10GB increments.

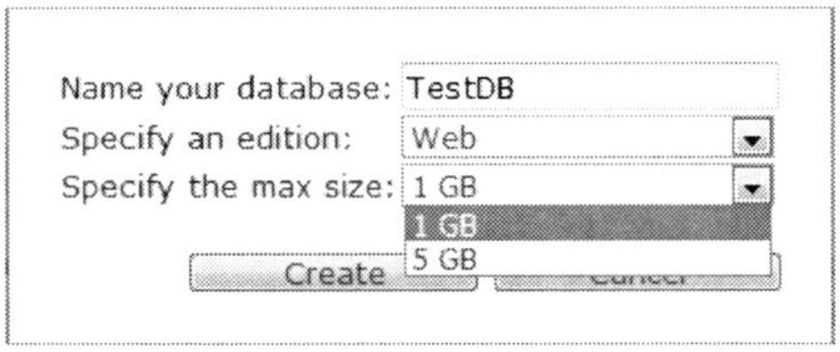

Figure 1-5. Creating a SQL Azure database

■ **Note** The monthly fee varies, depending on the size of the database. See the additional information later in this chapter and the complete pricing information on Microsoft's web site: www.microsoft.com/azure.

Using a T-SQL Command

Creating a new database using a T-SQL command is straightforward. Because a database in SQL Azure is managed by Microsoft, only a few options are available to you. In addition, you must be connected to the master database to create new databases.

To create a new database, log in using the administrator account (or any user with the dbmanager role), and run the following T-SQL command:

```
CREATE DATABASE mydatabase (MAXSIZE = 1 GB)
```

As previously discussed, the size of the database can be 1GB, 5GB, or 10GB–50GB. If the MAXSIZE parameter isn't defined, the size of the database is set to 1GB.

Configuring the Firewall

SQL Azure implements a firewall on your behalf. That's a benefit that helps protect your database. Indeed, the default firewall rule is that *no one* can connect. Allowing no connections by default is a good security practice, because it forces you to think through what IP addresses you wish to allow in.

Following these steps to add an IP address (or IP range) for a computer that needs access to the SQL Azure server:

1. On the Server Administration screen, click the Firewall Settings tab. This tab shows the firewall rules that are currently defined (see Figure 1-6).

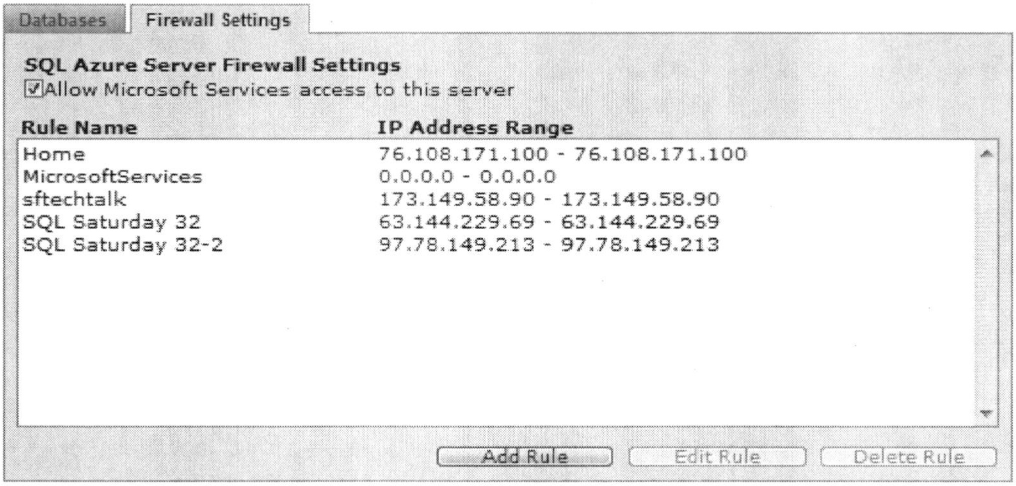

Figure 1-6. Firewall settings

2. Click Add Rule. Specify a name for this rule, and enter your IP address on the first line of the IP Range. Specify the same IP in the **to** field to limit access to a single IP (see Figure 1-7).

Figure 1-7. *Creating a firewall rule*

If for some reason the firewall rules aren't correctly configured, you see an error message saying so. Figure 1-8 shows the error message you get using SQL Server Management Studio if the firewall rules don't allow you to connect. The error message looks like a login failure, but the description of the error clearly indicates that the client with the given IP address isn't allowed to access the server.

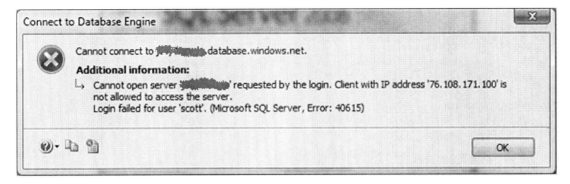

Figure 1-8. Firewall error

▪ **Note** When you're creating a firewall rule, you may need to wait a few minutes for the rule to take effect.

You can also view and edit firewall settings directly using T-SQL by connecting to the master database with the administrator account and using the following objects:

- sys.firewall_rules
- sp_set_firewall_rule
- sp_delete_firewall_rule

Now that you've configured your SQL Azure database, the fun can begin!

Connecting with SQL Server Management Studio

Follow these steps to connect to your SQL Azure database using SQL Server Management Studio:

1. You need to obtain the fully qualified server name of the SQL Azure database. Figure 1-9 shows the server information on the SQL Azure portal. The fully qualified server name is located above the Reset Password button.

▪ **Note** This example uses SQL Server 2008 SP1 Management Studio. Although you can connect to and manage SQL Azure using this release, additional features are available using the SQL Server 2008 R2 release, such as the ability to view database objects using the Object Browser.

---

2. Start SQL Server Management Studio. Click the Cancel button in the Login screen.

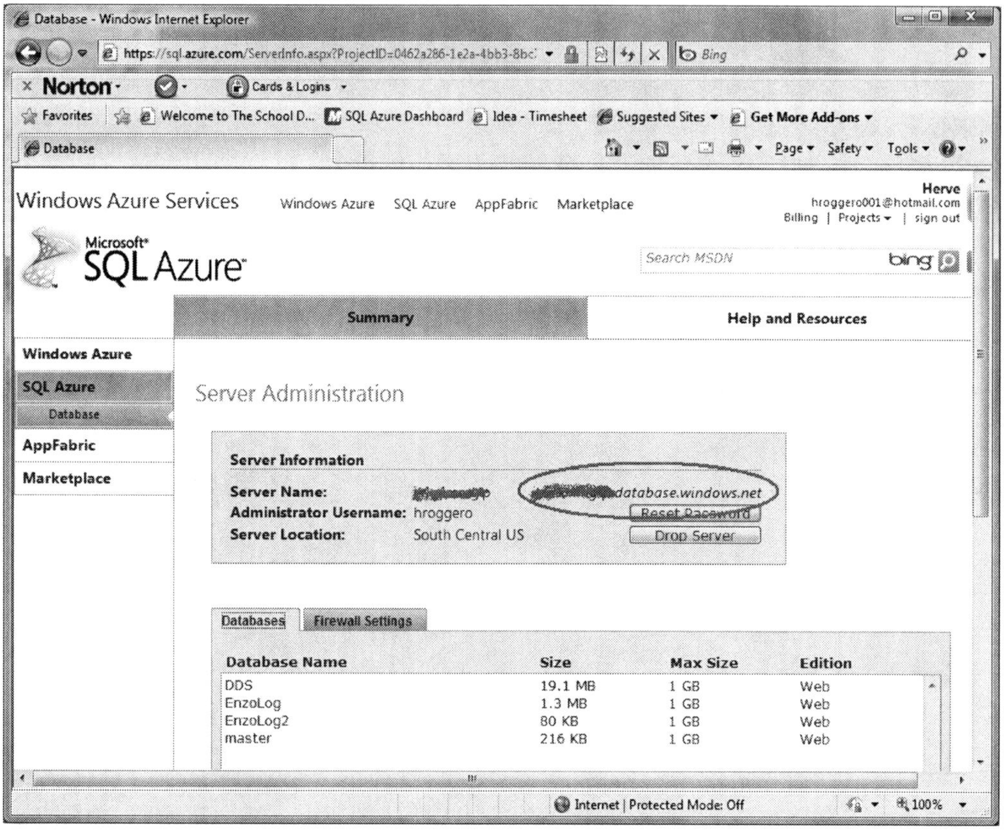

Figure 1-9. Obtaining the server name of your SQL Azure server

---

■ **Note** If you're using SQL Server Management Studio for SQL Server 2008 R2, you can log in using the first Login window. However, if you're using a previous version of SQL Server Management Studio, you need to click Cancel in the first Login window. The instructions provided in this section work for both editions.

---

3. Click the New Query button, or press Ctrl + N. A new Login screen opens (see Figure 1-10). In this window, enter the following information:

   • **Server name.** Enter the fully qualified server name.

   • **Authentication.** Select SQL Server Authentication.

   • Login. Type the administrator username (created previously).

   • **Password.** Type the password of the administrator account.

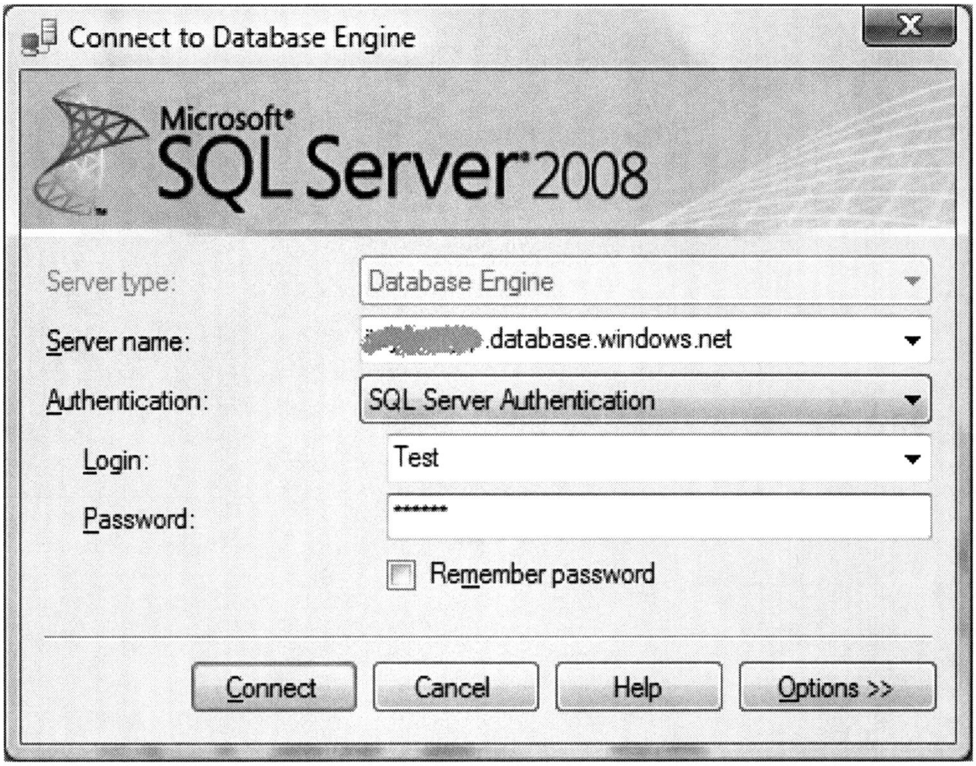

Figure 1-10. Logging in to a SQL Azure server

By default, clicking Connect authenticates you against the master database. If you want to connect to another database, click Options and type the desired database name in the "Connect to database" field, as shown in Figure 1-11. Note that you can't select the database name; the database name must be typed.

4. When you're ready, click Connect. A new query window opens, and you can execute T-SQL commands against your SQL Azure database.

■ **Note** After you connect to a database, the only way to use another database is to re-establish a connection and type the database name in the "Connect to database" field. The USE command doesn't work against SQL Azure to switch database contexts. Because a database can be physically located on any server, the only practical way to switch databases is to reconnect.

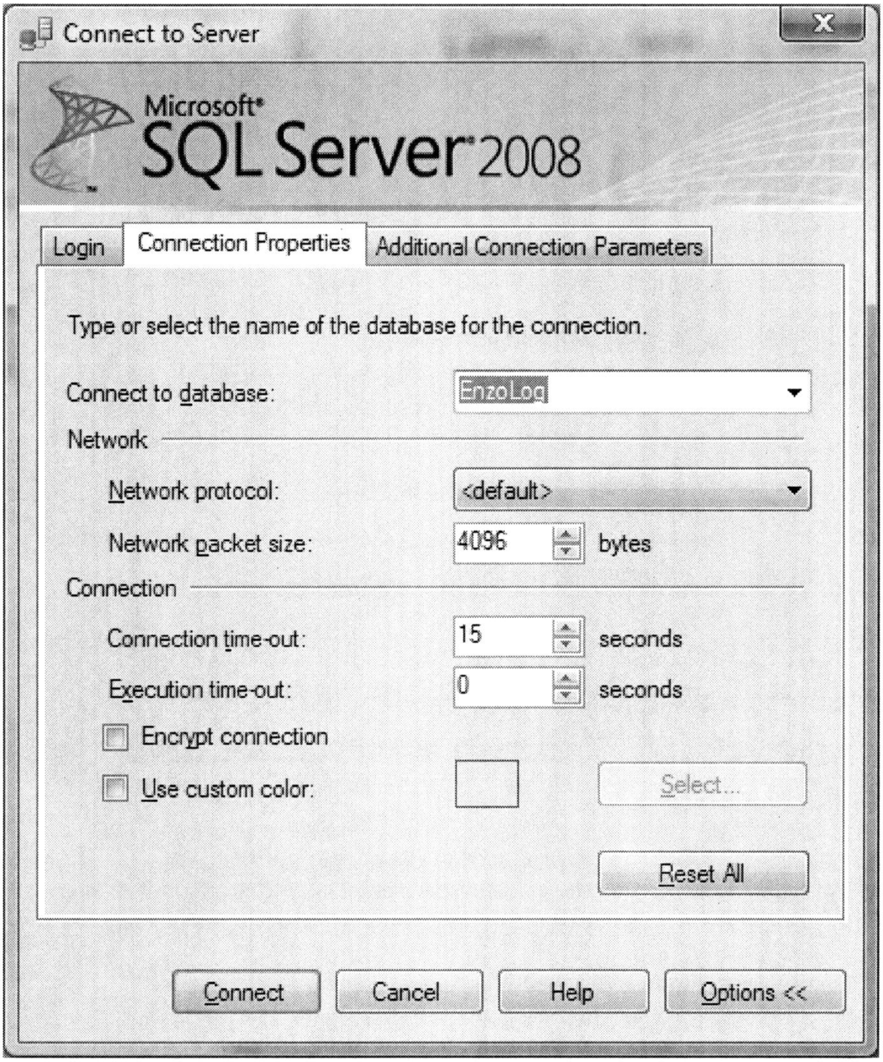

Figure 1-11. Connecting to a specific database other than master

Figure 1-12 shows the query window connected to SQL Azure, on which a simple command has been executed.

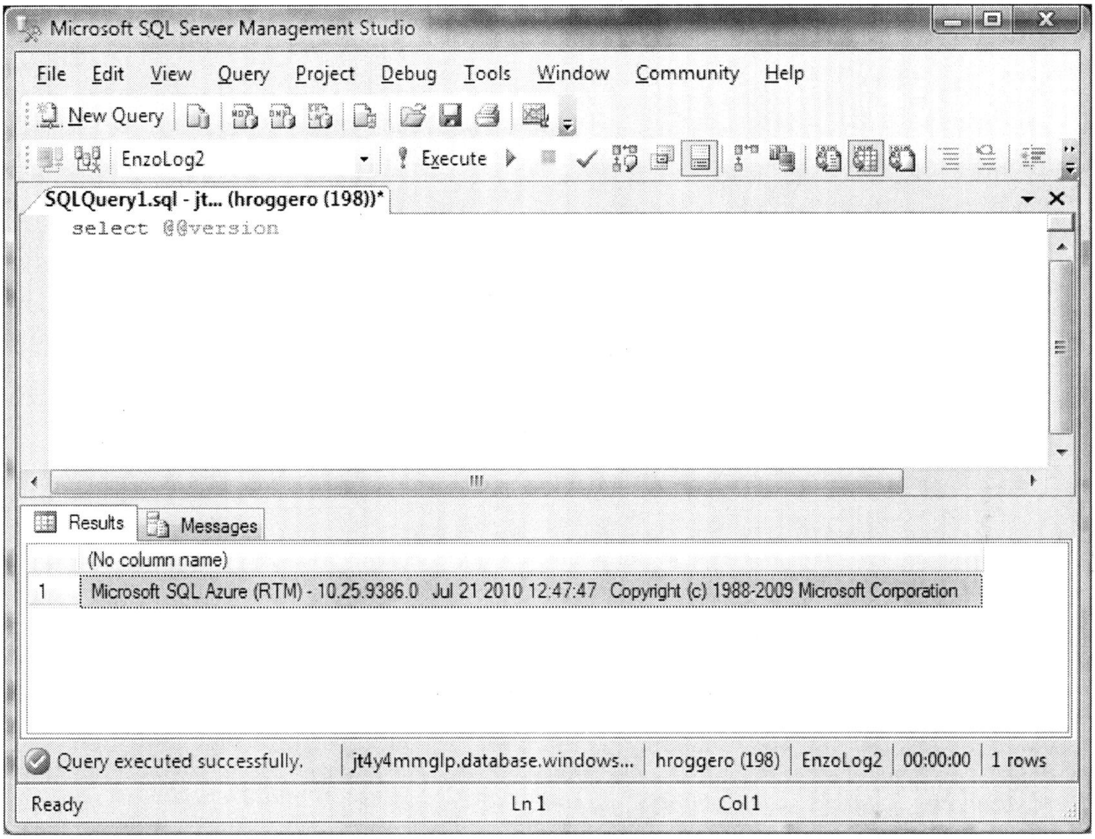

Figure 1-12. Running a simple T-SQL command on SQL Azure

Creating Logins and Users

With SQL Azure, the process of creating logins and users is mostly identical to that in SQL Server, although certain limitations apply. To create a new login, you must be connected to the master database. When you're connected, you create a login using the CREATE LOGIN command. Then, you need to create a user account in the user database and assign access rights to that account.

Creating a New Login

Connect to the master database using the administrator account (or any account with the loginmanager role granted), and run the following command:

```
CREATE LOGIN test WITH PASSWORD = 'T3stPwd001'
```

At this point, you should have a new login available called test. However, you can't log in until a user has been created. To verify that your login has been created, run the following command, for which the output is shown in Figure 1-13:

```
select * from sys.sql_logins
```

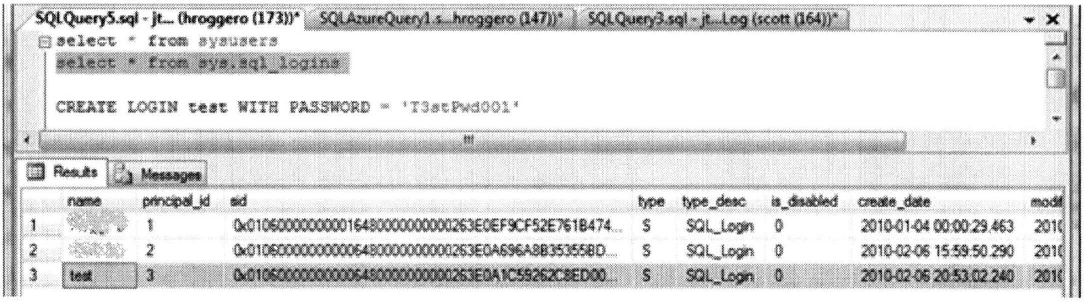

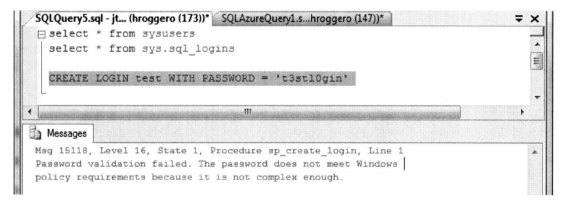

Figure 1-13. *Viewing a SQL login from the master database*

If you attempt to create the login account in a user database, you receive the error shown in Figure 1-14. The login must be created in the master database.

```
Messages
Msg 5001, Level 16, State 1, Line 1
User must be in the master database.
```

Figure 1-14. *Error when creating a login in a user database*

If your password isn't complex enough, you receive an error message similar to the one shown in Figure 1-15. Password complexity can't be turned off.

```
SQLQuery5.sql - jt... (hroggero (173))*    SQLAzureQuery1.s...hroggero (147))*

select * from sysusers
  select * from sys.sql_logins

    CREATE LOGIN test WITH PASSWORD = 't3stl0gin'


Messages
Msg 15118, Level 16, State 1, Procedure sp_create_login, Line 1
Password validation failed. The password does not meet Windows
policy requirements because it is not complex enough.
```

Figure 1-15. *Error when your password isn't complex enough*

■ **Note** Selecting a strong password is critical when you're running in a cloud environment, even if your database is used for development or test purposes. Strong passwords and firewall rules are important security defenses against attacks to your database. Chapter 4 reviews security in depth.

Creating a New User

You can now create a user account for your test login. To do so, connect to a user database using the administrator account (you can also create a user in the master database if this login should be able to connect to it), and run the following command:

```
CREATE USER test FROM LOGIN test
```

If you attempt to create a user without first creating the login account, you receive a message similar to the one shown in Figure 1-16.

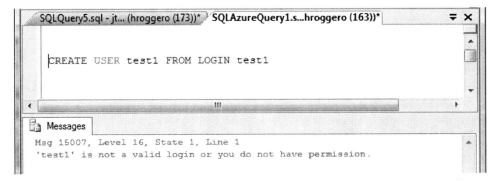

Figure 1-16. Error when creating a user without creating the login account first

Assigning Access Rights

So far, you've created the login account in the master database and the user account in the user database. But this user account hasn't been assigned any access rights.

To allow the test account to have unlimited access to the selected user database, you need to assign the user to the db_owner group:

```
EXEC sp_addrolemember 'db_owner', 'test'
```

At this point, you're ready to use the test account to create tables, views, stored procedures, and more.

■ **Note** In SQL Server, user accounts are automatically assigned to the public role. However, in SQL Azure the public role can't be assigned to user accounts for enhanced security. As a result, specific access rights must be granted in order to use a user account.

Understanding Billing for SQL Azure

SQL Azure is a pay-as-you-go model, which includes a monthly fee based on the cumulative number and size of your databases available daily, and a usage fee based on actual bandwidth usage. However, as of this writing, when the consuming application of a SQL Azure database is deployed as a Windows Azure application or service, and it belongs to the same geographic region as the database, the bandwidth fee is waived.

To view your current bandwidth consumption and the databases you've provisioned from a billing standpoint, you can run the following commands:

```
SELECT * FROM sys.database_usage      -- databases defined
SELECT * FROM sys.bandwidth_usage     -- bandwidth
```

The first statement returns the number of databases available per day of a specific type: Web or Business edition. This information is used to calculate your monthly fee. The second statement shows a breakdown of hourly consumption per database.

Figure 1-17 shows a sample output of the statement returning bandwidth consumption. This statement returns the following information:

- **time.** The hour for which the bandwidth applies. In this case, you're looking at a summary between the hours of 1 AM and 2 AM on January 22, 2010.

- **database_name.** The database for which the summary is available.

- direction. The direction of data movement. Egress shows outbound data, and Ingress shows inbound data.

- **class.** External if the data was transferred from an application external to Windows Azure (from a SQL Server Management Studio application, for example). If the data was transferred from Windows Azure, this column contains Internal.

- time_period. The time window in which the data was transferred.

- **quantity.** The amount of data transferred, in kilobytes (KB).

Visit `http://www.microsoft.com/windowsazure` for up-to-date pricing information.

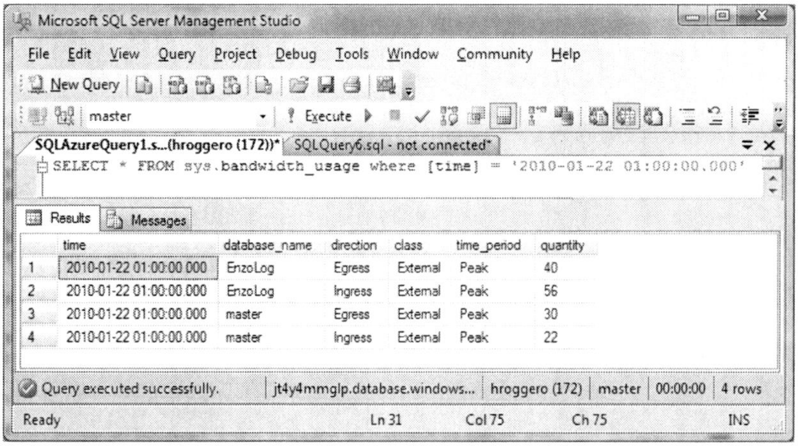

Figure 1-17. Hourly bandwidth consumption

Limitations in SQL Azure

As you've seen so far, creating databases and users requires manual scripting and switching database connections. The fundamental differences between SQL Server and SQL Azure lie in the basic design principals of cloud computing, in which performance, ease of use, and scalability must be carefully balanced. The fact that user databases can be located on different physical servers imposes natural limitations. In addition, designing applications and services against SQL Azure requires you to have a strong understanding of these limitations.

Security

Chapter 4 covers security in depth, but the following list summarizes important security considerations before you deploy your SQL Azure databases. From a security standpoint, you need to consider the following constraints:

- **Encryption.** Although SQL Azure uses SSL for data transfers, it doesn't support the data-encryption functions available in SQL Server. However, SQL Azure provides support for the existing hashing functions.

- **SSPI authentication.** SQL Azure only supports database logins. As a result, network logins using Security Support Provider Interface (SSPI) aren't supported.

- **Connection constraints.** In certain cases, the database connection is closed for one of the following reasons:

  - Excessive resource usage

  - Long-running query

  - Long-running single transaction

  - Idle connection

  - Failover due to server failure

- **Disallowed user names.** Certain user names can't be created for security reasons:

  - sa

  - admin

  - administrator

  - guest

  - root

- **Login name.** In certain cases, you may need to append the server name to the login name to correctly log in, in this format: [loginName]@[servername]. So, avoid using the arrobas character (@) in login names.

- **TCP port 1433.** Only TCP Port 1433 is allowed. It isn't possible to define another listening port for SQL Azure.

Backups

Backing up your SQL Azure database is somewhat different from backing up traditional SQL Server databases. You can't back up a SQL Azure database in the traditional sense, nor can you restore a SQL Server database in SQL Azure. You do, however, have the ability to create a transactionally consistent clone of a SQL Azure database. You can expect the following regarding backups:

- Backup/Restore operations. These operations aren't available. In addition, you may not attach or detach a SQL Azure database.

- Clone operations. You may create a clone of a SQL Azure database into another one using the `CREATE DATABASE` statement.

- Log files. You can't access the database log files, nor can you create a log backup.

Objects

Certain objects available in SQL Server aren't available in SQL Azure. If your applications depend heavily on these features, you may have difficulty using SQL Azure, and you may need to rethink your application design to accommodate these limitations. The following are some of the limitations that currently apply to SQL Azure:

- CLR. The .NET CLR isn't available in SQL Azure. As a result, you can't create extended stored procedures or extended functions.

- **System functions.** SQL Azure supports many system functions, including Aggregate functions and Ranking functions. However, SQL Azure doesn't support RowSet functions, including these:

  - `OPENQUERY`

  - `OPENXML`

  - `OPENROWSET`

  - `OPENDATASOURCE`

- **System stored procedures**. Only a small subset of system stored procedures are available in SQL Azure, in the following categories:

  - Catalog stored procedures

  - Database engine stored procedures

  - Security stored procedures

- **System tables**. None of the system tables are available.

- **System views**. A subset of system views is available; you can access some of them from the master database and others from user databases. The following are some of the system views available (for a complete list, refer to the online MSDN library for SQL Azure):

  - sys.sql_logins

- sys.views

- sys.databases

- sys.columns

- sys.objects

- **Heap tables**. SQL Azure doesn't allow the use of heap tables. All tables must have a primary |key.

Miscellaneous

In addition to the limitations outlined so far, additional components and options offered by SQL Server aren't available in SQL Azure. For the most part, these limitations shouldn't affect your application designs, but they're good to keep in mind:

- **Maximum number of databases**. You can create no more than four user databases.

- **Distributed transactions.** Although SQL transactions are supported, distributed transactions aren't supported across SQL Azure databases.

- **Collation.** SQL Azure only supports collation at the column level, or using an expression at execution time. Server- and database-level collations can't be changed and are set to `SQL_LATIN1_GENERAL_CP1_CI_AS`.

- **English language**. SQL Azure only supports the English language.

- **Database size**. You can only create databases of specific sizes, as outlined previously.

- **Database file placement**. You can't choose how the database files are deployed physically; you can't control filegroups, either. This is handled automatically by the Microsoft data center for optimum performance.

- **Trace flags**. Trace flags aren't available.

- **SQL Server configuration options**. None of the general SQL Server options are available, including CPU and I/O affinity.

- **Service Broker**. The Service Broker isn't available.

- **Global temporary tables**. The global temporary tables aren't available. However, you can use local temporary tables.

- **SQL Server Agent**. The SQL Server Agent isn't available.

Drivers and Protocols

You should also know that accessing SQL Azure can only be performed using specific libraries. This may be relevant if you don't use ADO.NET in your programming stack. For example, older versions of Delphi can't connect to SQL Azure. Here is a summary of the supported data libraries:

- **TDS version 7.3**. Any client using a TDS version prior to 7.3 isn't supported.

- **OLE DB**. Connecting with OLE DB isn't permitted.

- **Drivers and libraries**. The following drivers and libraries are allowed:

    - .NET Framework Data Provider for SQL Server from .NET 3.5 SP1

    - SQL Server 2008 Native Client ODBC driver

    - SQL Server 2008 driver for PHP version 1.1

Conclusion

This chapter focused on a fast-track overview of SQL Azure by providing a high-level introduction to cloud computing and how Microsoft is delivering its cloud offering. You also learned the major steps involved in creating an Azure account and how to get started in SQL Azure. You saw some important limitations of the SQL Azure platform, but keep in mind that Microsoft is releasing new versions of its cloud database every few months; as a result, some of these limitations will be lifted lover time.

CHAPTER 2

■ ■ ■

Design Considerations

In order to use cloud computing with the Azure platform beyond simple hosting, you must explore the vast array of options available to you when it comes to designing solutions. In addition to the design options presented in this chapter, you need a strong grasp of cloud computing's current shortcomings, which may affect your design choices.

Design Factors

Before reviewing various design patterns, let's start with some opportunities and limitations that impact your design choices. Keep in mind that although this book focuses primarily on SQL Azure, many of the concepts in this chapter apply to Azure development in general.

Offsite Storage

The Azure platform offers four distinct storage models, which were previously discussed in Chapter 1, "Blob, Table, Queue, and SQL Azure." Storing data in SQL Azure is similar to storing data in SQL Server. All you need to do is issue T-SQL statements and review some of the limitations of the syntax specific to SQL Azure, and off you go!

The ability to store data in SQL Azure using T-SQL offers unique opportunities. In many cases, you can easily extend or port certain types of applications in SQL Azure with no (or limited) modifications. This portability allows you either to implement solutions that directly depend on SQL Azure for storage, or to use a local database while using SQL Azure transparently for additional storage requirements (such as reporting).

However, keep in mind that you're limited to the amount of data you can store in a single SQL Azure database. At the moment, SQL Azure supports two editions: Web Edition (1GB or 5GB) and Business Edition (from 10GB to 50GB in 10GB increments). So, if your application needs to store more than 50GB of data, or if your database can benefit from a multithreaded data access layer, you need to consider splitting your data across multiple databases through a form of partitioning called a *shard*. You learn about shards later in this chapter and in more detail throughout this book.

High Availability

When designing applications, software developers and architects are usually concerned about high-availability requirements. SQL Azure uses a very elaborate topology that maximizes workload redistribution, transparency, and recovery. Figure 2-1 shows a high-level implementation of SQL Azure that gives a hint about how advanced the backend infrastructure must be.

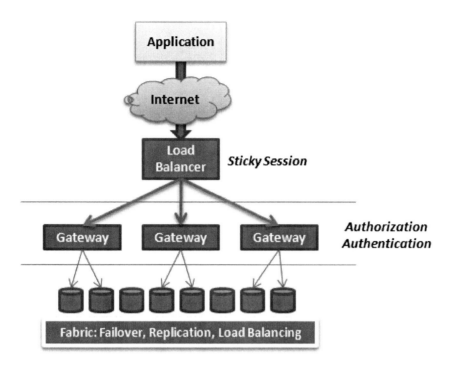

Figure 2-1. *SQL Azure topology*

Figure 2-1 illustrates that connections are made through a load balancer that determines which gateway should process the connection request. The gateway acts as a firewall by inspecting the request, performing authentication and authorization services, and forwarding the packets to an actual SQL Azure database. Because databases can be moved dynamically to ensure fair resource allocation, the gateway may alter the destination endpoint. The process is mostly transparent.

In addition, each SQL Azure database is replicated twice on different servers for redundancy. Behind the scenes, a replication topology ensures that a SQL Azure database exists on two other physical servers at all times. These two additional copies are totally transparent to consumers and can't be accessed.

■ **Note** SQL Azure offers 99.9% availability.

Performance

Performance of applications you write can be affected by two things: throttling and how you design the application. Microsoft has put *performance throttling* in place to prevent one client's applications from impacting another. (It's a good feature, not nearly so bad as it may sound.) Application design is something you control.

Throttling

SQL Azure runs in a multitenant environment, which implies that your databases share server resources with databases from other companies. As a result, the SQL Azure platform has implemented a throttling algorithm that prevents large queries from affecting other users from a performance standpoint. If your application issues a large query that could potentially affect other databases, your database connection is terminated.

In addition, to preserve valuable resources and control availability, SQL Azure disconnects idle sessions automatically. The session timeout is set to 30 minutes. When you're designing for SQL Azure, your application should account for automatic session recovery. This also means that performance testing in your development phase becomes more critical.

▓ **Note** In the context of SQL Azure, *throttling* means terminating the database connection. Whatever the reason for being throttled is, the outcome is the same: loss of database connection.

Application Design Considerations

When considering how to design your application to best take advantage of SQL Azure, you need to evaluate the following items:

- **Database roundtrips.** How many roundtrips are necessary to perform a specific function in your application? More database roundtrips mean a slower application, especially when the connection is made over an Internet link and is SSL encrypted.

- **Caching.** You can improve response time by caching resources on the client machine or storing temporary data closer to the consumer.

- **Property lazy loading.** In addition to reducing roundtrips, it's critical to load only the data that's absolutely necessary to perform the required functions. Lazy loading can help significantly in this area.

- **Asynchronous user interfaces.** When waiting is unavoidable, providing a responsive user interface can help. Multithreading can assist in providing more responsive applications.

- **Shards.** A *shard* is a way of splitting your data across multiple databases in a manner that is as transparent as possible to your application code, thus improving performance.

Designing an application for performance becomes much more important for cloud computing solutions that depend on remote storage. For more information on these topics and more, see Chapter 10.

SQL Data Sync Framework

The SQL Data Sync framework offers bidirectional data-synchronization capabilities between multiple data stores, including databases. SQL Data Sync uses the Microsoft Sync Framework, which isn't limited to database synchronization; you can use the framework to synchronize files over different platforms and networks.

Specifically as it relates to SQL Azure, you can use the Sync framework to provide an offline mode for your applications by keeping a local database synchronized with a SQL Azure database. And because the framework can synchronize data with multiple endpoints, you can design a shard, described later, in which all databases keep their data in sync transparently.

Direct vs. Serviced Connections

You may also consider developing Azure services to keep the database connection to a local network, and send the data back to the client using SOAP or REST messages. If your Azure services are deployed in the same region as your SQL Azure databases, the database connection is made from the same datacenter and performs much faster. However, sending data back to the consumer using SOAP or REST may not necessarily improve performance; you're now sending back XML instead of raw data packets, which implies a larger bandwidth footprint. Finally, you may consider writing stored procedures to keep some of the business logic as close to the data as possible.

Figure 2-2 shows the two different ways an application can retrieve data stored in a SQL Azure database. A direct connection can be established to the database from the application, in which case the application issues T-SQL statements to retrieve data. A serviced connection can be made by creating and deploying custom SOAP or REST services on Windows Azure, which in turn communicate to the database. In this case, the application requests data through web services deployed in Azure.

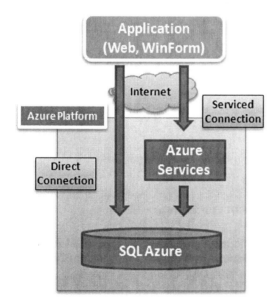

Figure 2-2. Data connection options

Keep in mind that you can design an application to use both connection methods. You may determine that your application needs to connect directly when archiving data, while using services to perform more complex functions.

■ **Note** Most of this chapter provides direct connection diagrams; however, many of the patterns presented would work just as well using a serviced connection to a Windows Azure service first.

Pricing

Pricing of a hosted environment isn't usually considered a factor when it comes to standard application design. However, in the case of cloud computing, including Azure, you need to keep in mind that your application's performance and overall design have a direct impact on your monthly costs.

For example, you incur network and processing fees whenever you deploy and use Azure services. Although this is true, at the time of this writing the data traffic between a Windows Azure application or service and a SQL Azure database is free within the same geographic location.

Pricing may affect your short-term application design choices, but you should keep in mind that Microsoft may change its pricing strategy at any time. As a result, although pricing is an important consideration especially for projects on limited budget, long-term viability of a design should be more important than short-term financial gains.

If you're designing an application to live in the Azure world and you depend on this application to generate revenue, you must ensure that your pricing model covers the resulting operational costs. For example, your application should be designed from the ground up with billing capabilities in mind if you intend to charge for its use.

Another factor related to pricing is that your SQL Azure database cost consists of a monthly fee and a usage fee. The monthly fee is prorated, so if you create a database at 1PM and drop it at 2PM the same day, you're charged a fraction of the monthly fee, plus the usage fee. The usage fee is strictly limited to bandwidth consumption: CPU utilization, I/O consumption, and your database's memory footprint aren't factors in the usage fee (see Figure 2-3). However, your database connection may be throttled if your CPU, I/O, and/or memory consumption reaches specific thresholds.

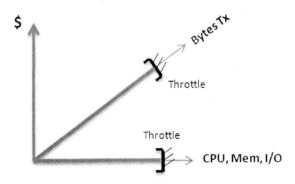

Figure 2-3. Pricing and resource throttling

In summary, you can consider moving certain CPU-intensive activities (within reason) on the SQL Azure database without being charged. You may, for instance, perform complex joins that use large datasets in a stored procedure and return a few summary rows to the consumer as a way to minimize your usage fee.

Security

It goes without saying that security may be a concern for certain types of applications; however, these concerns are similar to those that companies face when using traditional hosting facilities. The question that comes to mind when considering security is related to the lack of control over data privacy. In addition, certain limitations may prevent certain kinds of monitoring, which automatically rules out the use of SQL Azure for highly sensitive applications unless the sensitive data is fully encrypted on the client side.

As a result, encryption may become an important part of your design decision. And if you decide to encrypt your data, where will the encryption take place? Although the connection link is encrypted between your application code and SQL Azure, the data itself isn't encrypted when it's stored in SQL Azure. You may need to encrypt your data in your application code before sending it over the public Internet so that it's stored encrypted.

Encryption is good for data privacy, but it comes with a couple of downsides: slower performance and difficulty in searching for data. Heavy encryption can slow down an application, and it's notoriously difficult to search for data that is encrypted in a database.

Review of Design Factors

So far, you're seen a few considerations that can impact your design choices. Table 2-1 provides a summary. Some of the considerations are related to opportunities that you may be able to take advantage of; others are limitations imposed by the nature of cloud computing or specifically by the Azure platform.

As you design applications, make sure you evaluate whether specific Azure limitations discussed in this book still apply—the Azure platform is likely to change quickly in order to respond to customer demands.

Table 2-1. *Summary of design factors*

Opportunities	Limitations
Offsite storage	Limited amount of storage
Elastic cost	Performance
Instant provisioning	Backups
SQL Data Sync	Security concerns
High availability	

Design Patterns

Let's review the important design patterns that use SQL Azure. Before designing your first cloud application, you should read this section to become familiar with a few design options. Some of the advanced design patterns explained in this chapter can also provide significant business value, although they're more difficult to implement.

Note that for simplicity, the diagrams in this section show only a direct connection to SQL Azure. However, virtually all the patterns can be implemented using a serviced connection through Azure services.

Direct Connection

The *direct connection pattern*, shown in Figure 2-4, is perhaps the simplest form of connectivity to a SQL Azure database. The consumer can be either an application located in a corporation's network or a Windows Azure service connecting directly to the SQL Azure database.

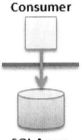

Figure 2-4. Direct connection pattern

As simple as it is, this may be one of the most widely used patterns, because it requires no special configuration or advanced integration technique. For example, a software as a service (SaaS) application may use this pattern; in this case, the consumer is the web site hosted in Azure (or on any other hosting provider). Alternatively, the consumer may be a smart device or a phone accessing records in SQL Azure.

Smart Branching

The *smart branching pattern* (see Figure 2-5) describes an application that contains sufficient logic to determine whether the data it needs to load is located in the cloud or in a local database. The logic to make this determination is either hardcoded in the application or driven from a configuration file. It may also be provided by a data access layer (DAL) engine that contains logic that fetches data either a local or a cloud database.

One of the uses for smart branching is to implement a form of caching in which the consumer caches parts of its data locally or fetches it from a cloud database whenever necessary. You can also use this pattern to implement a disconnected mode to your application, in case Internet connectivity becomes unavailable.

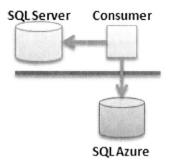

Figure 2-5. *Smart branching pattern*

Transparent Branching

Whereas smart branching depends on the consumer (or one of its components) to determine whether data is local or in the cloud, *transparent branching* (see Figure 2-6) removes this concern from the consumer. The consuming application no longer depends on routing logic and becomes oblivious to the ultimate location of the data.

This pattern is best implemented by applications that are difficult to modify or for which the cost of implementation is prohibitive. It can effectively be implemented in the form of extended stored procedures that have the knowledge to fetch data from a cloud data source. In essence, this pattern implements a DAL at the database layer.

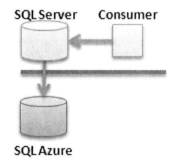

Figure 2-6. *Transparent branching pattern*

Sharding

So far, you've seen patterns that implement a single connection at a time. In a *shard* (see Figure 2-7), multiple databases can be accessed simultaneously in a read and/or write fashion and can be located in a mixed environment (local and cloud). However, keep in mind that the total availability of your shard depends partially on the availability of your local databases.

Shards are typically implemented when performance requirements are such that data access needs to be spread over multiple databases in a scale-out approach.

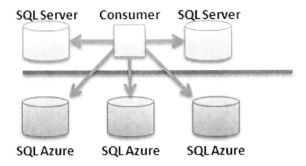

Figure 2-7. Shard pattern

Shard Concepts and Methods

Before visiting the shard patterns, let's analyze the various aspects of shard design. Some important concepts are explained here:

- **Decision rules**. Logic that determines without a doubt which database contains the interesting record(s). For example, *if Country = US, then connect to SQL Azure Database #1*. Rules can be static (hardcoded in C#, for example) or dynamic (stored in XML configuration files). Static rules tend to limit the ability to grow the shard easily, because adding a new database is likely to change the rules. Dynamic rules, on the other hand, may require the creation of a rule engine. Not all shard libraries use decision rules.

- **Round-robin.** A method that changes the database endpoint for every new connection (or other condition) in a consistent manner. For example, when accessing a group of five databases in a round-robin manner, the first connection is made to database 1, the second to database 2, and so on. Then, the sixth connection is made to database 1 again, and so forth. Round-robin methods avoid the creation of decision engines and attempt to spread the data and the load evenly across all databases involved in a shard.

- **Horizontal partition.** A collection of tables with similar schemas that represent an entire dataset when concatenated. For example, sales records can be split by country, where each country is stored in a separate table. You can create a horizontal partition by applying decision rules or using a round-robin method. When using a round-robin method, no logic helps identify which database contains the record of interest; so all databases must be searched.

- **Vertical partition.** A table schema split across multiple databases. As a result, a single record's columns are stored on multiple databases. Although this is considered a valid technique, vertical partitioning isn't explored in this book.

- **Mirrors.** An exact replica of a primary database (or a large portion of the primary database that is of interest). Databases in a mirror configuration obtain their data at roughly the same time using a synchronization mechanism like SQL Data Sync. For example, a mirror shard made of two databases, each of which has the Sales table, has the same number of records in each table at all times. Read operations are then simplified (no rules needed) because it doesn't matter which database you connect to; the Sales table contains the data you need in all the databases.

- **Shard definition.** A list of SQL Azure databases created in a server in Azure. The consumer application can automatically detect which databases are part of the shard by connecting to the master database. If all databases created are part of the shard, enumerating the records in sys.databases gives you all the databases in the shard.

- **Breadcrumbs.** A technique that leaves a small trace that can be used downstream for improved decisions. In this context, breadcrumbs can be added to datasets to indicate which database a record came from. This helps in determining which database to connect to in order to update a record and avoids spreading requests to all databases.

When using a shard, a consumer typically issues CRUD (create, read, update, and delete) operations. Each operation has unique properties depending on the approach chosen. Table 2-2 outlines some possible combinations of techniques to help you decide which sharding method is best for you. The left column describes the connection mechanism used by the shard, and the top row identifies the shard's storage mechanism.

Table 2-2. Shard access techniques

	Horizontal partitions	**Mirror**
Decision rules	Rules determine how equally records are spread in the shard. **Create:** Apply rules. **Read:** Connect to all databases with rules included as part of a WHERE clause, or choose a database based on the rules. Add breadcrumbs for update and delete operations. **Update:** Apply rules or use breadcrumbs, and possibly move records to another database if the column updated is part of the rule. **Delete:** Apply rules, or use breadcrumbs when possible.	This combination doesn't seem to provide a benefit. Mirrored databases aren't partitioned, and so no rule exists to find a record.
Round-robin	Records are placed randomly in	All records are copied to all databases.

Horizontal partitions	Mirror
databases based on the available connection. No logic can be applied to determine which database contains which records.	Use a single database (called the *primary database*) for writes.
Create: Insert a record in the current database.	**Create**: Insert a record in the primary database only.
Read: Connect to all databases, issue statements, and concatenate resultsets. Add breadcrumbs for update and delete operations.	**Read**: Connect to any database in a round-robin fashion.
Update: Connect to all databases (or use breadcrumbs), and apply updates using a primary ke.	**Update**: Update a record in the primary database only.
Delete: Same as update.	**Delete**: Delete a record in the primary database only.

Shards can be very difficult to implement. Make sure you test thoroughly when implementing shards. You can also look at some of the shard libraries that have been developed. The shard library found on CodePlex and explained further in this book (in Chapter 10) uses .NET 4.0; you can find it with its source code at `http://enzosqlshard.codeplex.com`. It uses round-robin as its access method. You can also look at another implementation of a shard library that uses `SQLAzureHelper`; this shard library uses decision rules as its access method and is provided by the SQL Azure Team (`http://blogs.msdn.com/b/sqlazure/`).

Read-Only Shards

Shards can be implemented in multiple ways. For example, you can create a read-only shard (ROS). Although the shard is fed from a database that accepts read/write operations, its records are read-only for consumers.

Figure 2-8 shows an example of a shard topology that consists of a local SQL Server to store its data with read and write access. The data is then replicated using the SQL Data Sync framework (or other method) to the actual shards, which are additional SQL Azure databases in the cloud. The consuming application then connects to the shard (in SQL Azure) to read the information as needed.

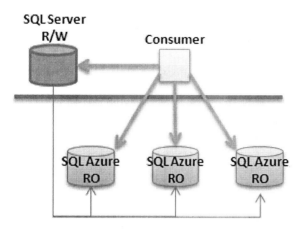

Figure 2-8. Read-only shard topology

In one scenario, the SQL Azure databases each contain the exact same copy of the data (mirror shard), so the consumer can connect to one of the SQL Azure databases (using a round-robin mechanism to spread the load, for example). This is perhaps the simpler implementation because all the records are copied to all the databases in the shard blindly. However, keep in mind that SQL Azure doesn't support distributed transactions; you may need to have a compensating mechanism in case some transactions commit and others don't.

Another implementation of the ROS consists of synchronizing the data using horizontal partitioning. In a horizontal partition, rules are applied to determine which database contains which data. For example, the SQL Data Synch service can be implemented to partition the data for US sales to one SQL Azure database and European sales to another. In this implementation, either the consumer knows about the horizontal partition and knows which database to connect to (by applying decision rules based on customer input), or it connects to all databases in the cloud by applying a WHERE clause on the country if necessary, avoiding the cost of running the decision engine that selects the correct database based on the established rules.

Read-Write Shards

In a read-write shard (RWS), all databases are considered read/write. In this case, you don't need to use a replication topology that uses the SQL Data Sync framework because there is a single copy of each record within the shard. Figure 2-9 shows a RWS topology.

Although a RWS removes the complexity of synchronizing data between databases, the consumer is responsible for directing all CRUD operations to the appropriate cloud database. This requires special considerations and advanced development techniques to accomplish, as previously discussed.

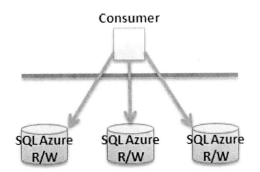

Figure 2-9. Multimaster shard topology

Offloading

In the offloading pattern, the primary consumer represents an existing onsite application with its own database; but a subset of its data (or the entire database) is replicated to a cloud database using SQL Data Sync (or another mechanism). The offloaded data can then be used by secondary consumers even if the primary database isn't accessible.

You can implement the offloading pattern in two ways, as shown in Figure 2-10. The primary database can be either the local SQL Server database or the cloud database. For example, a legacy application can use a local SQL Server database for its core needs. SQL Data Sync is then used to copy relevant or summary data in a cloud database. Finally, secondary consumers such as portable devices and PDAs can display live summary data by connecting to the cloud for their data source.

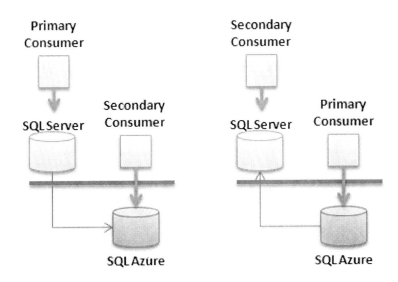

Figure 2-10. Offloading patterns

Aggregation

In its simplest form, the aggregation pattern provides a mechanism to collect data from multiple data providers into a SQL Azure database. The data providers can be geographically dispersed and not know about each other, but they must share a common knowledge of the schema so that, when aggregated, the data is still meaningful.

The aggregation patterns shown in Figure 2-11 use the direct connection pattern. You can use an aggregation pattern to provide a common repository of information, such as demographic information or global warming metrics collected from different countries. The key in this pattern is the ability to define a common schema that can be used by all providers and understood by the consumers. Because SQL Azure supports XML data types, you can also store certain columns in XML, which provides a mechanism to store slightly different information per customer.

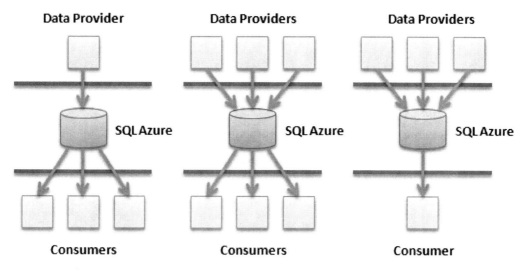

Figure 2-11. Aggregation patterns

Mirroring

The mirror pattern, shown in Figure 2-12, is a variation of the offloading pattern where the secondary consumer can be an external entity. In addition, this pattern implies that a two-way replication topology exists, so that changes in either database are replicated back to the other database. This pattern allows a *shared nothing* integration in which neither consumer has the authority to connect to the other consumer directly.

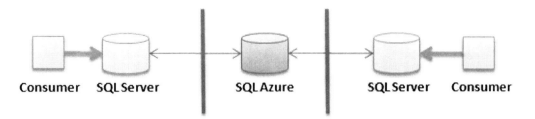

Figure 2-12. *Mirror pattern*

Combining Patterns

The previous design patterns provide the necessary basis to build systems with SQL Azure. Some of these patterns can be used as is, but you're very likely to combine patterns to deliver improved solutions. This section describes some useful combinations.

Transparent Branching + RWS

Figure 2-13 shows the transparent branching and the read-write shard patterns combined. This pattern can be used to offload into the cloud storage of historical data that an existing Enterprise Resource Planning (ERP) application generates. In this example, the shard provides a way to ensure high throughput by using asynchronous round-robin calls into SQL Azure databases.

This pattern offers the following advantages:

- **Transparent data transfer. In this case, the transparent branching pattern copies an existing application's data into cloud databases without changing a single line of code in the existing application.**

- **High performance.** To ensure high performance and throughput, the round-robin shard pattern is used along with asynchronous calls into the cloud.

- **Scalable.** When using a shard, it's very simple to expand it by adding a new SQL Azure database into the cloud. If implemented correctly, the shard automatically detects the new database and storage capacity, and throughput automatically increases.

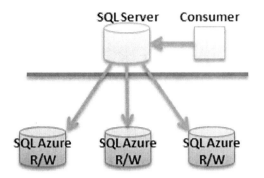

Figure 2-13. *Transparent branching + RWS patterns*

Cascading Aggregation

In cascading aggregation (see Figure 2-14), the aggregation pattern is applied serially to generate a summary database. The mechanism to copy (or move) data from one SQL Azure database to another must be accomplished using a high-level process, such as a worker process in Windows Azure.

For example, this pattern can be used to collect information from multiple SQL Azure databases into a single one used by a third party to monitor overall performance. A Windows Azure worker process can run a performance view provided by SQL Azure and store the data into another database. Although the SQL Azure databases being monitored for performance may have a totally different schema, the output of SQL Azure's performance data management view (DMV) is consistent. For example, the monitoring service can call sys.dm_exec_connections to monitor connection activity in various SQL Azure databases every 5 minutes and store the result in a separate SQL Azure database.

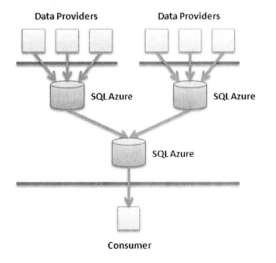

Figure 2-14. *Aggregation + MMS patterns*

Sample Design: Application SLA Monitoring

To put a few of the patterns in perspective, let's create a formal design around a system that monitors application performance service-level agreements (SLAs). In this design, a company already has a monitoring product that can audit activity in existing SQL Server databases at customer sites. Assume that the company that makes this monitoring product wants to extend its services by offering a SQL Azure storage mechanism so it can monitor customers' database SLAs centrally.

Pre-Azure Application Architecture

First, let's look at the existing application-monitoring product. It contains a module that monitors one or more SQL Servers in an enterprise and stores its results in another database located on the customer's network.

In this example, Company A has implemented the monitoring service against an existing ERP product to monitor access security and overall SLA. The monitoring application performs the auditing based on live activity on the internal SQL Server storing the ERP data. When certain statements take too long to execute, the monitoring service receives an alert and stores an audit record in the local auditing database, as shown in Figure 2-15.

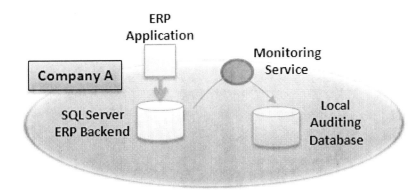

Figure 2-15. Onsite monitoring implementation

On a monthly basis, managers run reports to review the SLAs of the ERP system and can determine whether the ERP application is still performing according to predefined thresholds as specified in the ERP vendor contract. So far, the benefits of this implementation include the following:

- **Visibility. The customer has visibility into its internal database's performance.**

- **SLA management.** Measured SLAs can be used to negotiate contract terms with the ERP vendor.

However, the customer needs to store the auditing data internally and manage an extra SQL Server instance; this adds database management overhead, including making sure all security patches (operating system and database) are up to date. In addition, the local auditing database running on SQL Server isn't readily accessible to the ERP vendor, so the ERP vendor can't take proactive actions on any

SLA issues and must wait to be informed by the customer about serious performance issues. Finally, the customer doesn't know how its internal SLA measures compare to other customers running the same ERP product.

Azure Implementation

The monitoring provider has created an enhanced version of its monitoring system and includes an optional cloud storage option, in which the monitoring service can forward performance events in a centrally located database in the cloud. The monitoring provider has decided to implement an asynchronous smart branching pattern so that events can be stored in a SQL Azure database.

Figure 2-16 shows the implementation architecture that lets the monitoring service store data in a cloud database. Each monitoring service can now store SLA metrics in the cloud in addition to the local auditing database. Finally, the local auditing database is an option that customers may choose not to install. To support this feature, the monitoring provider has decided to implement a queuing mechanism in case the link to SQL Azure becomes unavailable.

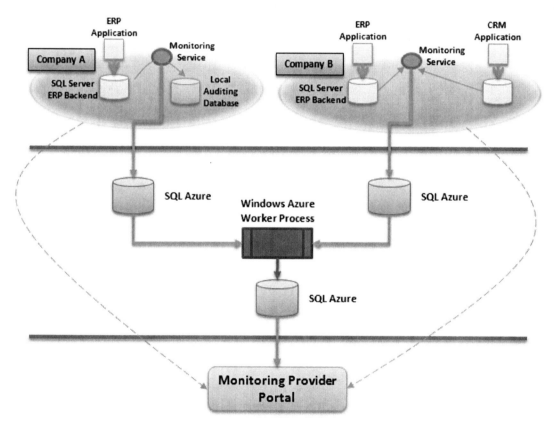

Figure 2-16. Azure monitoring implementation

The monitoring provider has also built a portal on which customers can monitor their SLAs. Customer B, for example, can now use the portal to monitor both its CRM and ERP application database SLAs. The customer can prepare reports and make them available to the ERP and CRM vendors for review online, with complete drilldown access to the statements from the same portal.

In this implementation, additional benefits include the following:

- **Improved sharing.** Sharing information with vendors becomes much easier because drilldown access to issues is provided through a cloud-enabled portal.

- **Local storage optional.** With the improved solution, customers may decide to implement the cloud storage only if they're short staffed to handle the necessary internal database-management activities.

- **External monitoring.** Customers A and B also have the ability to use the monitoring provider to proactively monitor their ERP products remotely with specific escalation procedures when the SLAs aren't met. The monitoring provider can, for example, manage performance issues directly with the ERP provider.

Other Considerations

This chapter has introduced many important design factors to help you design a solution that uses SQL Azure. Are few more concepts are worth a glance, such as blob data stores, edge data caching, and data encryption.

Blob Data Stores

Blobs are files that can be stored in Windows Azure. What is interesting about blobs is that they can be easily accessed through REST, there is no limit to the number of blobs that can be created, and each blob can contain as much as 50GB of data. As a result, blobs can be used as a backup and transfer mechanism between consumers.

A system can dump SQL Azure tables to files using the Bulk Copy Program (BCP), possibly compressing and/or encrypting the files beforehand, and store the blobs in Windows Azure.

Edge Data Caching

The chapter briefly mentioned caching earlier, but you should remember that caching may yield the most important performance gains in your application design. You can cache relatively static tables in memory, save them as blobs (or a form of in-memory storage) so that other caching systems use the same cache, and create a mechanism to refresh your data cache using queues in Azure.

Figure 2-17 shows an example of a design that creates a shared cache updated by two ERP systems. Each ERP systems uses the transparent branching pattern to update shared records in a SQL Azure database. At this point, however, the edge caches aren't aware of the change in data. At a specific interval (every 10 minutes, for example) a worker process in Windows Azure picks up the changes and stores them in blobs. The worker may decide to apply logic to the data and resolve conflicts, if any. Blobs are then created (or replaced) with the latest cache information that should be loaded. The edge cache refreshes its internal data by loading the blobs at specific intervals (every 5 minutes, for example) and replaces its internal content with the latest cache. If all edge caches are configured to run against a public atomic clock, all the caches are updated virtually at the same time.

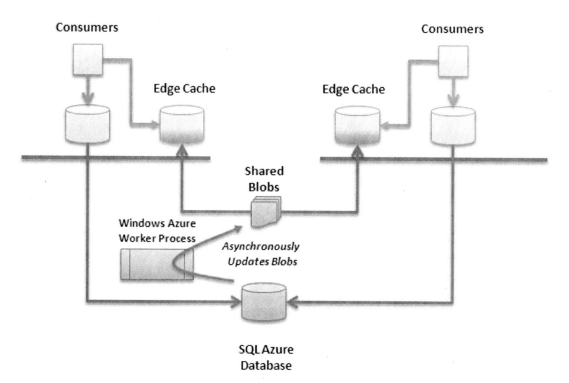

Figure 2-17. Shared *edge data* caching

Data Encryption

You can encrypt your data in two environments: onsite or in Windows Azure using a service. SQL Azure, as previously mentioned, doesn't support encryption at this time (although hashing is supported). If you need to encrypt Social Security numbers or phone numbers, you should consider where encryption makes sense.

Generally speaking, unless your application runs in a public environment where your private keys can be at risk, you should consider encrypting onsite before the data goes over the Internet. But if you need a way to decrypt in Windows Azure, or you need to encrypt and decrypt data across consumers that don't share keys, you probably need to encrypt your data in Windows Azure before storing it in SQL Azure.

Conclusion

This chapter reviewed many design concepts that are unique to distributed computing and for which cloud computing is a natural playground. Remember that designing cloud applications can be as simple as connecting to a SQL Azure database from your onsite applications or as complex as necessary (with distributed edge caches and shards) for enterprise-wide systems.

The chapter provided multiple parameters that you should consider when designing your application, each of which can significantly impact your final design, such as performance, billing, security, storage options, and throttling. You should consider creating two or more cloud-based designs and review them with other designers to discuss pros and cons before making your final selection. And if you have the time, build a proof-of-concept to validate your assumptions and measure how effective the solution will be.

CHAPTER 3

■ ■ ■

Setting Up and Configuring

The first two chapters of this book have provided an introductory look at cloud-based computing and how similar a cloud database is to a regular database. Although there are many similarities, you've also seen some of the differences between a cloud database and a local database. Chapter 6 discusses many more of these differences in greater detail.

Chapter 2 also took an in-depth look at the design patterns and factors that companies must take into account when considering moving to a cloud computing architecture. Deciding to move to a cloud computing solution isn't cut and dried; you must consider many options when designing cloud solutions. The rest of the book, including this chapter, builds on the information from Chapter 2.

Before you get started with the Azure platform, you must first register for an Azure account. After the account is created, you have access to all of Azure's features and functionality. This chapter shows you the account options, walks you through creating an Azure account, and then introduces you to options and T-SQL syntax statements you can use to create, modify, and delete important types of objects in SQL Azure, such as databases, users, and stored procedures. You also spend a few pages looking at how to connect to a SQL Azure database from different environments.

Creating Your Azure Account

Creating an Azure account is simple, but it takes quite a few steps because of the amount of information required. To begin setting up your Azure account, open your browser and go to www.microsoft.com/windowsazure/offers. This URL takes you to the Windows Azure Platform Offers page, shown in Figure 3-1. This page lists several packages based on your usage (transactions, connections, and so on) and storage. You can see detailed information about each package by clicking the View Details button in the comparison table on the page.

It's highly recommend that you select the Introductory Special package to begin working with Azure. With this package, you get the following at no charge:

- 25 hours of small compute instance, 500MB of storage, and 10,000 storage transactions on Windows Azure

- 1 Web Edition database on SQL Azure

- 100,000 access control transactions and 2 service bus connections on AppFabric

- 500MB in and 500MB out for data transfer (per region)

45

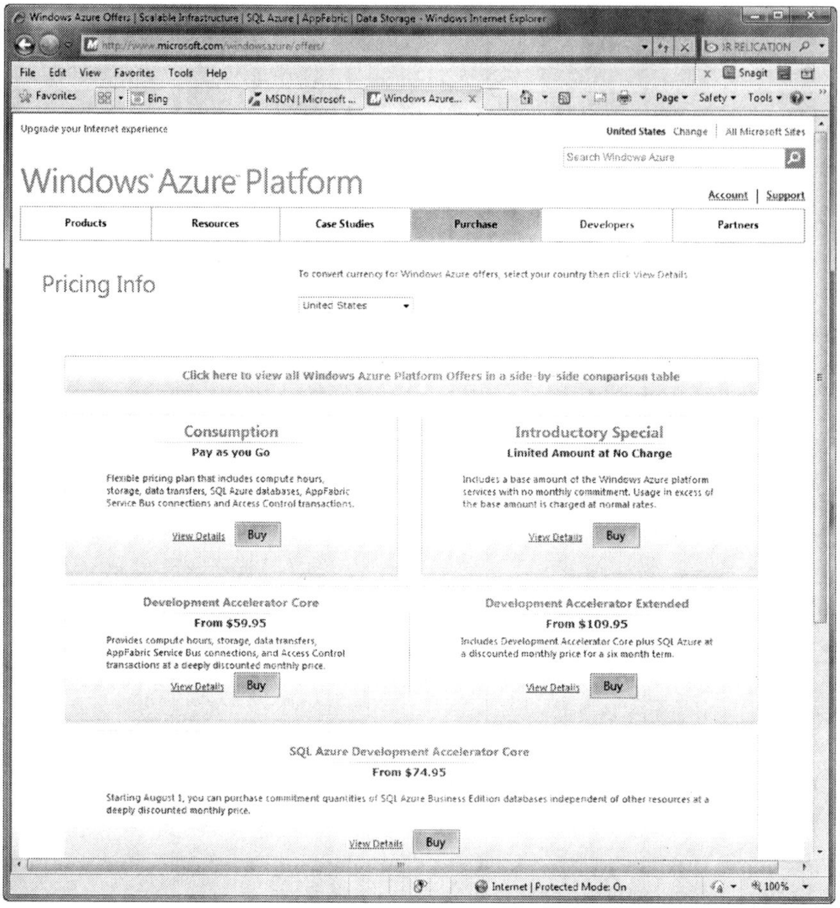

Figure 3-1. Azure offers

■ **Note** The Introductory Special offer, per the details of the offer, ends on October 31, 2010. Standard rates will apply after that date. It's unknown at the time of this writing whether a free or "lite" version will continue to be offered. Standard rates are based on storage, computer, AppFabric transactions, and data transfers. You can find information regarding the exact standard rates by clicking the Details button for any of the offers.

To sign up for an Azure account, you must have a Windows Live ID. Clicking the Buy button prompts you to sign in with that ID. After you've signed in, creating your account is a four-step process:

1. Creating Your Profile. This step asks you to enter your contact and business information and then select the location that will use the Azure service so it can determine the services available as well as calculate tax.

2. Billing Information. After the introductory special ends, you begin to be billed for using Azure services. This step asks you to enter your billing information, including payment options and payment information.

3. Service Activation. This step lets you to create a meaningful subscription name and define a service administrator (the individual who is responsible for setting up and managing your service). The service administrator is created/assigned by the account owner (the individual defined in the main contact profile).

4. Confirmation. In this step, you provide additional information regarding the activation of your Azure service.

The Confirmation page tells you that an e-mail has been sent to your Windows Live ID e-mail address. This e-mail contains a link to the Microsoft Online Services Customer Portal, with the following instructions:

1. Click the link, and log in with your Windows Live ID.

2. In the Customer Portal, open the Subscriptions page, and locate your subscription.

3. In the Actions list for your subscription, select Activate Now, and then click the Go button.

At this point, your service is activated and ready to go.

Managing Your Azure Projects

Now you're getting to the meat of Azure. After reading all the information in the last two chapters, and working through setup and activation in this chapter, the time has come to start getting your hands dirty. From here on out, it's hands-on.

To access your SQL Azure Portal projects, go to `https://sql.azure.com/`. Your browser displays the SQL Azure Summary page, which shows all your SQL Azure projects. The page lists each project's name (which you created during the activation process) and the account and service administrators, as shown in Figure 3-2.

The projects listed on the Summary page are those you've created or those you've been given access to via the account administrator. At this point, you can't do much; but you'll fix that in the following sections as you walk you through administering your SQL Azure server.

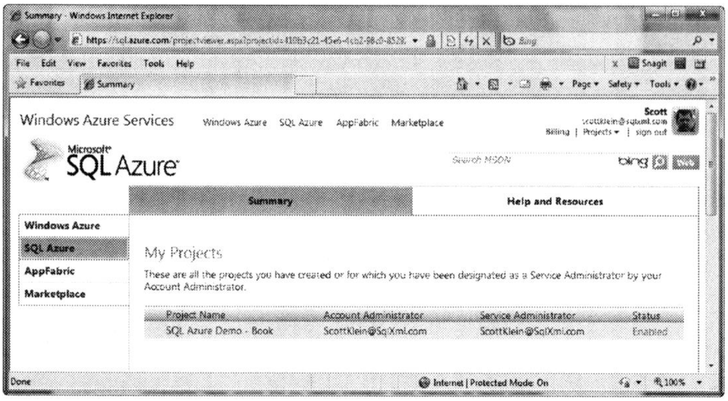

Figure 3-2. SQL Azure Summary page

Azure Server Administration

Administering your SQL Azure projects is easy. Go ahead and click the project you created in the Summary window. You're prompted to enter a username and password. (You see how this information is used in a moment.) After you enter your username and password, you're presented with the SQL Azure Server Administration portal, shown in Figure 3-3.

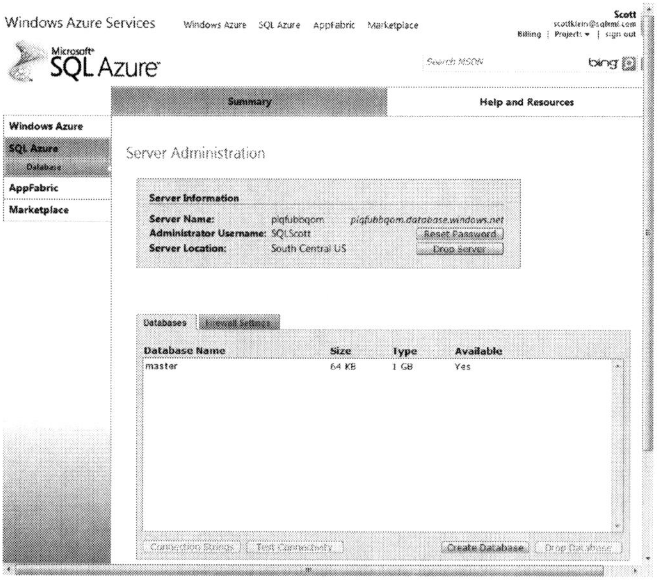

Figure 3-3. Server Administration portal

The Server Administration portal displays three categories of information that are vital to administering, connecting to, and working with SQL Azure. You see information about your server, including its name and location. You also have two tabs: one showing your firewall settings and the other listing your databases.

Server Information

The Server Information box is at the top of the Summary tab. Figure 3-3 shows that box in context, and Figure 3-4 focuses in so you can read the details.

Server Information

Server Name:	plqfubbqom plqfubbqom.database.windows.net
Administrator Username:	SQLScott [Reset Password]
Server Location:	South Central US [Drop Server]

Figure 3-4. Server Information

The Server Information box displays the following:

- **Server Name.** The fully qualified domain name (FQDN) of your logical database server—a physical machine name that resolves to an IP address at the Microsoft data center. This is *not* the database server name. When a connection is made to this IP address, your connection is routed to the physical database server based on your login name and the database (master, for example).

- **Administrator Username.** The name you entered in the pop-up dialog when you clicked the project name in Figure 3-2. Whenever you connect to SQL Azure, for example through SQL Server Management Studio, this is the username you use, along with the associated password.

- **Server Location.** The geo location where your Azure server resides. As of this writing, there are seven locations: Anywhere Asia, Anywhere Europe, Anywhere US, North Central US, North Europe, South Central US, and Southeast Asia.

Microsoft recommends that when creating your logical servers, you should put them in the same geo location. If you don't, you incur data charges. For example, if you put your Windows Azure web application in the North Central US location and your SQL Azure database in the South Central US location, you incur data-transfer and other transactional charges. If your application and database are located in the same geo location, you don't incur these charges. Another reason to put your application and database in the same geo location is performance. However, spreading your services across geo locations helps with redundancy.

A quick note about the Drop Server button in the Server Information box: dropping a SQL Azure server deletes all databases associated with the server and removes the server from your account. When you drop a server, you're informed that dropping the server can't be undone and asked whether you want to continue. If you choose to continue, no databases can be recovered, and you must start the server-creation process all over again, including creating a new administrator and selecting the location.

Firewall Settings

Because your databases are located in places you physically can't get to or control, Microsoft has implemented a mechanism to help protect your data. This protection mechanism is the SQL Azure firewall, which prevents restricted access to all your databases until you physically specify which computers have permission. Access to your SQL Azure databases is based on the originating IP address that makes a request.

To grant access to your SQL Azure databases, you specify a range of acceptable IP addresses in the Server Administration portal on the Firewall Settings tab, shown in Figure 3-5. IP address ranges are defined by rules that allow you to specify multiple firewall setting entries. For example, you can define an IP address range for your home as well as one for your office. If you attend a conference, you can define an additional rule and IP address that let you connect from that specific location. Also notice the "Allow Microsoft Services access to this server" check box on the Firewall Settings tab; it allows internal communication between Windows Azure services and SQL Azure databases.

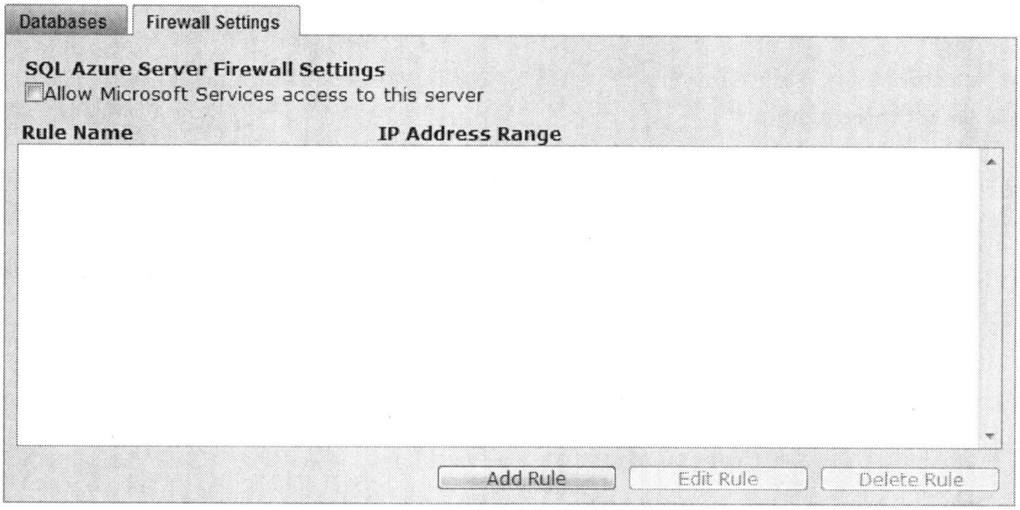

Figure 3-5. Firewall Settings tab

To add a firewall rule, click the Add Rule button on the Firewall Settings tab to display the Add Firewall Rule dialog, shown in Figure 3-6. You're asked to specify the rule name and the IP address range. Firewall rule names must be unique, and there is no limit to the number of rules you can have.

Entering the IP Range is simple because the dialog tells you what your IP address is. Figure 3-6 uses the same value for the range's start and ending values to indicate that only the single specified address should be allowed to access the database. You can enter a range of IP address if you want multiple computers to access SQL Azure.

After you've entered your firewall rule information, click the Submit button. Your new rule is added to the Firewall Settings tab, as shown in Figure 3-7. As the note in Figure 3-6 states, it may be up to 5 minutes before your rule takes effect and you can connect to SQL Azure (although I have never had it take more than 1 minute to take affect). After that, you can edit and delete the rule.

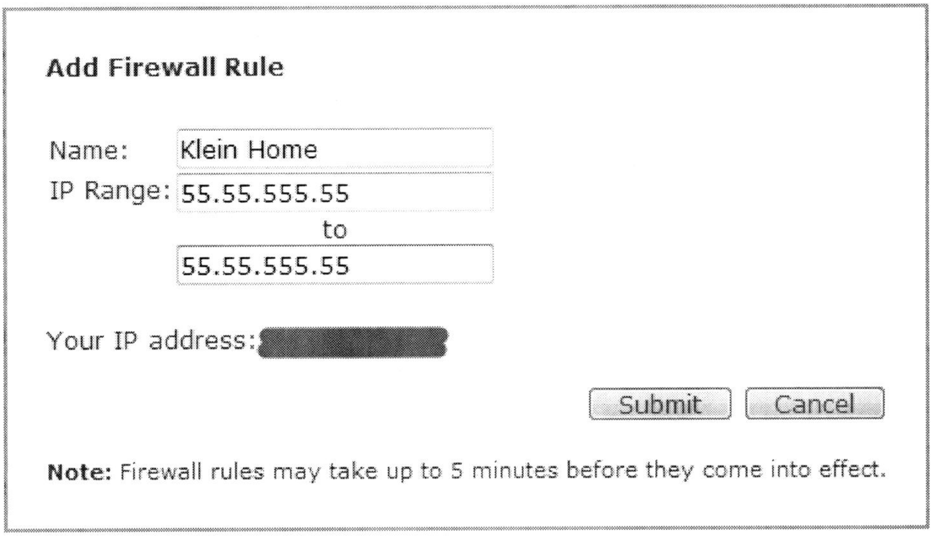

Add Firewall Rule

Name: Klein Home

IP Range: 55.55.555.55

to

55.55.555.55

Your IP address:

[Submit] [Cancel]

Note: Firewall rules may take up to 5 minutes before they come into effect.

Figure 3-6. Adding a firewall rule

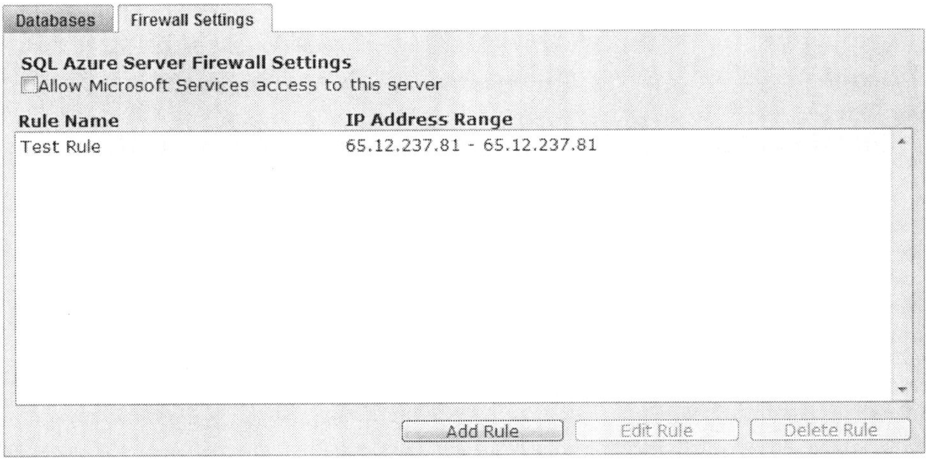

| Databases | Firewall Settings |

SQL Azure Server Firewall Settings
☐ Allow Microsoft Services access to this server

Rule Name	IP Address Range
Test Rule	65.12.237.81 - 65.12.237.81

[Add Rule] [Edit Rule] [Delete Rule]

Figure 3-7. New firewall rule

Databases

The Databases tab is first in the Server Administration portal, but the chapter discussed the Firewall Settings tab before it because even though you can create databases, you can't connect to them without defining a firewall rule and an IP address range. Now that you've defined your firewall rules, let's create a database and connect to it.

The Databases tab makes it very easy to create and manage SQL Azure databases. Click the Create Database button on the Databases tab to bring up the dialog shown in Figure 3-8. This dialog asks you to enter the name of the database, the database edition (Web or Business), and the database's maximum size. Web database editions are available in 1 GB and 5 GB; the Business edition provides sizes ranging from 10 GB to 50 GB, in increments of 10.

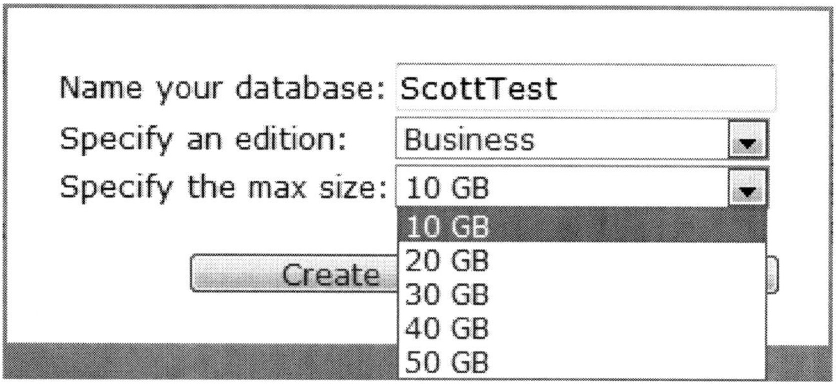

Figure 3-8. Create Database dialog

■ **Note** You're free to pick any database size. But if you use more space than you select, you're charged for the next biggest size. For example, if you initially select a 20 GB database, and after a few months your data grows to 22GB, you then begin to be charged for the 30 GB maximum size.

After you've entered the database name, edition, and maximum size, click the Create button. Your database is now be listed on the Databases tab, along with the database's current size, type (or maximum size), and availability. (See Figure 3-9.)

From the SQL Azure Server Administration portal and the Databases tab, you can also drop existing databases and test connectivity to databases. To test connectivity, select a database from the list, and click the Test Connectivity button. Doing so opens the Database Connectivity Test dialog, which asks you to specify your username and password to connect to the selected database. Enter the appropriate username and password, and click Connect. If the connection is successful, the dialog lets you know, as shown in figure 3-10.

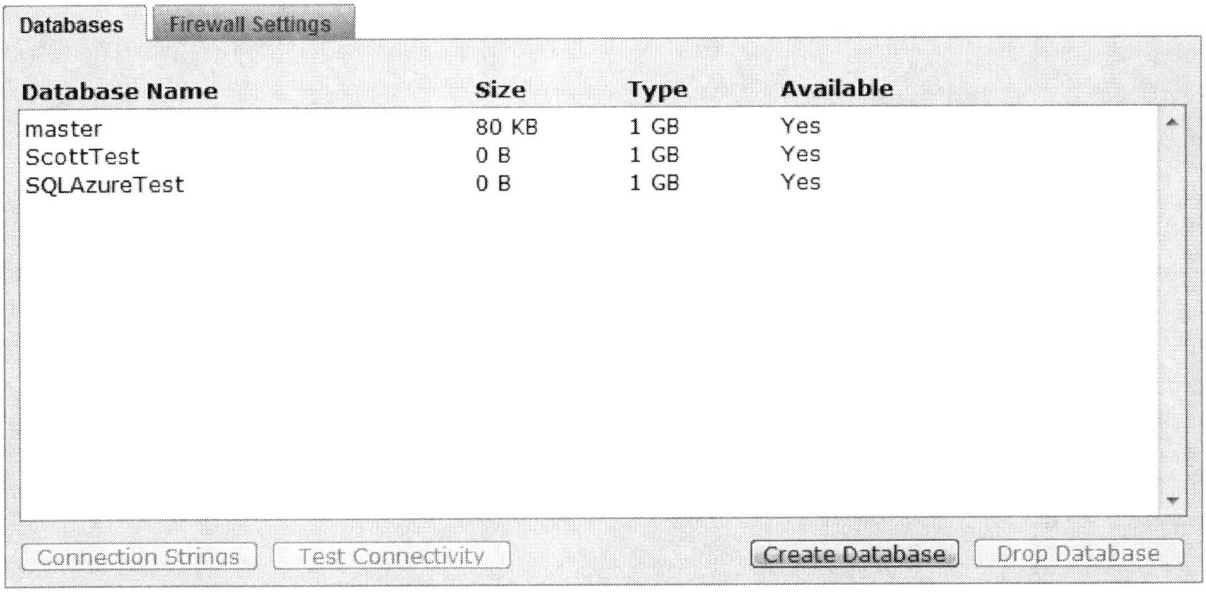

Databases	Firewall Settings			
Database Name		**Size**	**Type**	**Available**
master		80 KB	1 GB	Yes
ScottTest		0 B	1 GB	Yes
SQLAzureTest		0 B	1 GB	Yes

Connection Strings	Test Connectivity		Create Database	Drop Database

Figure 3-9. Database list

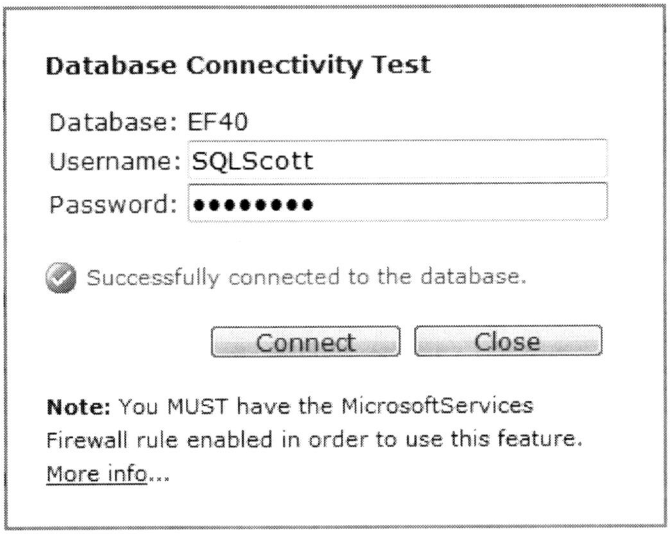

Database Connectivity Test

Database: EF40

Username: SQLScott

Password: ●●●●●●●●

✅ Successfully connected to the database.

Connect	Close

Note: You MUST have the MicrosoftServices Firewall rule enabled in order to use this feature.

More info...

Figure 3-10. Successful database connectivity test

At this point, you've created a database and walked through how to create and manage your databases. Let's move on to how to connect to your databases through SQL Server Management Studio (SSMS) and how to create databases and users via T-SQL.

Now that you've defined your firewall rules and settings, you can create and access SQL Azure databases. Let's do that now.

Creating Databases, Logins, and Users

This section provides a quick and high-level overview of using T-SQL syntax to create databases and users. Chapter 6 goes into an in-depth discussion of the full T-SQL syntax available in SQL Azure to create database objects, such as stored procedures and tables, as well as programming in SQL Azure.

You've walked through how to create and manage databases using the SQL Azure Portal, but now let's use SQL Server Management Studio (SSMS) to create and manage a database. This book uses SQL Server 2008 R2 throughout for the examples. As explained in Chapter 1, you can also use SQL Server 2008, but you must connect via a query window.

Fire up SQL Server 2008 R2, and enter the FQDN of the database server name in the "Server name" box when the Connect to Server dialog appears (see Figure 3-11). Enter the administrator login name and password, and click Connect. You're now connected to SQL Azure.

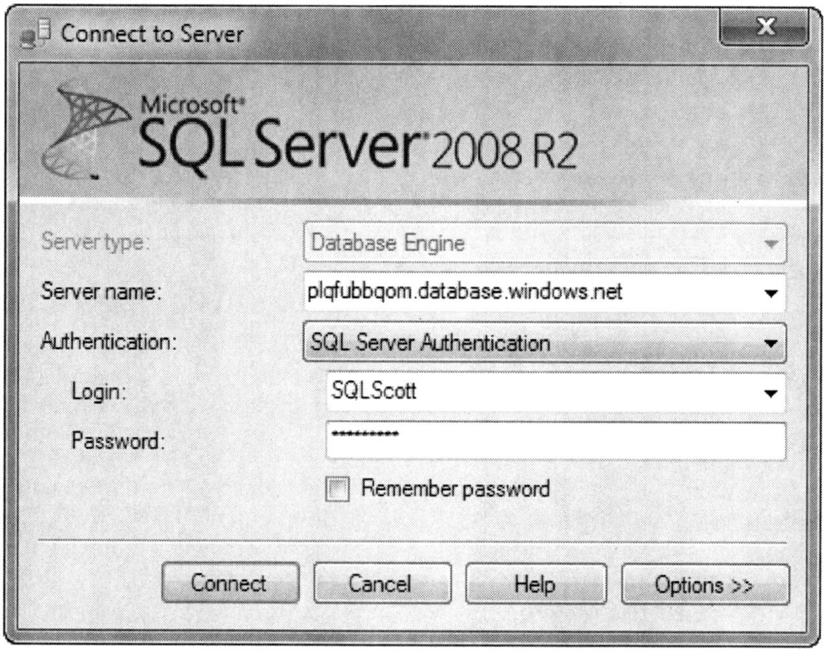

Figure 3-11. Connecting to SQL Azure via SSMS

At this juncture, the only database available to you is the master database, unless you've created databases via the SQL Azure Portal. Let's spend a few minutes discussing how to create databases and other objects using T-SQL. Some of this information was covered briefly in Chapter 1, but this section reviews it as a primer for upcoming chapters.

Databases

When you create databases in a non-Azure environment, you have to know and specify a lot in the `CREATE` statement. For example, you must provide the path and physical object names of the database and log files, as well as the database size and optionally the maximum size and file growth. A `CREATE DATABASE` statement in a non-Azure environment might look like the following:

```
CREATE DATABASE [MyDatabase] ON  PRIMARY
```
(NAME = N'MyDatabase', FILENAME = N'C:\Program Files\Microsoft SQL Server\MSSQL10.MSSQLSERVER\MSSQL\DATA\MyDatabase.mdf' , SIZE = 32768KB , MAXSIZE = UNLIMITED, FILEGROWTH = 1024KB)
 LOG ON
(NAME = N'MyDatabase_log', FILENAME = N'C:\Program Files\Microsoft SQL Server\MSSQL10.MSSQLSERVER\MSSQL\DATA\MyDatabase_log.ldf' , SIZE = 92864KB , MAXSIZE = 2048GB
, FILEGROWTH = 10%)
```
GO
```

As you've learned in the past few chapters, with Azure you don't have to worry about hardware and where objects are located and how hardware is provisioned, which makes statements such `CREATE DATABASE` much simpler. In Chapter 1, you learned that you must connect to the master database first; then, all you need to do is issue the following statement:

```
CREATE DATABASE MyDatabase
```

You can optionally supply two parameters with the `CREATE DATABASE` statement: `MAXSIZE`, which specifies the maximum size of the database; and `EDITION`, which specifies the edition of the database (Web or Business). Here's an example:

```
CREATE DATABASE MyDatabase (MAXSIZE= 10 GB, EDITION= 'Business')
```

In the current release of SQL Azure, two database sizes are available for the Web edition: 1GB and 5GB. For the Business edition, available sizes range from 10GB to 50GB, in increments of 10GB. If `MAXSIZE` is set to a value of 1GB or 5GB and `EDITION` isn't specified, the database edition is automatically set to Web. If `MAXSIZE` is set to a value between 10BG and 50GB and `EDITION` isn't specified, the database edition is automatically set to Business. If neither `MAXSIZE` nor `EDITION` is specified, a Web database of 1GB is created.

SQL Azure doesn't support additional arguments that you're used to using when working with SQL in a local environment. For example, SQL Azure doesn't support parameters that relate to working with physical files, such as `filespec` and `filegroup`. You also can't attach or detach a database. Other unsupported arguments are covered in depth in Appendix B.

Logins and Users

Now that you've created a database, you need to grant access to other users. This section discusses creating logins and users, and allowing others to access the SQL Azure environment. Creating logins and users is similar to doing so locally; but as you found out when creating databases, there are T-SQL limitations.

When granting access to another user, you must first create the login for that user. Then, you create the user based on that login. A login is used for authentication; a user account is used for database access and permission validation.

Logins

When creating logins and users, you must be connected to the master database. You then can use the `CREATE LOGIN` command as follows:

```
CREATE LOGIN loginname WITH PASSWORD = 'password'
```

You must use the `WITH PASSWORD` option and specify a password. Several options you may be used to from using SQL Server locally aren't support in SQL Azure, such as `DEFAULT_DATABASE` and `DEFAULT_LANGUAGE`. Chapter 6 discusses the `CREATE LOGIN` command in more detail.

Users

Now that you've created a login, let's create a user based on it. This is also simple. The syntax is nearly equivalent to the local syntax:

```
CREATE USER username
```

This syntax works if there is a login with the same name. For example, the following is valid:

```
CREATE LOGIN myuser WITH PASSWORD = 'T3stPwd001'
CREATE USER myuser
```

However, the following fails:

```
CREATE LOGIN myuser WITH PASSWORD = 'T3stPwd001'
CREATE USER myotheruser
```

You must use the `FROM LOGIN` clause when creating a user whose username differs from that of the login name:

```
CREATE USER username FROM LOGIN loginname
```

Thus, the correct syntax is the following:

```
CREATE LOGIN myuser WITH PASSWORD = 'T3stPwd001'
CREATE USER myotheruser FROM LOGIN myuser
```

■ **Note** SQL Azure doesn't support GUEST accounts. When you create a user, it must be based on an existing login.

OK, enough about creating databases, users, and logins. Chapter 6 talks more about SQL Azure–specific T-SQL syntax when it discusses programming with SQL Azure in detail. Let's wrap up this chapter with a simple example of how to connect an application to a SQL Azure database.

Connecting to a SQL Azure Database

You have to hand it to Microsoft for going above and beyond in some areas of Azure. The fact that it provides you with connection strings to use in your applications is just plain cool. If you flip back to Figure 3-3, notice the button labeled, appropriately enough, Connection Strings. As soon as you select a database in the list, the Connection Strings button becomes enabled. Clicking it brings up the dialog shown in Figure 3-12, which provides you with two connections strings (one .NET and the other ODBC) to use in your applications to connect to the selected SQL Azure database.

Figure 3-12. *SQL Azure connection strings*

This section uses the ADO.NET connection string to create an ADO.NET 4.0 Entity Framework application. You also use Visual Studio 2010, which at the time of this writing is a release candidate and available to everyone, and which should be available by the time this book is in your hands.

Before you start building your application, you need a database with data in it. Based on what you've learned in this chapter, create a new SQL Azure database named EFAzure. Next, open the SQL file for this chapter called CreateContactTable.sql, and run that script against the EFAzure database. The script creates a single table called Contact and inserts about a dozen contact records.

The examples in the following two sections illustrate connecting to a SQL Azure database and querying the database for contact records. The first example uses the ADO.NET connection string shown in Figure 3-12, and the second uses the ADO.NET 4.0 Entity Framework. You have many options to connect to a SQL Azure database, and this chapter shows you simple examples; later chapters show more detailed examples.

Connecting Using ADO.NET

In this first example, you build a simple Windows Forms application and use ADO.NET to query the EFAzure SQL Azure database. Follow these steps:

1. Open Visual Studio 2010, and create a new Windows Forms Application project.

2. Open Form1 in design mode, and place a button and a ListBox on the form.

3. Double-click the button to view its Click event, and enter the following code. Copy the ADO.NET connection string for your database from the dialog shown in Figure 3-12, and use it to replace the bolded section shown in the code:

```
using (SqlConnection conn = new
SqlConnection("Server=tcp:servername.database.windows.net;Database=EFAzure;User
ID=userid;Password=mypassword;Trusted_Connection=False;Encrypt=True;"))
{

    try
    {
        SqlCommand cmd = new SqlCommand(@"SELECT FirstName, LastName
            FROM Contact
            ORDER BY LastName", conn);
        cmd.Connection.Open();
        SqlDataReader rdr = cmd.ExecuteReader();
        while (rdr.Read())
```

```
        {
            listBox1.Items.Add(String.Format("{0} {1}", rdr[0], rdr[1]));
        }
    }
    catch (Exception ex)
    {
        MessageBox.Show(ex.Message.ToString());
    }
}
```

When the code is in place, run the application. When Form1 appears, click the button; doing so should quickly display in the list box the first name and last name of the contacts from the Contact table. As you can see, the code is the same as if you were querying a local SQL Server database, except for the connection string.

Connecting from the Entity Framework

This example uses the ADO.NET Entity Framework and lets it handle your connection. Follow these steps:

1. Fire up Visual Studio 2010, and create a new Windows Forms Application project. For this simple example, you can use whatever project name you like.

2. Right-click the project in the Solution Explorer window, and select Add → New Item from the context menu. Doing so brings up the Add New Item dialog.

3. Select the ADO.NET Entity Data Model data template, as shown in Figure 3-13.

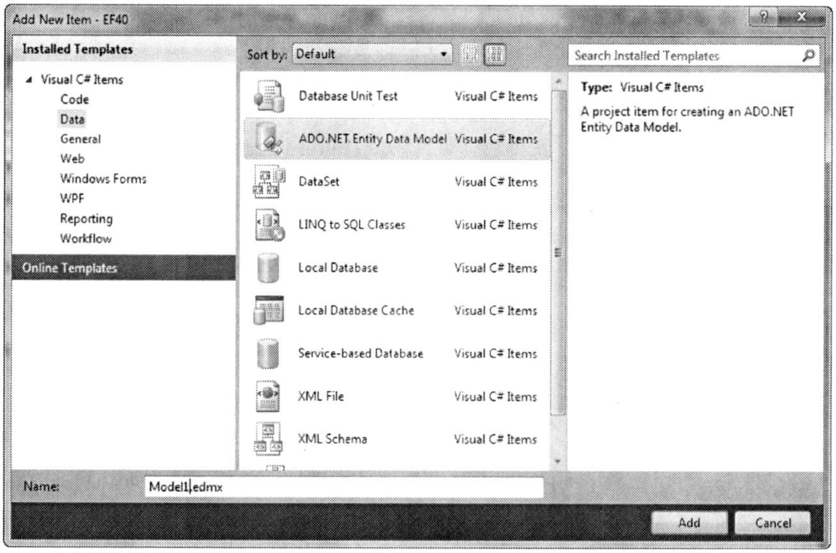

Figure 3-13. Adding an ADO.NET entity data model

4. Accept the default name of Model1 and click the Add button, which starts the Entity Data Model Wizard.

5. The first page of wizard is the Choose Model Contents page, which lets you create a conceptual model of your database by reverse-engineering an existing database. Or, you can start with an empty model and build your conceptual model by hand first. For this example, select the Generate From Database option, and click Next.

■ **Note** This section doesn't go deep into the ADO.NET Entity Framework. For more information about the Entity Framework, see *Pro ADO.NET 4.0 Entity Framework* by Scott Klein (Apress, 2010).

---

6. Next is the Choose Your Data Connection page. You need to create a connection to your new EFAzure database, so click the New Connection button. Doing so brings up the Connection Properties dialog, which you've probably seen before; it lets you define a connection that your application uses to connect to the specified database.

7. In the Connection Properties dialog, click the Change button to open the Choose Data Source dialog shown in Figure 3-14.

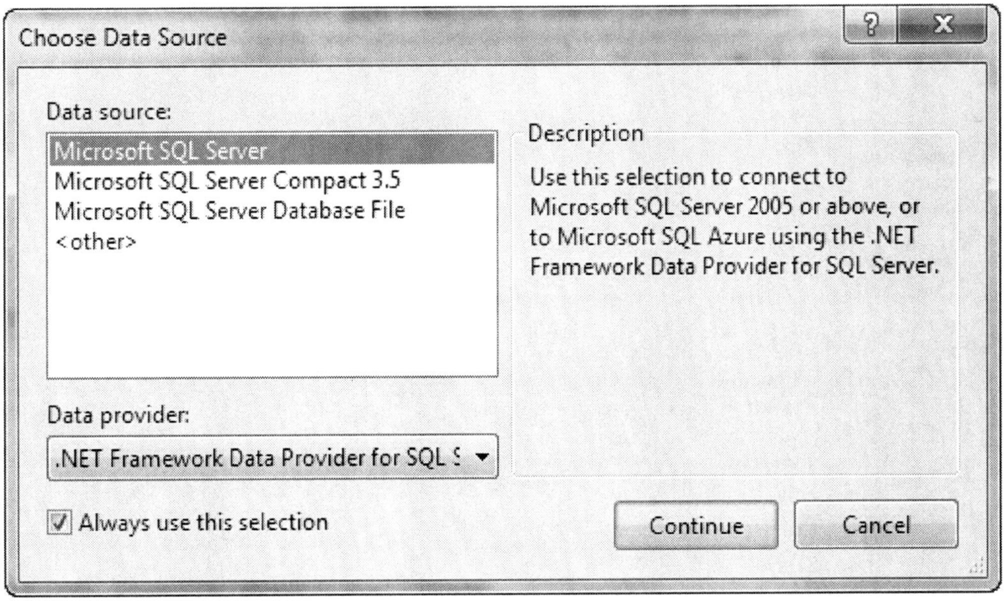

Figure 3-14. Selecting the data source

8. Select Microsoft SQL Server from the list of data sources, and click Continue to return to the Connection Properties dialog.

9. Enter the server name and the administrator username and password, and select the EFAzure database (see Figure 3-15). The server name is the logical name of the server (FQDN); you can get that piece of information from the SQL Azure Portal in the Server Information section, shown earlier in Figure 3-4.

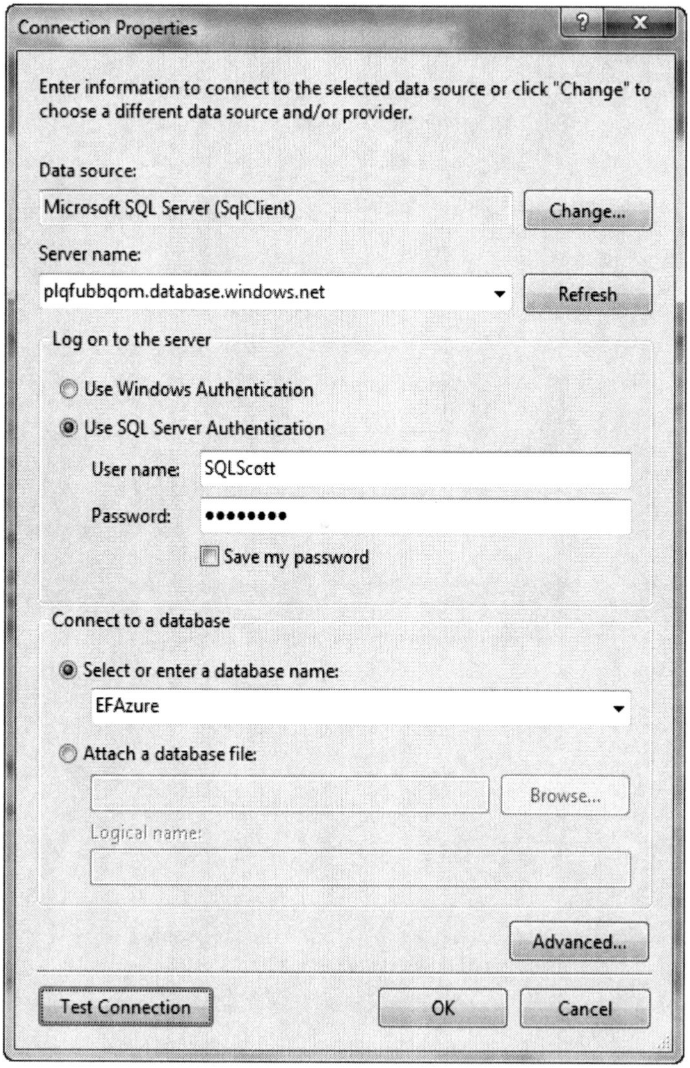

Figure 3-15. *The completed Connection Properties dialog*

10. To ensure that your connection works, click the Test Connection button. If you entered everything correctly and the firewall settings are correct, you get a message stating that the test connection succeeded.

11. Click OK in the Connection Properties dialog. Doing so takes you back to the Entity Data Model Wizard's Choose Your Data Connection page.

12. Your connection has been defined, and you're ready to proceed. You may need to select whether to include the sensitive data in the connection string or to exclude it. For the sake of this example, select the include option (see Figure 3-16). Keep the other default settings, and click Next.

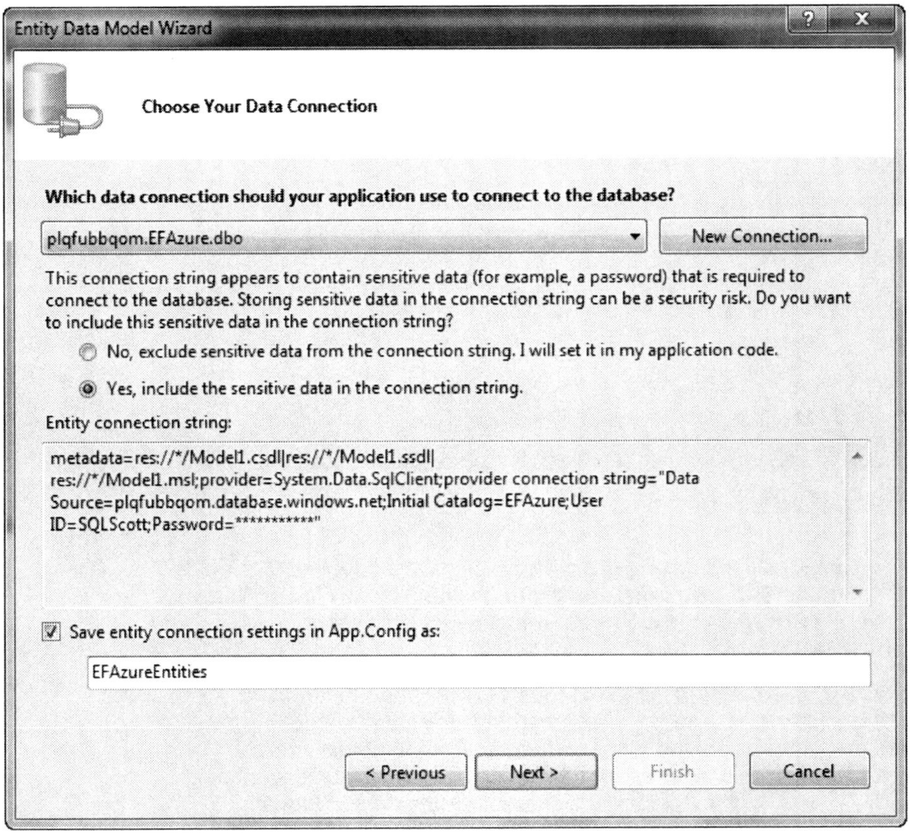

Figure 3-16. The completed Choose Your Data Connection wizard page

13. The next step of the Entity Data Model Wizard allows you to select the objects from your database that you want to include in your conceptual model (see Figure 3-17). You see nodes for Views and Stored Procedures; but because you didn't create any, you can't select anything. Select the Contact table, and click Finish.

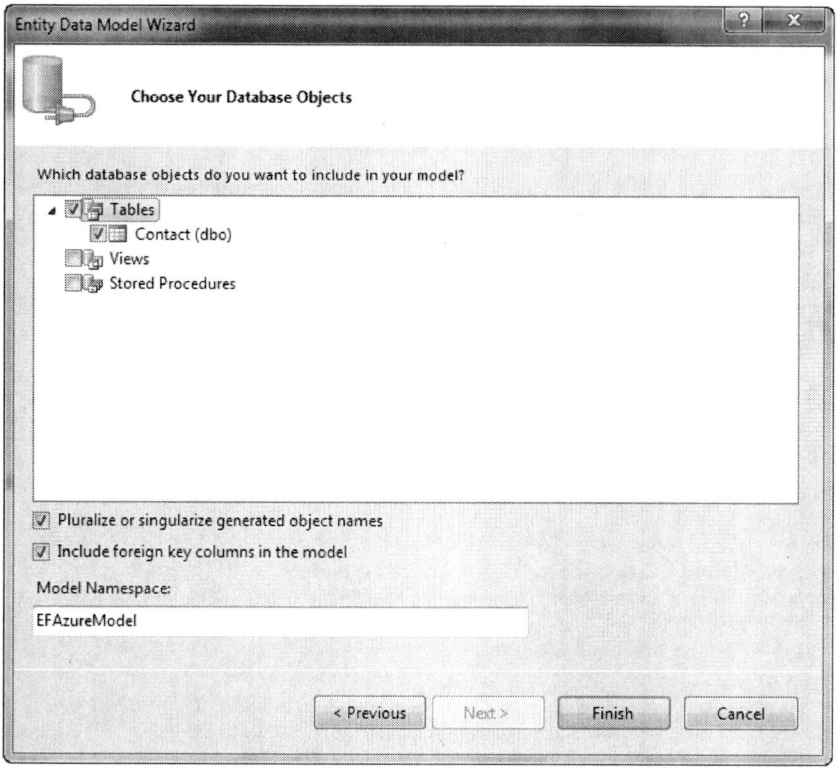

Figure 3-17. Selecting database objects

14. The Entity Data Model Wizard creates your conceptual model and displays it in the Visual Studio IDE. You won't work with this directly, so close it. You do need the form, so open it in Design view and place a ListBox on it, leaving the default name listbox1.

15. Double-click the form (not the ListBox) to display the code-behind and create the form's Load event. You want to do something very simple: load the contacts from the Contact table into the list box when the form loads. (In normal circumstances, this wouldn't be a good idea; but because the table contains only a few contacts, and this example is demonstrating the functionality of querying an Azure database, you can let it slide.) In the Load event, enter the following code:

```
using (EFAzureEntities context = new EFAzureEntities())
{
    var query = from con in context.Contacts
                select con;

    foreach (var cont in query)
    {
```

```
        listBox1.Items.Add(cont.FirstName);
    }
}
```

Again, this book isn't focused on the Entity Framework, but here's a quick explanation of what this code does (you use the Entity Framework in a couple more places in this book). The first line creates an instance of the EFAzureEntities class. This class lets you work with database objects in terms of .NET object-oriented objects. You then use the Language Integrated Query (LINQ) language technology (in this case, LINQ to Entities) to query the Contact table and fill the list box with the first names of all the contacts, as shown in Figure 3-18.

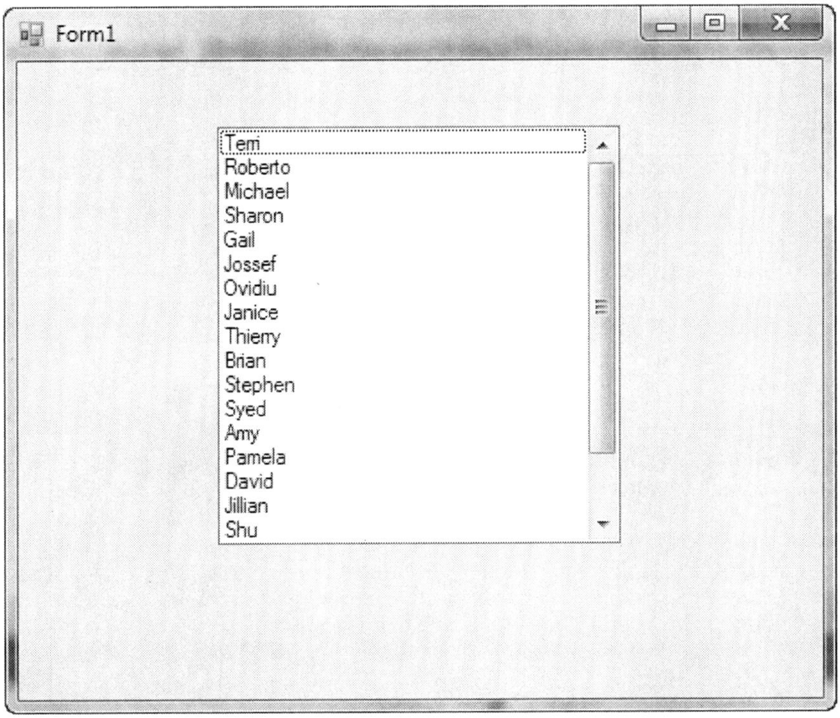

Figure 3-18. Completed Form With Data From SQL Azure.

And there you have it; you've successfully queried the cloud. Yes, this is a simple example, but its purpose is to illustrate how easy it is to connect to SQL Azure, create and populate a database, and create an application that queries the database.

Conclusion

This chapter walked through a brief introduction to creating and configuring you Azure account. You learned how to maintain and administer your SQL Azure Portal, from creating databases to maintaining security via the built-in firewall settings that allow you to specify who can connect to those databases.

You also saw how to create databases of different editions and sizes, as well as how to create databases through T-SQL statements.

You then created a simple application that connected to your SQL Azure database and returned data to a form. With this foundation, you can move on to more detailed and advanced topics such as security, which is discussed next.

CHAPTER 4

■ ■ ■

Security

Compared to other systems in most corporations, database environments receive very little attention when it comes to security, with a few exceptions such as the banking sector. The reason is that databases are considered well within the boundaries of internal networks, which are considered secured and usually inaccessible directly from the Internet.

With the advent of SQL Azure and most Database as a Service solutions, the focus on database security rises all the way to the top for two primary reasons: you're no longer in control of your data, and the data is directly accessible from the Internet. As a result, it becomes even more important to take advantage of all the capabilities of SQL Azure and understand its limitations.

Overview

Before diving in to the specifics of SQL Azure, let's look at a general security framework to assess how Database as a Service can impact you. The following discussion is based on the basic security principles encapsulated by confidentiality, integrity, and availability (CIA). This is referred to as the *CIA triad* and is one of the most accepted forms of security categorization. SQL Azure shifts the balance of the CIA triad from traditional SQL Server installations.

Confidentiality

Confidentiality is the ability to ensure that data can be accessed only by authorized users. It's about protecting your data from prying eyes or from inadvertent leakage by using multiple technologies, including the following:

- **Encryption**. Creates a *ciphertext* (encrypted information) that can be decrypted through the use of a shared key or a certificate

- **Hashing**. Generates a ciphertext that can't be decrypted (typically used for password storage)

- **Access control**. Controls access to data based on contextual information

- **Authentication**. Controls who can access the database and which objects in the database a user can access

- **Firewall**. Uses technology to limit network connectivity to a list of known machines

SQL Azure offers new features, such as a firewall (as previously discussed); however, it doesn't yet support data encryption natively (such as Transparent Data Encryption [TDE] and field-level encryption), which places more emphasis on the other confidentiality techniques.

SQL Server, on the other hand, doesn't provide a native firewall (although it's possible to purchase after-market database firewalls), but it offers strong encryption capabilities. Finally, both SQL Server and SQL Azure offer hashing capabilities.

Because SQL Azure doesn't provide native encryption, your code needs to do all the hard work. Not to worry! In this chapter, you see how to implement hashing and encryption using C# and how to store the ciphertext in SQL Azure (or SQL Server, for that matter).

Integrity

Data *integrity* refers to the objective of ensuring that information is modified only by authorized users. Integrity of data can be compromised in multiple ways, such as a malicious SQL Injection attack or the unintentional execution of a TRUNCATE statement on a table, wiping out all the records. You can implement integrity measures in a database as follows:

- **Authorization**. Controls who can change what data

- **Backup**. Creates a transactionally consistent database snapshot from which data can be recovered

- **Roles-based access**. Provides the minimum access rights to different roles in a company, such as developers and support

- **Auditing**. Tracks database access and data changes to provide an audit trail for forensic analysis

From an integrity standpoint, SQL Azure doesn't yet provide the same capabilities as SQL Server. SQL Azure does deliver strong authorization capabilities, similar to SQL Server 2008. However, regular database backups and activity auditing aren't available as of this writing. Microsoft is building new backup mechanisms for SQL Azure, above and beyond the BCP (Bulk Copy Program) operations available now. See Chapter 5 for more information about how to back up your data in SQL Azure.

Availability

Availability ensures service uptime so your data can be accessed when it's needed. Designing highly available systems can be very complex and requires advanced knowledge in multiple areas including disk configuration, system administration, disaster-recovery locations, and more. The following are some of the technologies involved in high availability:

- **Redundant disks**. Can recover from the loss of a disk spindle. Usually involves a RAID configuration.

- **Redundant networks**. Can survive the loss of multiple network components, such as a network card or a router.

- **Redundant services**. Can survive the interruption of services such as security and databases. An example is the use of Microsoft Cluster Service.

- **Redundant hardware**. Can survive the loss of machine hardware, such as a CPU or a memory chip.

- **Scalability**. Delivers information at near constant speed under load.

- **DOS prevention**. Prevents successful denial of service (DoS) attacks that would otherwise prevent data availability.

In addition to ensuring redundancy of infrastructure components, you need to understand the recovery objectives of your business to determine how to best implement your availability requirements.

SQL Azure offers a unique platform because all the areas just listed are automatically provided for. SQL Azure offers a 99.9% availability guarantee through its service-level agreement (SLA). In order to deliver this high availability, SQL Azure transparently keeps two additional standby databases for each user database you create. If anything happens to one of your user databases, one of the two backups takes over within a few seconds; you may not even notice the failover process. SQL Azure also provides automatic handling of DoS attacks.

SQL Azure accomplishes failover using the architecture shown in Figure 4-1. You interact with a proxy that directs your request to whichever of your databases is current. The standby databases aren't accessible to you.

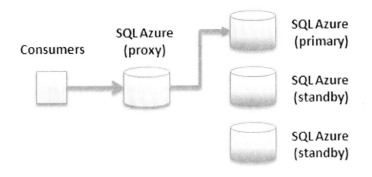

Figure 4-1. SQL Azure's standby database architecture

■ **Note** In terms of availability, SQL Azure far surpasses SQL Server; SQL Azure is built on a scalable and highly available platform that doesn't require configuration or tuning. None of the typical SQL Server configuration settings are available in SQL Azure (such as CPU Affinity, Replication, Log Shipping, and so on).

Let's take an example of a project that needs to deploy a new application with high availability requirements. The following items would need to be planned for in a traditional SQL Server installation but are provided to you automatically with SQL Azure:

- **Clustered SQL Server instance**. Install and configure Microsoft Cluster Service and SQL Server instances in an active/active or active/passive configuration.

- **RAID configuration**. Purchase new disks and hardware to install and configure a RAID 10 (or RAID 0+1) disk array (for disk redundancy and performance).

- **Disaster-recovery server**. Purchase similar hardware and configure it at a disaster-recovery site.

- **Replication topology**. Create a mechanism to transfer the data from the primary site to the secondary site using log shipping, replication, disk-level replication, or another technique, depending on your needs.

- **Database tuning**. In larger systems, tuning SQL Server for high performance can be very difficult and involves CPU and I/O affinitization, degree of parallelism, and many other considerations.

- **Testing**. Plan and execute a disaster-recovery plan once a year, to make sure it's working as intended.

And of course, you must consider the costs associated with all these activities, the time it takes to plan and execute such a project, and the specialized resources needed to implement a highly available database environment.

By now, you can see that although SQL Azure falls short in certain areas of security, it excels in others, especially its availability model. Deploying a highly available SQL Azure database is quick and extremely simple.

Securing Your Data

Let's dive into some specifics and code examples to show how to secure your data in SQL Azure. You may need to secure specific columns in your database that contain sensitive information, such as Social Security numbers or credit card numbers. Certain applications store patient data, which can fall under compliance review, and as such may need to be encrypted as well. As hinted previously, not all security mechanisms are currently available, so this section focuses on what SQL Azure provides and on ways to mitigate the missing features. Regarding data encryption, because SQL Azure provides none, you see how to implement your own security classes to simplify data encryption in your projects.

▨ **Note** The examples that follow use a database script called `Security.sql` and a Visual Studio 2008 project called `SQLAzureSecurity.sln`. You can run the SQL script on your local SQL Server database if you don't have a Windows Azure account yet.

This chapter uses a few classes and methods to demonstrate how to use encryption, hashing, and other techniques. Figure 4-2 shows the objects being used. The `Encryption` class performs the actual encryption and returns a `CipherText` structure; the `UserProperties` class uses extension methods from the `Extensions` class and a helper method in the `Util` class. The `CDatabase` class returns the database connection string.

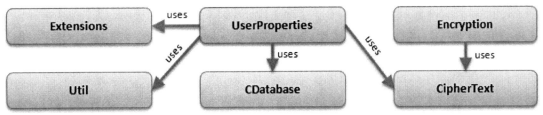

Figure 4-2. *Object model used in the examples*

Encryption

As mentioned previously, data encryption isn't available. Why? Because SQL Azure doesn't support X.509 certificates yet. Certificates are necessary for many encryption-related features, such as Transparent Data Encryption (TDE), column-level encryption, and certain T-SQL commands, such as FOR ENCRYPTION and SIGNBYCERT.

However, SQL Azure requires the use of SSL encryption for its communication. This means your sensitive data is always transmitted safely between your clients and your SQL Azure database. There is nothing you need to do to enable SSL encryption; it's required and automatically enforced by SQL Azure. If an application tries to connect to SQL Azure and the application doesn't support SSL, the connection request fails.

But SSL doesn't encrypt data at rest; it only encrypts data in transit. How can you protect your data when it's stored in SQL Azure? Because SQL Azure doesn't support encryption natively, you must encrypt and decrypt your data in the application code.

The Security.sql script contains the following T-SQL statement:

```
1. CREATE TABLE UserProperties
2. (
3.    ID int identity(1,1) PRIMARY KEY,        -- identity of the record
4.    PropertyName nvarchar(255) NOT NULL,     -- name of the property
5.    Value varbinary(max) NOT NULL,           -- encrypted value
6.    Vector binary(16) NOT NULL,              -- vector of encrypted value
7.    LastUpdated datetime NOT NULL,           -- date of last modification
8.    Token binary(32) NOT NULL                -- record hash
9. )
```

Each record contains a property name (line 4) that can be used as a search key and an encrypted value (line 5). The value itself is a binary data type, which lends itself well to encryption. A vector is used for additional security; this column is explained shortly. The Token and LastUpdated columns are addressed later when discussing hashing.

The following C# code shows how to encrypt a string value using the Advanced Encryption Standard (AES) algorithm; you can easily add support for Triple Data Encryption Standard (3DES) or other algorithms. It uses a shared secret to create the ciphertext and returns a byte array. The byte array is stored later in the Value column in the database:

```
1. /// <summary>
2. /// A result structure that stores the encrypted value
3. /// and its associated vector
4. /// </summary>
5. public struct CipherText
6. {
7.     public byte[] cipher;
8.     public byte[] vector;
```

```
9. }
10.
11. /// <summary>
12. /// The encryption class that encapsulates the complexity behind encrypting
13. /// and decrypting values
14. /// </summary>
15. public class Encryption
16. {
17.     private byte[] _SECRET_KEY_ = new byte[] { 160, 225, 229, 3,
18.         148, 219, 67, 89, 247, 133, 213, 26, 129, 160, 235, 41,
19.         42, 177, 202, 251, 38, 56, 232, 90, 54, 88, 158, 169,
20.         200, 24, 19, 27 };
21.
22./// <summary>
23./// Encrypt using AES
24./// </summary>
25./// <param name="value">The string to encrypt</param>
26.public CipherText EncryptAES(string value)
27.{
28.     // Prepare variables...
29.     byte[] buffer = UTF8Encoding.UTF8.GetBytes(value);
30.     CipherText ct = new CipherText();
31.     System.Security.Cryptography.Aes aes = null;
32.     ICryptoTransform transform = null;
33.
34.     // Create the AES object
35.     aes = System.Security.Cryptography.Aes.Create();
36.     aes.GenerateIV();
37.     aes.Key = _SECRET_KEY_;
38.
39.     // Create the encryption object
40.     transform = aes.CreateEncryptor();
41.
42.     // Encrypt and store the result in the structure
43.     ct.cipher = transform.TransformFinalBlock(buffer, 0, buffer.Length);
44.     // Save the vector used for future use
45.     ct.vector = aes.IV;
46.
47.     return ct;
48.     }
49.}
```

The CipherText structure (line 5) is used as a return value. Each encrypted byte array comes with its initialization vector, which is a security mechanism that prevents dictionary attacks on your database. The Encryption class contains an EncryptAES method that performs the actual encryption of a string value; this method returns CipherText.

Because AES requires a secret key, you created one in the form of a byte array on line 17. The secret key must be 32 bytes in length. You can easily generate your own by using the GenerateKey method provided by the Aes class provided by .NET.

On line 29, you transform the string value to its byte representation using UTF-8 encoding. UTF-8 encoding is very practical because it automatically chooses between ASCII and Unicode based on the input value.

You declare the AES object on line 31 and instantiate it on line 35 using the static `Create()` method on the `Aes` class. This method creates the vector automatically on line 36 and sets the private key discussed earlier.

On line 40, you create a cryptographic object using the `CreateEncryptor()` method. A call to its `TransformFinalBlock()` method does the trick and outputs a variable-length byte array that you store in the `CipherText` structure instance on line 43. You save the previously generated vector as well and return the structure on line 47.

That was simple, right? Now all you have to do is store the `CipherText` content in the UserProperties table. But before doing this, let's discuss hashing.

■ **Note** This example uses AES, but other algorithms are available with the .NET framework. Because you also use an initialization vector, running the same code over and over yields different output, given the same input. That makes the encrypted value harder to crack. The Visual Studio Solution provided includes additional methods to decrypt data.

Hashing

Hashing isn't nearly as complicated as you've seen so far. And although you can store the values you've encrypted so far in the database, in this example you hash all the columns of the rows (except the ID value) to make sure they're unchanged. Why? The answer goes back to the integrity concern of the CIA triad discussed earlier. You want a way to tell whether your data has been modified outside of your code. Encrypting your secret value makes it virtually impossible to break the confidentiality aspect of the triad, but someone can still update the PropertyName column—or, worse, the Value column. Hashing doesn't prevent data from being modified, but you have a way to detect whether it was changed without your authorization.

To simplify the code, start by creating a couple of extension methods. Extension methods are a handy way to extend the methods available to a class (or data type) even if you don't have the original source code. Here you can see how to declare an extension method on the `string` and `DateTime` data types:

```
1.  public static class Extensions
2.  {
3.      public static byte[] GetBytes(this string value)
4.      {
5.          byte[] buffer = UTF8Encoding.UTF8.GetBytes(value);
6.          return buffer;
7.      }
8.
9.      public static byte[] GetBytes(this DateTime value)
10.     {
11.         return value.ToString().GetBytes();
12.     }
13. }
```

This code adds a `GetBytes()` method to the `string` and `DateTime` data types. You also create a utility class that allows you to create a hash value based on a collection of byte arrays. The following code shows that class:

```
1.  public class Util
```

```
2.  {
3.  /// <summary>
4.  /// Computes a hash value based on an array of byte arrays
5.  /// </summary>
6.  /// <param name="bytes">Array of byte arrays</param>
7.  public static byte[] ComputeHash(params byte[][] bytes)
8.  {
9.      SHA256 sha = SHA256Managed.Create();
10.     MemoryStream ms = new MemoryStream();
11.
12.     for (int i = 0; i < bytes.Length; i++)
13.     ms.Write(bytes[i], 0, bytes[i].Length);
14.
15.     ms.Flush();
16.     ms.Position = 0;
17.
18.     return sha.ComputeHash(ms);
19.     }
20. }
```

This Util class is very handy shortly. Note on line 7 the declaration of the variable as params byte[][]; this means each parameter passed to this method must be a byte array. You declare a memory stream, loop on each byte-array variable, and append it to the memory stream on line 13. Finally, you return the computed hash of the memory stream on line 18. You see how to call this method shortly.

The UserProperties class is next, in the following example, and makes the actual call to the SQL Azure database. It takes two input parameters: the property name to save and its encrypted value stored in the CipherText structure. On line 13, you retrieve the connection string from another class and open the database connection on line 15. You then create the command object, specifying a call to a stored procedure. The code for the stored procedure is provided later. The hash value is then created on line 39; as you can see, you call the ComputeHash method just reviewed by passing each stored procedure parameter as a byte array. This is where you use both the extension methods created earlier and the hashing method. After the hash result is calculated, you pass it into the last stored procedure parameter on line 45:

```
1.  using System.Data.SqlDbType;
2.  public class UserProperties
3.  {
4.
5.      /// <summary>
6.      /// Saves a property value in a SQL Azure database
7.      /// </summary>
8.      /// <param name="propertyName">The property name</param>
9.      /// <param name="ct">The CipherText structure to save</param>
10.     public static void Save(string propertyName, CipherText ct)
11.     {
12.         using (SqlConnection sqlConn =
13.                     new SqlConnection(CDatabase.ConnectionString))
14.         {
15.             sqlConn.Open();
16.
17.             using (SqlCommand sqlCmd = new SqlCommand())
18.             {
19.
```

```
20.                DateTime dateUpdated = DateTime.Now;
21.
22.                sqlCmd.Connection = sqlConn;
23.                sqlCmd.CommandType = System.Data.CommandType.StoredProcedure;
24.                sqlCmd.CommandText = "proc_SaveProperty";
25.                sqlCmd.Parameters.Add("name", NVarChar, 255);
26.                sqlCmd.Parameters.Add("value", VarBinary, int.MaxValue);
27.                sqlCmd.Parameters.Add("vector", VarBinary, 16);
28.                sqlCmd.Parameters.Add("lastUpdated", DateTime);
29.                sqlCmd.Parameters.Add("hash", VarBinary, 32);
30.                sqlCmd.Parameters[0].Value = propertyName;
31.                sqlCmd.Parameters[1].Value = ct.cipher;
32.                sqlCmd.Parameters[2].Value = ct.vector;
33.                sqlCmd.Parameters[3].Value = dateUpdated;
34.
35.                // Calculate the hash of this record...
36.                // We pass the list of values that should be hashed
37.                // If any of these values changes in the database,
38.                // recalculating the hash would yield a different result
39.                byte[] hash = Util.ComputeHash(
40.                    propertyName.GetBytes(),
41.                    ct.cipher,
42.                    ct.vector,
43.                    dateUpdated.GetBytes());
44.
45.                sqlCmd.Parameters[4].Value = hash;
46.
47.                int res = sqlCmd.ExecuteNonQuery();
48.
49.            }
50.
51.            sqlConn.Close();
52.
53.        }
54.    }
55.
56. }
```

As promised, following is the code for the stored procedure. You create a stored procedure because it allows you to provide additional security from an access-control standpoint. As you see later, you create a schema that contains the tables and a separate schema for the stored procedures that access the tables. This provides greater control over your database security. You review schemas later in this chapter:

```
IF (Exists(SELECT * FROM sys.sysobjects WHERE Name = 'proc_SaveProperty' AND Type = 'P'))
    DROP PROC proc_SaveProperty

GO

-- SELECT * FROM UserProperties
CREATE PROC proc_SaveProperty
    @name nvarchar(255),
    @value varbinary(max),
    @vector binary(16),
```

•

```
    @lastUpdated datetime,
    @hash binary(32)
AS


IF (Exists(SELECT * FROM UserProperties WHERE PropertyName = @name))
BEGIN
    UPDATE UserProperties SET
        Value = @value,
        Vector = @vector,
        LastUpdated = @lastUpdated,
        Token = @hash
    WHERE
        PropertyName = @name
END
ELSE
BEGIN
    INSERT INTO UserProperties
        (PropertyName, Value, Vector, LastUpdated, Token)
    VALUES (
        @name,
        @value,
        @vector,
        @lastUpdated,
        @hash )
END
```

This stored procedure performs both updates and inserts depending on the property name. Note the use of varbinary(max); because you don't know how long the encrypted value will be, you allow large but variable binary objects to be stored. However, the vector is always 16 bytes in length and the hash 32.

Running the Save() method on the UserProperties class creates a record in the UserProperties table. The following code shows how to call the Save method:

```
1.    class Program
2.    {
3.        static void Main(string[] args)
4.        {
5.            // Declare the encryption object and encrypt our secret value
6.            Encryption e = new Encryption();
7.            CipherText ct = e.EncryptAES("secret value goes here...");
8.
9.            UserProperties.Save("MySecret", ct);
10.
11.       }
12.   }
```

Figure 4-3 shows the content of the table. The Value column is your encrypted value, the Vector is the @vector variable from the stored procedure, and the Token column is the calculated hash passed as the @hash variable.

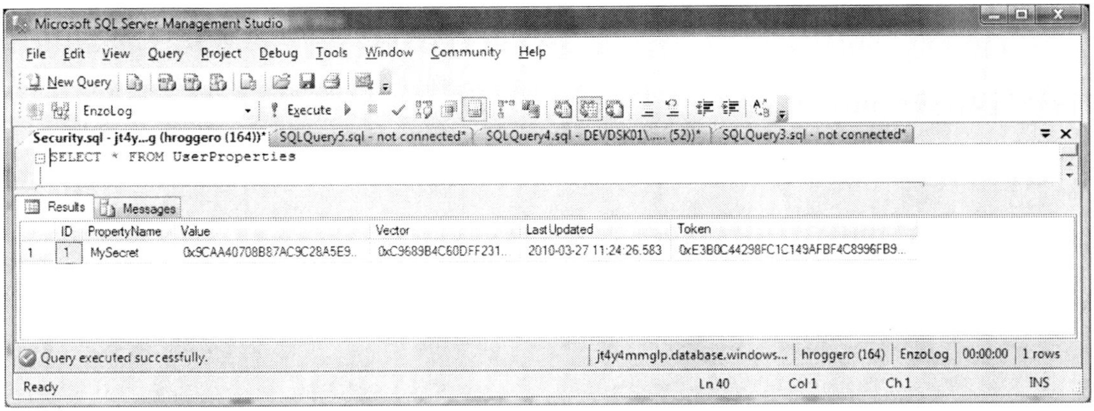

Figure 4-3. Record with the encrypted value, a hash, and a vector

Last but not least, you should know that SQL Server and SQL Azure both support hashing natively. Unfortunately, support for hashing in both database platforms is limited to the MD5 and SHA-1 algorithms. The hashing method used in the C# code shown previously uses SHA-256 as its algorithm, which is much stronger. Here is a quick example of how to compute an SHA-1 hash in SQL:

```
SELECT HASHBYTES('sha1', 'MySecret')
```

The output of HASHBYTES() is a byte array as well:

```
0xEABBEC6F31804EB968E2FAEAAEF150546A595FC3
```

So far, you've seen a way to encrypt sensitive information for confidentiality, hashed certain columns of a record for increased integrity, and deployed in Azure for strong availability. As you can see, developing encryption and hashing routines can be very complex and requires a strong command of the programming language. You may find it beneficial to create a generic encryption library, like the one shown in the previous examples, that can be reused across projects.

Certificates

As discussed previously, SQL Azure doesn't support X.509 certificates, although you can deploy X.509 certificates in Windows Azure. Your client code (either hosted on your company's network or in Windows Azure) can use certificates to encrypt and decrypt values. The use of certificates implies that you're encrypting using a public/private key pair. The public key is used to encrypt data, and the private key is used to decrypt data.

■ **Note** For more information on how to deploy X.509 certificates in Windows Azure, visit the MSDN blog http://blogs.msdn.com/jnak and look at the January 2010 archive. The blog entry by Jim Nakashima contains detailed instructions.

You can easily create a self-signed certificate using the MakeCert.exe utility. To create a certificate on your machines, run the following command at a command line. You need to execute this statement as an Administrator or the command will fail:

```
makecert -ss root -pe -r -n "CN=BlueSyntaxTest" -sky Exchange -sr LocalMachine
```

Here is a brief overview of the options used to create this certificate:

- -ss root stores the certificate in the root certificate store.

- -pe marks the private key exportable.

- -r creates a self-signed certificate (meaning that it wasn't issued by a root certificate authority (CA) like Thawte).

- -n "CN=..." specifies the subject's name of the certificate.

- -sky Exchange specifies that the certificate is used for encryption.

- -sr LocalMachine specifies that the certificate store location as LocalMachine.

■ **Note** Make sure you run this statement as an Administrator, or you'll get an error that looks like this:

```
Error:Save encoded certificate to store failed => 0x5 (5).
```

To verify that your certificate was properly installed, open mmc.exe. Select File→ Add/Remove Snap In. Then, select Certificates, click Add, choose Computer, and click OK. Expand the tree on the left to view the certificates under Trusted Root Certification Authorities. Figure 4-4 shows the BlueSyntaxTest certificate that was created with the earlier command.

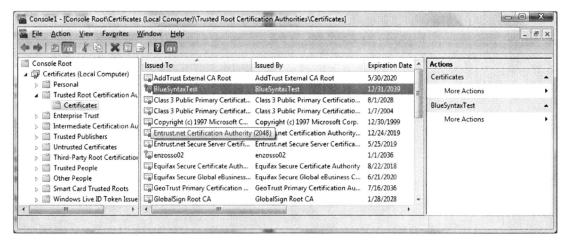

Figure 4-4. Viewing certificates on your machine

Now that you have a certificate installed, you can search for and locate it with code. Usually, a certificate is searched for by its unique identifier (*thumbprint*) or by its *common name* (CN). To view the thumbprint of your certificate, double-click the certificate, select the Details tab, and scroll down until you see the Thumbprint property, as shown in Figure 4-5.

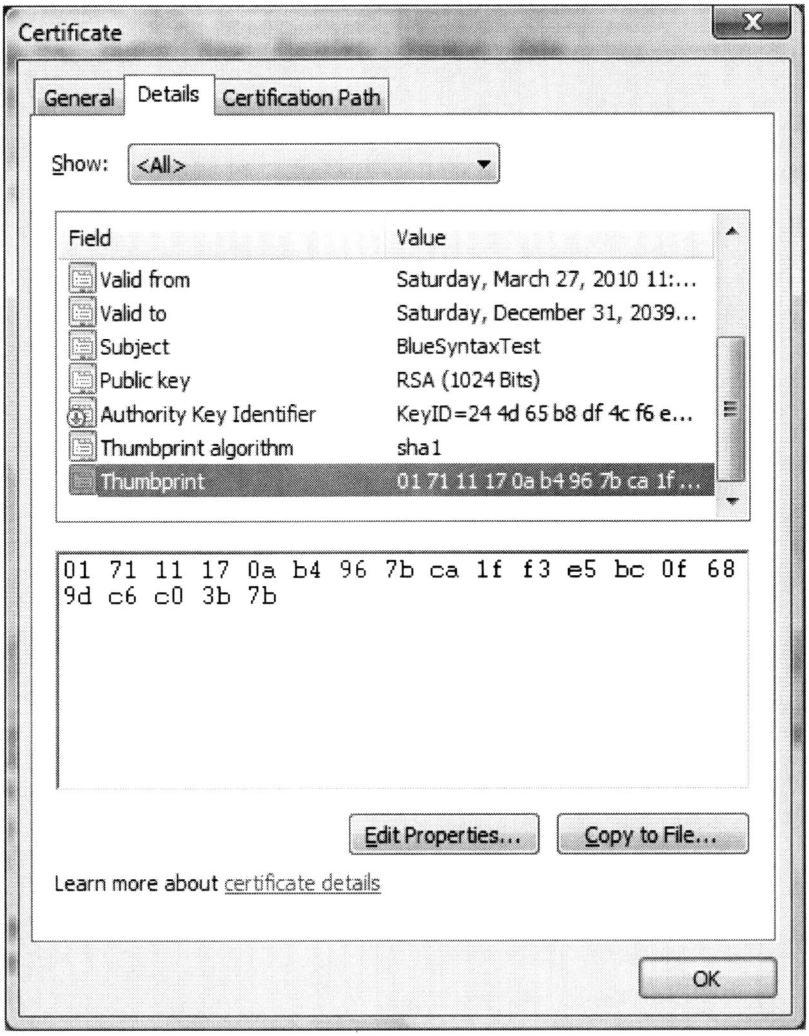

Figure 4-5. Obtaining a certificate's thumbprint

You can select the thumbprint and copy it into a string variable. The following code shows a new private variable and a new method in the Encryption class you saw earlier. Line 1 contains the thumbprint as seen in Figure 4-5, line 13 opens the root certificate store on LocalMachine, and line 17 instantiates an X.509 object by searching the thumbprint. Note that the Find method returns a collection; you're interested in the first certificate because only one will match this thumbprint. On line

24, you create the RSA encryption object and call its Encrypt method on line 27. Because encrypting with RSA automatically incorporates a vector, there is no need to keep track of it. So, the CipherText vector variable is set to 0:

```
1.   private string _THUMBPRINT_ =
2.      "01 71 11 17 0a b4 96 7b ca 1f f3 e5 bc 0f 68 9d c6 c0 3b 7b";
3.
4.          /// <summary>
5.          /// Encrypts a string value using a self-signed certificate
6.          /// </summary>
7.          /// <param name="value">The value to encrypt</param>
8.          /// <returns></returns>
9.          public CipherText EncryptByCert(string value)
10.         {
11.             byte[] buffer = UTF8Encoding.UTF8.GetBytes(value);
12.
13.             X509Store store = new X509Store(StoreName.Root,
14.                 StoreLocation.LocalMachine);
15.             store.Open(OpenFlags.ReadOnly);
16.
17.             X509Certificate2 x509 =
18.                 store.Certificates.Find(
19.                 X509FindType.FindByThumbprint,
20.                 _THUMBPRINT_, true)[0];
21.
22.             store.Close();
23.
24.             RSACryptoServiceProvider rsaEncrypt = null;
25.             rsaEncrypt = (RSACryptoServiceProvider)x509.PublicKey.Key;
26.
27.             byte[] encryptedBytes = rsaEncrypt.Encrypt(buffer, false);
28.
29.             CipherText ct = new CipherText();
30.             ct.cipher = encryptedBytes;
31.             ct.vector = new byte[] {0, 0, 0, 0, 0, 0, 0, 0, 0,
32.                 0, 0, 0, 0, 0, 0, 0};
33.
34.             return ct;
35.         }
```

The decryption code is shown next and is very similar to the preceding example. You make a call to Decrypt instead of Encrypt on the RSA object:

```
1.          public string DecryptByCert(CipherText ct)
2.          {
3.              X509Store store = new X509Store(StoreName.Root,
4.                  StoreLocation.LocalMachine);
5.              store.Open(OpenFlags.ReadOnly);
6.
7.              X509Certificate2 x509 =
8.                  store.Certificates.Find(
9.                  X509FindType.FindByThumbprint,
10.                 _THUMBPRINT_, true)[0];
11.
11.             store.Close();
```

```
12.
13.              RSACryptoServiceProvider rsaEncrypt = null;
14.              rsaEncrypt = (RSACryptoServiceProvider)x509.PrivateKey;
15.
16.              byte[] bytes = rsaEncrypt.Decrypt(ct.cipher, false);
17.
18.              return UTF8Encoding.UTF8.GetString(bytes);
19.          }
```

The following code calls the RSA encryption routine and saves to the UserProperties table as previously described. The table now contains two records. Note that the length of the ciphertext is much greater with the certificate encryption approach:

```
1.    class Program
2.    {
3.        static void Main(string[] args)
4.        {
5.            // Declare the encryption object and encrypt our secret value
6.            Encryption e = new Encryption();
7.            CipherText ct = e.EncryptAES("secret value goes here...");
8.            CipherText ct2 = e.EncryptByCert("another secret!!!");
9.
10.           UserProperties.Save("MySecret", ct);
11.           UserProperties.Save("MySecret2", ct2);
12.
13.        }
14.    }
```

Access Control

So far, you've spent a lot of time encrypting and hashing values for increased confidentiality and integrity. However, another important aspect of the CIA triad is access control. This section reviews two subcategories of access control: authentication (also referred to as AUTHN) and authorization (AUTHZ).

Authentication (AUTHN)

AUTHN is a process that verifies you're indeed who you say you are. In SQL Server, the AUTHN process is done through one of two mechanisms: network credentials (or Security Support Provider Interface [SSPI]) or SQL Server credentials. Connection strings must specify which AUTHN is being used. And when you use SQL Server AUTHN, a password must be provided before attempting to connect, either by a user at runtime or in a configuration file.

Keep the following items in mind when you're considering AUTHN with SQL Azure:

- **No network authentication**. Because SQL Azure isn't on your network, network AUTHN isn't available. This further means you must use SQL AUTHN at all times and that you must store passwords in your applications (in configuration files, preferably). You may want to store your passwords encrypted. Although you can encrypt sections of your configuration files in Windows using the aspnet_regiis.exe utility, this option isn't available in Windows Azure. So, you can use one of the encryption methods presented earlier to encrypt and decrypt the SQL Azure connection string if necessary.

- **Strong passwords**. SQL Azure requires the use of strong passwords. This option can't be disabled, which is a good thing. A strong password must be at least eight characters long; must combine letters, numbers, and symbols; and can't be a word found in a dictionary.

- **Login name limitations**. Certain login names aren't available, such as sa, admin and guest. These logins can't be created. You should also refrain from using the @ symbol in your login names; this symbol is used to separate a user name from a machine name, which may be needed at times.

Authorization (AUTHZ)

Authorization gives you the ability to control who can perform which actions after being authenticated. It's important to define a good AUTHZ model early in your development cycle, because changing access-control strategy can be relatively difficult.

Generally speaking, a strong AUTHZ model defines which users can access which objects in the database. This is typically performed in SQL Azure and SQL Server by defining relationships between logins, users, schemas, and rights.

Creating Logins and Users

In SQL Azure, you must be connected to the master database to manage your logins. The CREATE LOGIN T-SQL statement is partially supported. Also, remember that you must use a strong password when creating logins.

SQL Azure offers two new roles:

- **LoginManager role**. Grants a user the ability to create new logins in the master database

- **DBManager role**. Grants a user the ability to create new databases from the master database

The following code shows how to create a login and grant that login the LoginManager role:

```
CREATE LOGIN MyTestLogin WITH PASSWORD='MyT3stLogin'
GO
CREATE USER MyTestLoginUser FROM LOGIN MyTestLogin
GO
EXEC sp_addrolemember 'loginmanager', MyTestLoginUser
GO
```

Note that CREATE USER statement creates a user in the master database because you haven't connected to another database. Creating the MyTestLogin user in the master database is precisely what you want because you can only create login accounts from the master database.

To allow the MyTestLogin account to also access another database, connect to the desired database in SQL Azure using another login and run the CREATE USER statement again. Now the MyTestLogin account can connect to another database.

Schemas

A *schema* is a container that holds database objects; schemas reside inside a database. Schemas are part of the three-part naming convention of database objects; they're considered namespaces. Each object in a schema must have a unique name.

By default, objects created are owned by the DBO schema. For example, the CREATE TABLE statement showed previously for the UserProperties table uses DBO as the schema owner (schema_id is always 1 for DBO). See Figure 4-6.

Right now, the new user MyTestLoginUser can't read from this table. Attempting to issue a SELECT statement against UserProperties returns a SELECT permission denied error. So, you have a choice: you can either give that user account SELECT permission or create a schema for that user and assign the SELECT permission to the schema.

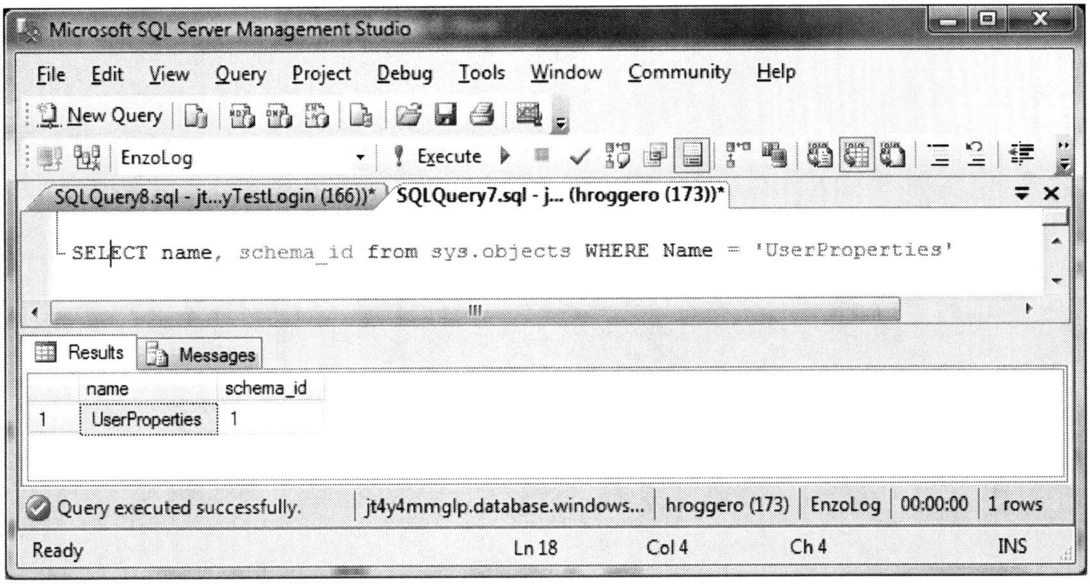

Figure 4-6. Viewing an object's schema ownership

It's usually much easier to manage access rights through schemas instead of users directly. To do this properly, you need to change the ownership of the UserProperties table to a new schema (other than DBO) and then assign access rights to the schema.

To create a new schema, you must be connected to the desired user database where MyTestLoginUser has been created. Then, run the following statement:

```
CREATE SCHEMA MyReadOnlySchema AUTHORIZATION DBO
```

At this point, a schema as been created; it's owned by DBO. You now need to change the ownership of the UserProperties table to MyReadOnlySchema:

```
ALTER SCHEMA MyReadOnlySchema TRANSFER DBO.UserProperties
```

The table now belongs to the schema, as shown in Figure 4-7.

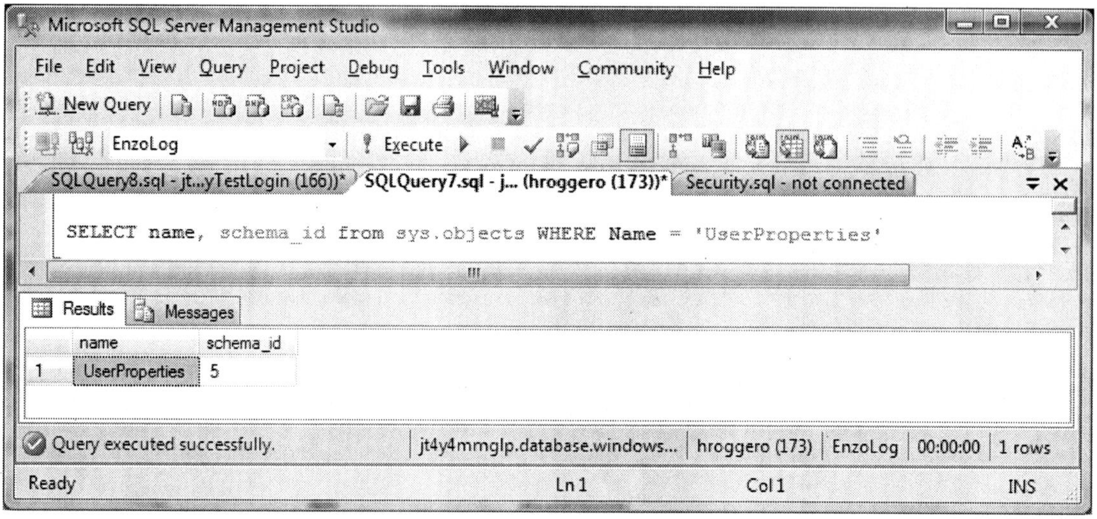

Figure 4-7. *Viewing the new schema owner*

However, you aren't done just yet. MyTestLoginUser can no longer see the table. Issuing a select statement on the table returns an Invalid object name message, as shown in Figure 4-8.

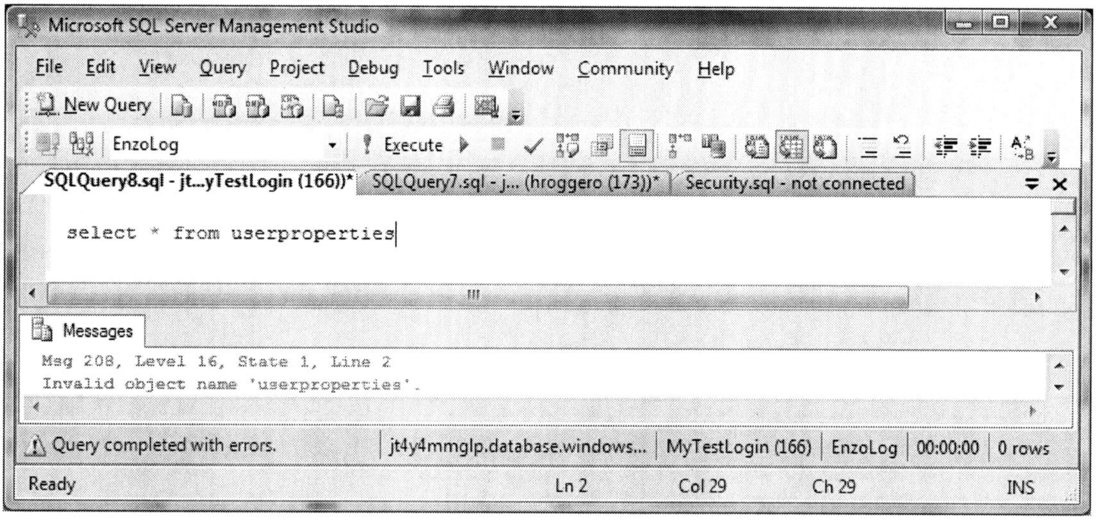

Figure 4-8. *Error when the user can't see an object*

The default schema of MyTestLoginUser is DBO, as shown in Figure 4-9. The default schema of a user is the schema that's used if none is specified in a T-SQL statement. To make it easier on developers, change the default schema to MyReadOnlySchema, so it doesn't have to be specified in T-SQL statements.

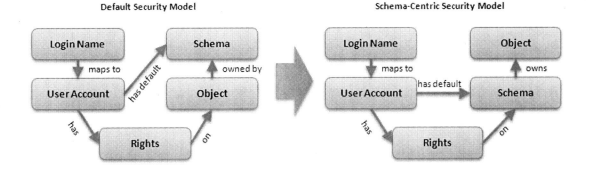

```
Microsoft SQL Server Management Studio
File   Edit   View   Query   Project   Debug   Tools   Window   Community   Help
New Query
EnzoLog                    ! Execute
```

SQLQuery8.sql - jt...yTestLogin (169))* SQLQuery7.sql - j... (hroggero (173))* Security.sql - not connected

```
SELECT name, default_schema_name FROM sys.database_principals
WHERE Name = 'MyTestLoginUser'
```

Results | Messages

	name	default_schema_name
1	MyTestLoginUser	dbo

Query executed successfully.   jt4y4mmglp.database.windows... MyTestLogin (169) EnzoLog 00:00:00 1 rows

Ready   Ln 4   Col 62   Ch 62   INS

Figure 4-9. Schema owner of a login

To change the user's default schema, you need to execute this statement:
```
ALTER USER MyTestLoginUser WITH DEFAULT_SCHEMA = MyReadOnlySchema
```
Now that the user has MyReadOnlySchema as its default schema, it can see the objects owned by
that schema directly, without having to specify the object owner. However, you haven't set the access
rights yet. Let's grant SELECT rights to MyTestLoginUser:
```
GRANT SELECT ON SCHEMA :: MyReadOnlySchema TO MyTestLoginUser
```
The following statement works again for the MyTestLoginUser account:
```
SELECT * FROM UserProperties
```
Why did you go through all this trouble? Because creating your own schemas is a great way to
simplify access control by granting rights to schemas instead of objects directly. In a way, schemas can
be used as a group, like a Windows Group, on which rights are granted or denied.

Figure 4-10 shows how you've switched the security model around for greater flexibility and control.

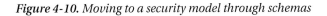

Figure 4-10. Moving to a security model through schemas

Firewall

SQL Azure comes with its own firewall, which you can configure directly from the SQL Azure portal, as previously covered in Chapter 3. You can also view and change firewall rules in T-SQL. Let's take a quick look at the available SQL statements.

■ **Note** You need to be connected to the master database to view or change firewall rules. At least one connection rule must be added to the firewall through the SQL Azure portal before a connection can be made.

To view the current firewall rules, execute this statement:

```
SELECT * FROM sys.firewall_rules
```

You can see that each rule has a name; the name is used as a unique key. The `sp_set_firewall_rule` command allows you to add a new rule.

It may take a few minutes for the new rules to take effect. For example, the following statement adds a new rule called NewRule. Notice that the first parameter must be a Unicode string:

```
sp_set_firewall_rule N'NewRule', '192.168.1.1', '192.168.1.10'
```

To delete a rule, run the following statement:

```
sp_delete_firewall_rule N'NewRule'
```

Compliance

Although cloud computing creates new challenges for organizations from a risk-management standpoint, Microsoft's cloud data centers undergo multiple audits and assessments based on their local regulations. In order to facilitate its compliance audits and assessment, Microsoft created the Operational Compliance team, which designed a common compliance framework for its operations.

According to Microsoft, its cloud computing infrastructure is compliant with multiple regulations including PCI, Health Insurance Portability and Accountability Act (HIPAA), and Sarbanes-Oxley. It also has achieved numerous certifications, including

- ISO/IEC 27001:2005

- SAS 70 Type I and II

■ **Note** For more information about Microsoft's compliance initiatives, visit www.globalfoundationservices.com.

Conclusion

Security in the cloud is a complex topic and involves careful analysis of your requirements and design options. This chapter covered the basics of the CIA triad and classified security options in terms of confidentiality, integrity, and availability.

You also reviewed how to plan for strong encryption and hashing in your Visual Studio applications. Finally, keep in mind that schema separation can be very useful and should be implemented early in your development cycles.

By now, you should understand the many options available to you in order to secure you data in SQL Azure and be aware of some of the limitations of the SQL Azure platform. Keep in mind, however, that some of those limitations are likely to be either removed or mitigated at some point in the future as Microsoft provides additional updates to its SQL Azure platform.

CHAPTER 5

■ ■ ■

Data Migration and Backup Strategies

When companies talk about their research into or experiences with the Azure technology—specifically the SQL side of Azure—two of their most frequent concerns (aside from security) are migrating local databases and data into the cloud, and backup strategies. Until Azure came around, databases were housed locally (and they still are): they're contained within the walls of the company or in a data center. Moving to the Azure platform, and SQL Azure, means moving and storing all or a portion of your data into the cloud.

Chapter 4 talked at length about security concerns, considerations, and best practices regarding storing your precious data in the cloud. Moving data into the cloud is a decision that you shouldn't and can't take lightly. But after you make the decision to utilize SQL Azure, the question becomes, how do you get your data into the cloud? As nice as it would be if moving your local database into SQL Azure was seamless, it isn't as cut-and-dried as you may think. You do you have several options available, all of which are viable; but you must consider things beyond just moving the data, such as costs from data transfers.

After your data is in the cloud, further questions arise regarding the backup strategies that are common with local databases. In SQL Azure, gone are the concepts of backup devices and backing up and restoring databases. As shocking as this may sound, remember that Microsoft is managing the hardware behind the scenes. For now, there are no such things as drives, devices, and so on.

In this chapter we will discuss the different migration tools, strategies and concepts for moving your database and data into the cloud and examples which illustrate how these tools are used. We'll then discuss a recently added feature to SQL Azure which allows the backup, or "copy" of a SQL Azure database.

Migrating Databases and Data to SQL Azure

So you want to move one or more of your applications and their databases to the cloud. It's a noble idea. More than likely, you're in the same category as countless others who are looking into moving applications into the cloud: you don't want to start from scratch. You'd rather migrate an existing application to the cloud, but you aren't sure about the steps necessary to do so, or the technologies available to help in the process. This section discusses three tools from Microsoft and come with SQL Server:

- Generate and Publish Scripts Wizard
- SQL Server Integration Services
- Bcp utility

In addition to these three tools, we will also briefly mention a free utility found on CodePlex called the SQL Azure Migration Wizard which provides a wizard-driven interface to walk you through migrating your database and data to SQL Azure.

The examples in this chapter use SQL Server 2008 R2 Community Technology Preview (CTP), which at the time of this writing is available from Microsoft's MSDN site. These examples also work with SQL Server 2008, although some the screens may be a bit different.

You may wonder why the SQL Server Import and Export Wizard isn't listed here. The answer is that the SQL Server Import and Export Wizard isn't supported for SQL Azure yet. Microsoft is working on it. No timeframe has been given as to when the Import/Export Wizard will support SQL Azure, but support is definitely in the works.

The database you use in these examples is TechBio, which you can download from the Apress web site for this book. This sample database is a mini version of the TechBio database that is behind the TechBio application found in the download for this book.

Generate and Publish Scripts Wizard

The Generate and Publish Scripts Wizard is used to create T-SQL scripts for SQL Server databases and/or related objects within the selected database. You have probably used this wizard, so this section doesn't walk through it step by step; instead, the section briefly highlights a few steps in the wizard and points out the options necessary to effectively work with SQL Azure.

SQL Server 2008 R2 comes with the ability to script an on-premises database for the SQL Azure environment. Because many haven't moved to SQL Server 2008 R2, the examples in this section use the version prior to R2, which is the original release of SQL Server 2008.

One of the differences between SQL Server 2008 R2 and SQL Server 2008 (pertaining to object scripting) is a setting in the Advanced Scripting Options dialog as you go through the wizard. This dialog includes two properties you can set regarding the version of SQL Server for which you're scripting database objects: Script for Server Version and "Script for the database engine type." The Script for Server Version option lists the version of SQL Server that the Generate and Publish Scripts wizard supports, which ranges from SQL Server 2000 to SQL Server 2008 R2.

The "Script for the database engine type" property has two options you can choose from: "Stand-alone instance" and "SQL Azure database." The "SQL Azure database" option only works with the SQL Server 2008 R2 Server version. For example, if you set the Script for Server version to SQL Server 2008 (non R2) and then set the "Script for the database engine type" property to "SQL Azure database," the Script for Server version property value automatically changes to SQL Server 2008 R2.

The Generate and Publish Scripts Wizard does a really nice job of appropriately scripting objects for SQL Azure. The wizard checks for unsupported syntax and data types, and checks for primary keys on each table. Thus, the following example sets SQL for Server Version to SQL Server 2008 (non R2) for several reasons. First, many people aren't using SQL Server 2008 R2 and therefore don't have the option to script for SQL Azure. Second, this exercise shows you what steps are needed to get a script ready to run in SQL Azure.

Starting the Wizard

To start the Generate and Publish Scripts Wizard in SQL Server Management Studio (SSMS), open Object Explorer and expand the Databases node. Select a database, right-click it, and then select Generate Scripts from the context menu.

On the wizard's Introduction page for SQL Server 2008 R2, you're informed that you must follow four steps to complete this wizard:

1. Select database objects.

2. Specify scripting or publishing objects.

3. Review selections.

4. Generate scripts.

The following sections work through these steps.

Choosing Target Objects

To select your target database objects, follow these steps:

1. On the Introduction page of the Generate and Publish Scripts Wizard, click Next.

2. On the Choose Objects page (see Figure 5-1), select the "Select specific database objects" option, because for the purposes of this example, you simply want to select a few objects to migrate.

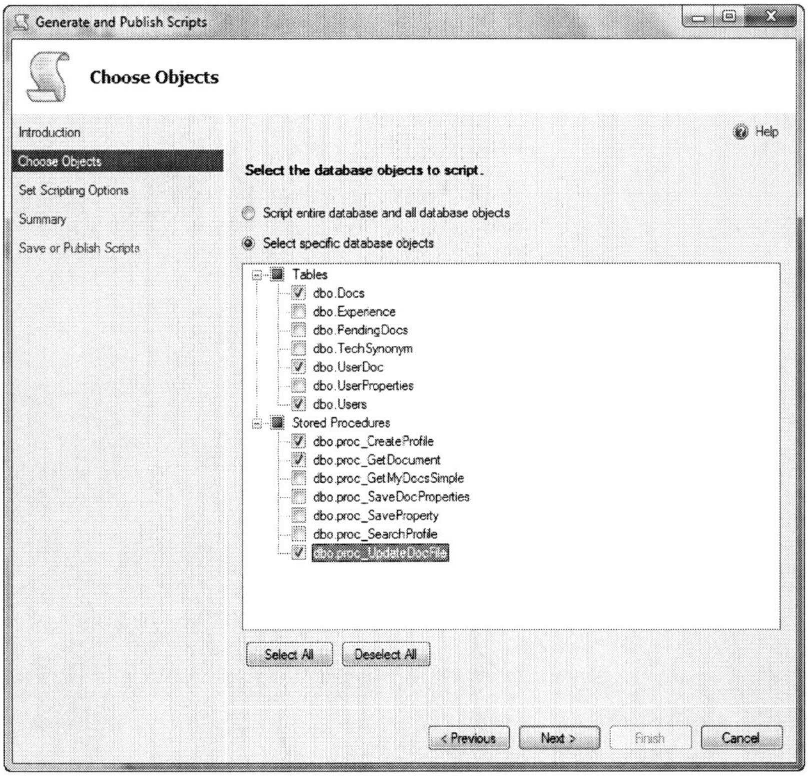

Figure 5-1. Choosing objects to migrate into script form

3. In the list of objects in Figure 5-1, expand the Tables and Stored Procedures nodes, and select the following objects:

- Tables: Docs, UserDoc, and Users

- Stored procedures: proc_CreateProfile, proc_GetDocument, and proc_UpdateDocFile

4. Click Next on the Choose Objects page.

5. On the Set Scripting Objects page, select the "Save to new query window" option shown in Figure 5-2, and then click the Advanced button.

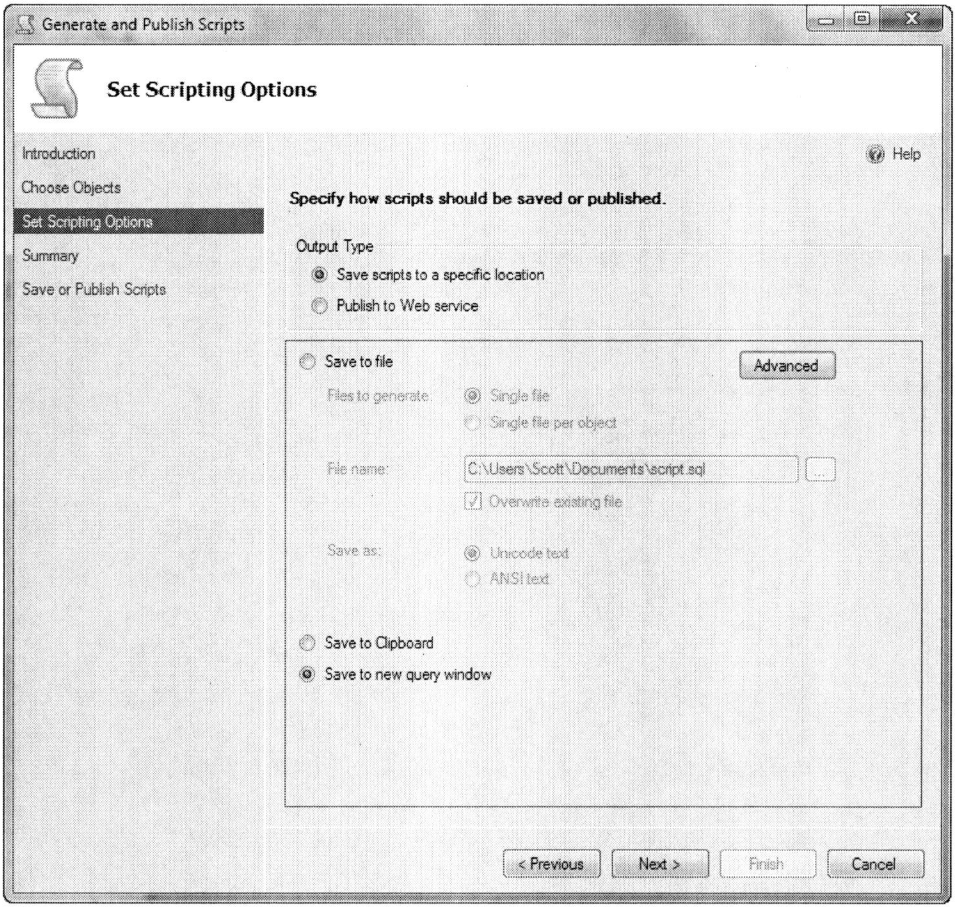

Figure 5-2. Scripting options

Setting Advanced Options

Clicking the Advanced button brings up the Advanced Scripting Options dialog shown in Figure 5-3. Follow these steps:

1. In the Advanced Scripting Options dialog, set the following options:

   - Convert UDDTs to Base Types = True

   - Script Extended Properties = False

   - Script Logins = False

   - Script USE DATABASE = False

   - Types of data to script = Schema and data

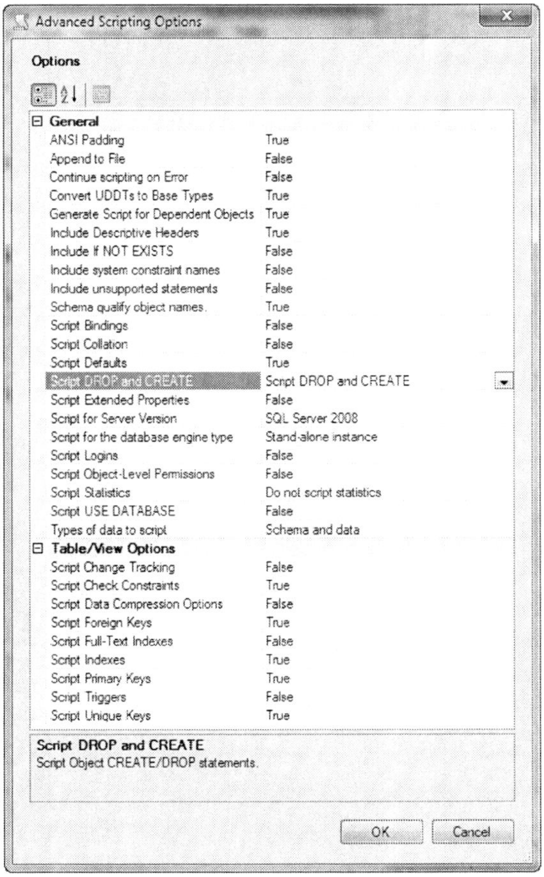

Figure 5-3. Advanced Scripting Options dialog

You can also set the Script DROP and CREATE option to Script DROP and CREATE, as shown in Figure 5-3, but that option isn't required for SQL Azure.

2. Click OK in the Advanced Scripting Options dialog, and then click Next in the Generate Scripts wizard.

Saving and Publishing

Complete the wizard with these steps:

1. On the wizard's Summary page, review your selections, and then click Next. The T-SQL script is generated, and you're taken to the Save or Publish Scripts page (see Figure 5-4).

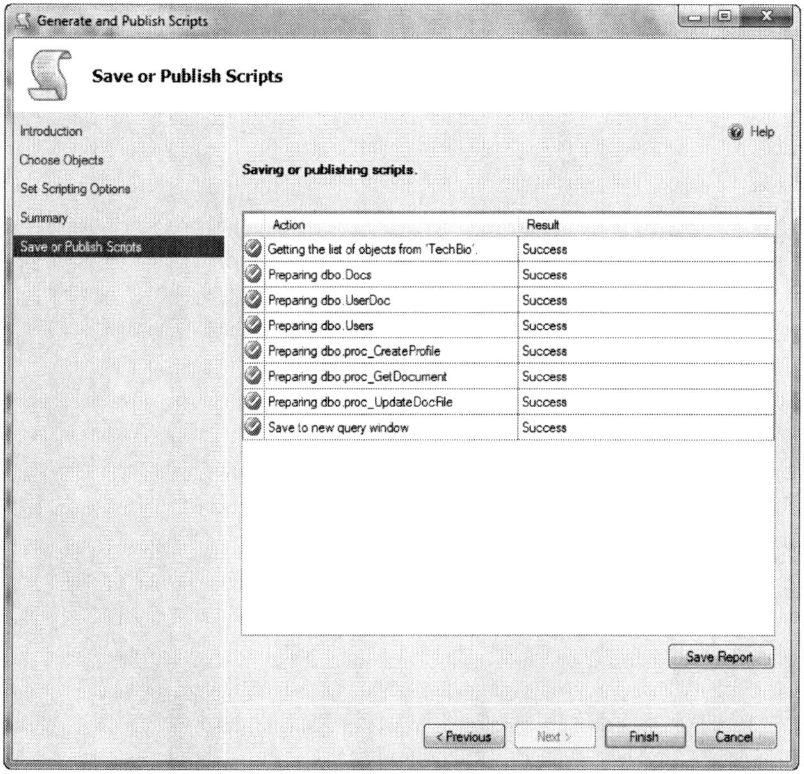

Figure 5-4. Completed Scripted Process

2. Click Finish. At this point your script is finished and is displayed in a query window in SSMS.

Reviewing the Generated Script

Open the file you created, and let's take a quick look at the generated T-SQL. The following snippet from what you see shows the creation of three tables and three stored procedures, and a few INSERT statements that add rows of data to some of the tables. Except for the things you told the script-generation wizard to ignore, the following T-SQL looks like all other object creation T-SQL you typically deal with on a daily basis:

```
/****** Object:  Table [dbo].[Users]     Script Date: 03/31/2010 23:39:20 ******/
SET ANSI_NULLS ON
GO
SET QUOTED_IDENTIFIER ON
GO
SET ANSI_PADDING ON
GO
CREATE TABLE [dbo].[Users](
      [ID] [int] IDENTITY(1,1) NOT NULL,
    [Name] [nvarchar](50) NULL,
    [NTUserName] [nvarchar](128) NULL,
    [Domain] [nvarchar](50) NOT NULL,
    [Intro] [nvarchar](100) NULL,
    [Title] [nvarchar](50) NOT NULL,
    [State] [nvarchar](10) NOT NULL,
    [Country] [nvarchar](100) NULL,
    [PWD] [varbinary](100) NULL,
    [rowguid] [uniqueidentifier] DEFAULT NEWSEQUENTIALID()
PRIMARY KEY CLUSTERED
(
    [ID] ASC
)WITH (PAD_INDEX  = OFF, STATISTICS_NORECOMPUTE  = OFF,
IGNORE_DUP_KEY = OFF, ALLOW_ROW_LOCKS  = ON,
ALLOW_PAGE_LOCKS  = ON) ON [PRIMARY]
) ON [PRIMARY]
GO
SET ANSI_PADDING OFF
GO

SET IDENTITY_INSERT [dbo].[Users] ON
INSERT [dbo].[Users] ([ID], [Name], [NTUserName], [Domain], [Intro], [Title],
    [State], [Country], [PWD])
VALUES (1, N'Herve Roggero', N'hroggero', N'PYNLOGIC',
N'Enterprise and Azure Architect; Speaker. Expert knowledge in C#. Prev. mgmt exp.',
N'Azure Architect', N'FL', N'US',
0xE8F97FBA9104D1EA5047948E6DFB67FACD9F5B73)

INSERT [dbo].[Users] ([ID], [Name], [NTUserName], [Domain], [Intro], [Title],
    [State], [Country], [PWD])
VALUES (2, N'Jim Mullis', N'jmullis', N'PYNLOGIC',
N'Expert in software development. C++; Oracle; SQL Server DBA', N'', N'FL', N'US',
0xE8F97FBA9104D1EA5047948E6DFB67FACD9F5B73)

INSERT [dbo].[Users] ([ID], [Name], [NTUserName], [Domain], [Intro], [Title],
```

```
        [State], [Country], [PWD])
VALUES (3, N'Scott Klein', N'sklein', N'',
N'Expert in software development. MVP SQL Server. Author. Speaker.',
N'Architect', N'FL', N'US', 0xE8F97FBA9104D1EA5047948E6DFB67FACD9F5B73)
SET IDENTITY_INSERT [dbo].[Users] OFF

/****** Object:  StoredProcedure [dbo].[proc_CreateProfile]
Script Date: 03/31/2010 23:39:21 ******/
SET ANSI_NULLS ON
GO
SET QUOTED_IDENTIFIER ON
GO
CREATE PROCEDURE [dbo].[proc_CreateProfile]
    @uid [nvarchar](50),
    @pwd [nvarchar](50),
    @name [nvarchar](50),
    @title [nvarchar](50),
    @country [nvarchar](50),
    @state [nvarchar](20),
    @rowguid uniqueidentifier
WITH RECOMPILE, ENCRYPTION
AS
DECLARE @password varbinary(100)
SET @password = HASHBYTES('sha1', @pwd)

-- Make sure the UID is not already taken...
IF (Exists(SELECT TOP 1 * FROM Users WHERE NTUserName = @uid))
BEGIN
    RAISERROR(N'0x001 - User ID already in use', 16, 1)
END
ELSE
BEGIN
    INSERT INTO Users
        (Name, NTUserName, Domain, Intro, Title, State, Country, PWD, rowguid)
    VALUES
        (@name, @uid, '', '', @title, @state, @country, @password, @rowguid)
 END
GO
```

Notice that the script enables several options, such as ANSI_NULL and ANSI_PADDING. Then, the script creates the Users table. This table has an IDENTITY column as well as a rowguid column that uses the uniqueidentifier database. The rowguid column also has a default on it, which uses the NEWSEQUENTIALID() function to automatically generate new GUIDs. This table is created on the PRIMARY file group, followed by the setting of several table options via the WITH clause.

Further down in the script, several stored procedures are created, one of which is shown in the preceding code snippet. proc_CreateProfile is a standard stored procedure that accepts several input parameters and uses the WITH option to specify procedure options: in this case, RECOMPILE (to indicate that the database engine doesn't need to cache a plan for this procedure and to compile the procedure at runtime) and ENCRYPTION (indicating that SQL Server converts the text of this stored procedure to an obfuscated format).

Fixing the Script

Because you selected to script for SQL Server 2008, the script includes some syntax and statements that aren't supported in SQL Azure. Figure 5-5 shows some of the errors you see if you try to run the script as generated.

```
Messages
Msg 40508, Level 16, State 1, Line 1
USE statement is not supported to switch between databases. Use a new connection to connect to a different Database.
Msg 40517, Level 16, State 1, Line 17
Keyword or statement option 'pad_index' is not supported in this version of SQL Server.
Msg 1088, Level 16, State 11, Line 1
Cannot find the object "dbo.Docs" because it does not exist or you do not have permissions.
Msg 40517, Level 16, State 1, Line 17
Keyword or statement option 'pad_index' is not supported in this version of SQL Server.
Msg 1088, Level 16, State 11, Line 1
Cannot find the object "dbo.Users" because it does not exist or you do not have permissions.
Msg 40514, Level 16, State 6, Line 3
'Filegroup reference and partitioning scheme' is not supported in this version of SQL Server.
Msg 208, Level 16, State 1, Line 2
Invalid object name 'dbo.UserDoc'.
```

Figure 5-5. SQL Azure execution errors

Another problem is that SQL Azure doesn't support *heap tables*. A heap table is one without a clustered index. SQL Azure currently supports only clustered tables. Here's what to do:

1. Delete all instances of SET ANSI_NULLS ON.

2. Delete all instances of ON [PRIMARY].

3. Delete all instance of PAD_INDEX = OFF as well as ALLOW_ROW_LOCKS = ON and ALLOW_PAGE_LOCKS = ON.

4. In the Users table, modify the rowguid column, changing DEFAULT NEWSEQUENTIALID() to NULL.

5. In the stored procedure, remove the ENCRYPTION clause.

6. Add a clustered index to any heap tables.

Appendix B discusses the need for these changes in detail. For now, here's a quick explanation:

- ON [PRIMARY] isn't needed because, as you learned in Chapters 1 and 2, SQL Azure hides all hardware-specific access and information. There is no concept of PRIMARY or file groups because disk space is handled by Microsoft, so this option isn't required.

- According to SQL Server Books Online (BOL) you can remove the entire WITH clause that contains the table options. However, the only table options you really need to remove are those listed in step 3 (PAD_INDEX, ALLOW_ROW_LOCKS, and ALLOW_PAGE_LOCKS).

- The NEWSEQUENTIALID() function isn't supported in SQL Azure because there is no CLR support in SQL Azure, and thus all CLR-based types aren't supported. The NEWSEQUENTIALID() return value is one of those types. Also, the ENCRYPTION option isn't supported because SQL Azure as a whole doesn't yet support encryption.

- SQL Azure doesn't support heap tables. Thus, you need to change any heap table into a clustered table by adding a clustered index. (Interestingly, if you execute one statement at a time, you can, in fact, *create* a heap table. However, any inserts into that table fail.)

A word about the final item in the list. The syntax for defining a clustered index looks like this:

```
CREATE TABLE [dbo].[UserDocs]
(
    [UserID] [int] NOT NULL,
    [DocID] [int] NOT NULL
PRIMARY KEY CLUSTERED
(
    [UserID], [DocID] ASC
)
)
```

One of the things the SQL Azure documentation suggests, and which is listed earlier, is to set the Convert UDDTs to Base Types property to True. This is because user-defined types aren't supported in SQL Azure.

After you make the changes just described to your SQL script, it should look like the following:

```
/****** Object:  Table [dbo].[Users]    Script Date: 03/31/2010 23:39:20 ******/
SET QUOTED_IDENTIFIER ON
GO
SET ANSI_PADDING ON
GO
CREATE TABLE [dbo].[Users](
    [ID] [int] IDENTITY(1,1) NOT NULL,
    [Name] [nvarchar](50) NULL,
    [NTUserName] [nvarchar](128) NULL,
    [Domain] [nvarchar](50) NOT NULL,
    [Intro] [nvarchar](100) NULL,
    [Title] [nvarchar](50) NOT NULL,
    [State] [nvarchar](10) NOT NULL,
    [Country] [nvarchar](100) NULL,
    [PWD] [varbinary](100) NULL,
    [rowguid] [uniqueidentifier] NULL
PRIMARY KEY CLUSTERED
(
    [ID] ASC
)WITH (STATISTICS_NORECOMPUTE  = OFF, IGNORE_DUP_KEY = OFF)
)
GO
SET ANSI_PADDING OFF
GO

SET IDENTITY_INSERT [dbo].[Users] ON
INSERT [dbo].[Users] ([ID], [Name], [NTUserName], [Domain], [Intro], [Title],
    [State], [Country], [PWD])
```

```sql
VALUES (1, N'Herve Roggero', N'hroggero', N'PYNLOGIC',
N'Enterprise and Azure Architect; Speaker. Expert knowledge in C#. Prev. mgmt exp.',
N'Azure Architect', N'FL', N'US',
0xE8F97FBA9104D1EA5047948E6DFB67FACD9F5B73)

INSERT [dbo].[Users] ([ID], [Name], [NTUserName], [Domain], [Intro], [Title],
    [State], [Country], [PWD])
VALUES (2, N'Jim Mullis', N'jmullis', N'PYNLOGIC',
N'Expert in software development. C++; Oracle; SQL Server DBA', N'', N'FL', N'US',
0xE8F97FBA9104D1EA5047948E6DFB67FACD9F5B73)

INSERT [dbo].[Users] ([ID], [Name], [NTUserName], [Domain], [Intro], [Title],
    [State], [Country], [PWD])
VALUES (3, N'Scott Klein', N'sklein', N'',
N'Expert in software development. MVP SQL Server. Author. Speaker.',
N'Architect', N'FL', N'US', 0xE8F97FBA9104D1EA5047948E6DFB67FACD9F5B73)
SET IDENTITY_INSERT [dbo].[Users] OFF

/****** Object:  StoredProcedure [dbo].[proc_CreateProfile]
Script Date: 03/31/2010 23:39:21 ******/
SET QUOTED_IDENTIFIER ON
GO
CREATE PROCEDURE [dbo].[proc_CreateProfile]
    @uid [nvarchar](50),
    @pwd [nvarchar](50),
    @name [nvarchar](50),
    @title [nvarchar](50),
    @country [nvarchar](50),
    @state [nvarchar](20),
    @rowguid uniqueidentifier
WITH RECOMPILE
AS
DECLARE @password varbinary(100)
SET @password = HASHBYTES('sha1', @pwd)

-- Make sure the UID is not already taken...
IF (Exists(SELECT TOP 1 * FROM Users WHERE NTUserName = @uid))
BEGIN
    RAISERROR(N'0x001 - User ID already in use', 16, 1)
END
ELSE
BEGIN
    INSERT INTO Users
        (Name, NTUserName, Domain, Intro, Title, State, Country, PWD, rowguid)
    VALUES
        (@name, @uid, '', '', @title, @state, @country, @password, @rowguid)
 END
GO
```

Now that you've made the necessary corrections, you're ready to create your objects in a SQL Azure database.

Executing the Script Against an Azure Database

You don't have a SQL Azure database to run the script against, so let's create one now:

1. Connect to your SQL Azure instance (refer to Chapter 2 for reference if needed), making sure you're connecting to the master database.

2. Open a new query window, and use the syntax discussed in Chapter 2 to create your SQL Azure database. Name it TechBio, because this is the name the examples use throughout this chapter.

3. Click over to the generated script. This query window is currently connected to your local SQL instance, so you need to change it to your SQL Azure instance and the database you just created. Right-click anywhere in the script, and select Connection → Change Connection from the context menu.

4. In the Connect to Database Engine dialog, enter the information for your SQL Azure instance, and enter the name of the database you just created on the Connection Properties tab.

5. Click Connect.

You now have your script, a database, and a connection to that database. Click the Execute button. Your script should run and create the tables, procedures, and data in your SQL Azure Database.

The SQL Server Generate and Publish Script wizard is a great way to start understanding the required changes that need to be made when migrating to SQL Azure. With this foundation, let's discuss one of the other options, SQL Server Integration Services.

SQL Server Integration Services

SQL Server Integration Services (SSIS) is a data-integration and workflow-solutions platform, providing ETL (Extract, Transformation, Load) solutions for data warehousing as well as extractions and transformations. With its graphical tools and wizards, developers often find that SSIS is a quick solution for moving data between a source and destination. As such, it's a great choice for migrating data between a local database and a SQL Azure database. Notice, however, that the previous sentence says *data*. When you're using SSIS, the database and tables must already exist in SQL Azure.

▓ **Note** Volumes of information (books, articles, online help, and so on) are available about SSIS. This section isn't intended to be an SSIS primer. If you're unfamiliar with SSIS, this section provides enough information to give you a foundation and get you started.

If you're familiar at any level with SSIS, you're probably wondering why it has the limitation of only moving data. Several SSIS tasks can provide the functionality of moving objects as well data, such as the Transfer SQL Server Objects task. When asked about this task, Microsoft replied that SSIS relies on SMO (SQL **Server Management Objects**) for this task, and SMO doesn't currently support SQL Azure. In addition, some of the SSIS connection managers use SMO and therefore are limited when dealing with objects. Thus, the current solution is to create databases and tables using straight SQL and then use SSIS to do the actual data transfer. The following section illustrates how to use SSIS move migrate your data from on-premise SQL to SQL Azure.

Creating an Integration Services Project

To create your project, follow these steps:

1. Fire up Business Intelligence Development Studio (BIDS) by choosing Programs → Microsoft SQL Server 2008 → Business Intelligence Development Studio.

2. When BIDS opens and the New Project dialog displays, select Business Intelligence Projects from the list of project types, and then select Integration Services Project, as shown in Figure 5-6. Click OK.

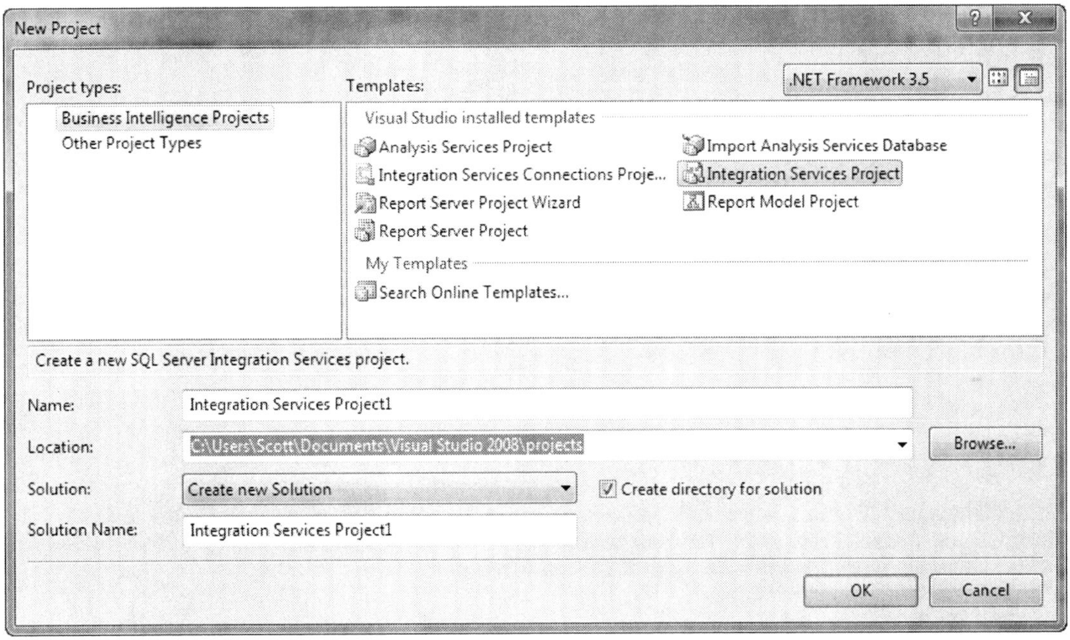

Figure 5-6. Creating a new SSIS project

You now see an SSIS package designer surface. This surface has several tabs along the top: Control Flow, Data Flow, Event Handlers, and Package Explorer, shown in Figure 5-7. This example uses the Control Flow and Data Flow tabs.

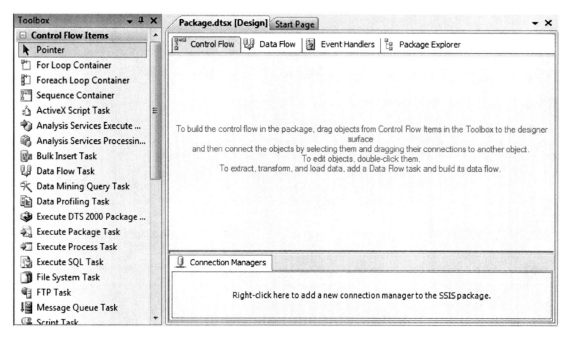

Figure 5-7. *SSIS Designer*

In Visual Studio, select View → Toolbox. The Toolbox contains a plethora of what are called *tasks*, which are control and data-flow elements that define units of work that are contained and preformed within a package. You use a few of these tasks to migrate the data from your local database to your SQL Azure database.

Clearing Any Preexisting Data

Let's clear any data that exists in the SQL Azure database so you can start with a clean slate. In SSMS, open a new query connecting to the TechBio database, and delete the data from the UserDocs, Users, and Docs tables by executing the following DELETE statements:

```
DELETE FROM UserDocs
DELETE FROM Docs
DELETE FROM Users
```

All three of those tables should now contain no data, as shown in Figure 5-8.

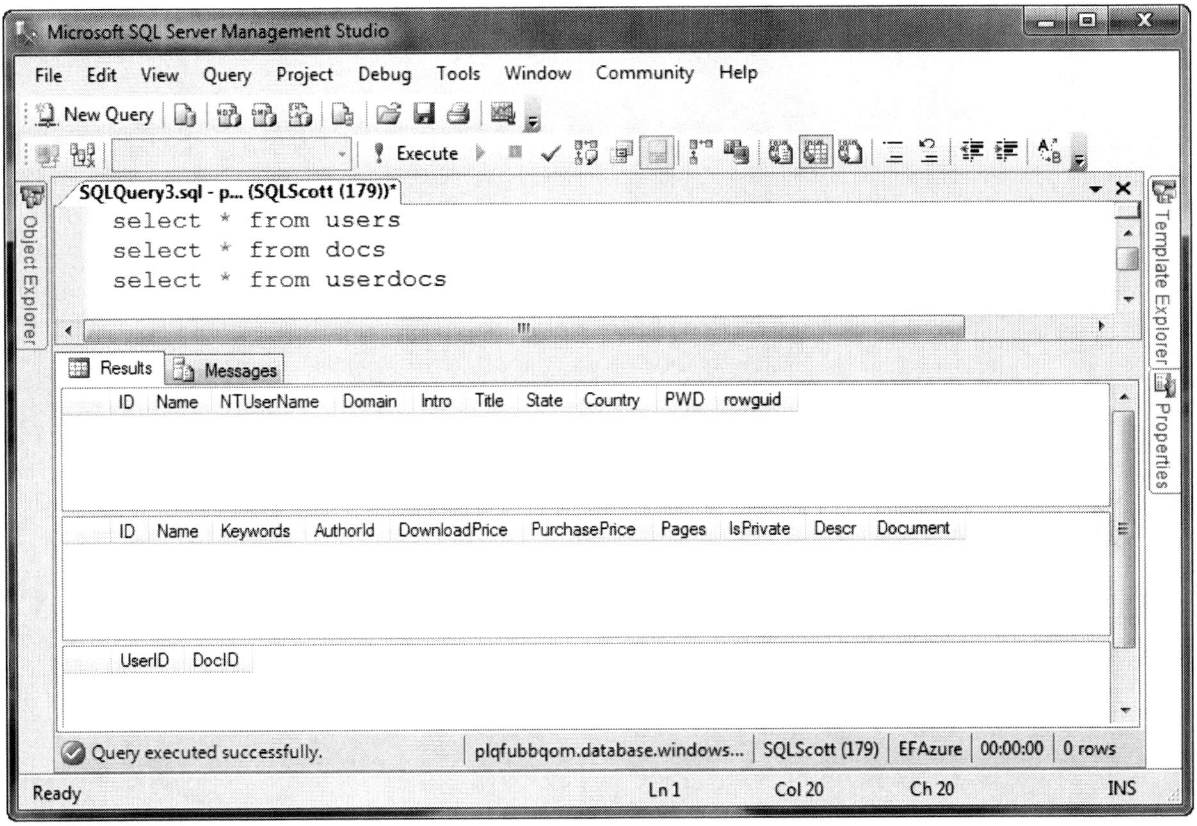

Figure 5-8. Checking for existing data

Building a Migration Package

Let's start building an SSIS package to migrate your data. Follow these steps:

1. In the SSIS package designer, select the Control Flow tab, and drag an Execute SQL task and three data flow tasks from the Toolbox onto the Control Flow designer.

2. Right-click Execute SQL task, and select Edit from the context menu. The Execute SQL Task Editor opens.

3. Change the task name to **Clear Data**, leave the Connection Type as OLE DB, and leave the SQLSourceType as Direct Input.

4. In the Connection property, select <New connection>, as shown in Figure 5-9. The Connection Manager dialog opens (see Figure 5-10).

101

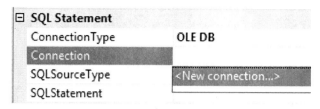

Figure 5-9. *Adding a new connection*

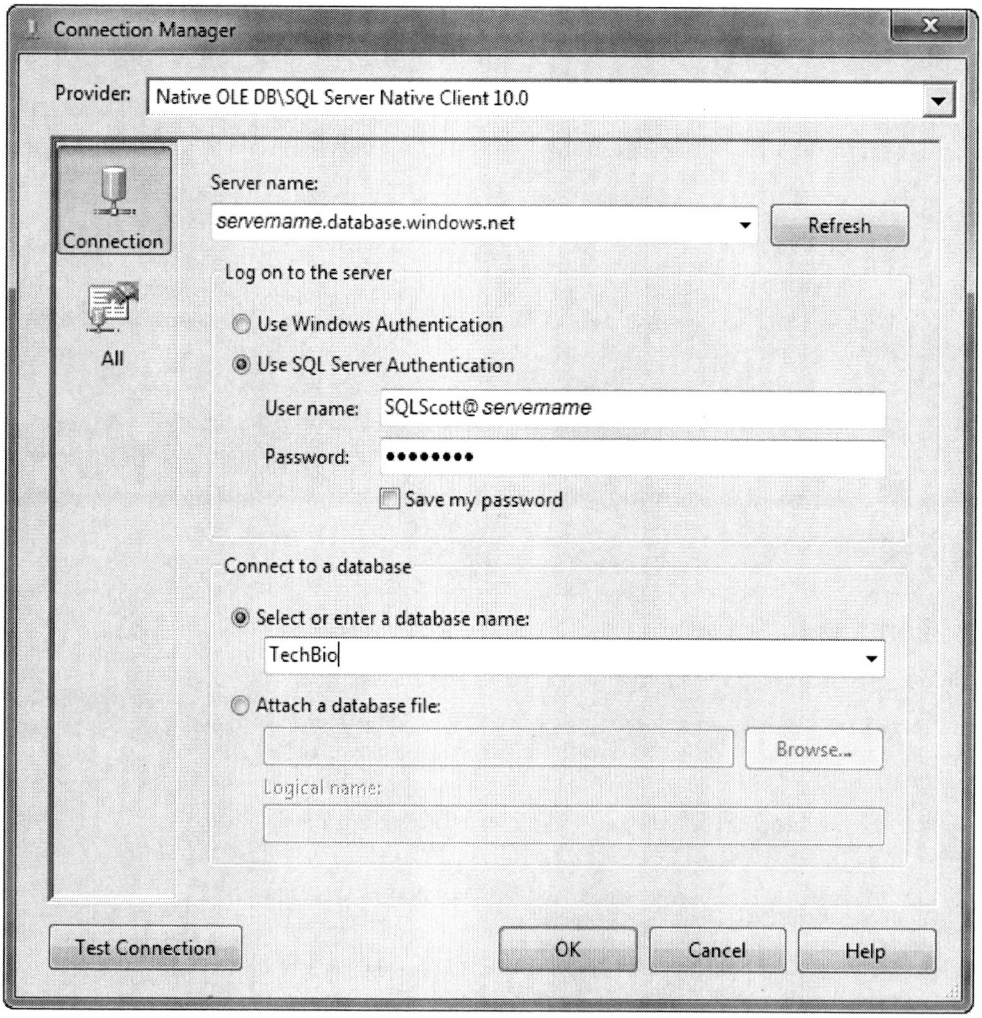

Figure 5-10. *Entering the connection information*

5. In the Connection Manager dialog, enter the server name of your SQL Azure server, select Use SQL Authentication, and enter your SQL Azure username and password. The username must be in the format *username@server* where *username* is your Administrator username or a valid SQL Azure username and *server* is the first part of the server name (the piece prior to .database.windows.net).

6. In the "Select or enter a database name" field, the OLE DB provider doesn't return a list of databases. No big deal: type in the name **TechBio**.

7. Click the Test Connection button. If you've entered everything correctly and your firewall is set up, your test connection succeeds.

8. Click OK in the Connection Manager dialog.

9. Back in the Execute SQL Task Editor, click the ellipsis button in the SQLStatement property to display a small Enter SQL Query dialog in which to enter one or more T-SQL statements. Enter the following DELETE statements, which clear out the data from the previous example. (This isn't critical, but it gives you a clean slate to start with.)

```
DELETE FROM UserDocs
DELETE FROM Users
DELETE FROM Docs
```

10. Click OK in the Enter SQL Query dialog. The Execute SQL Task Editor dialog should look like Figure 5-11. Click OK.

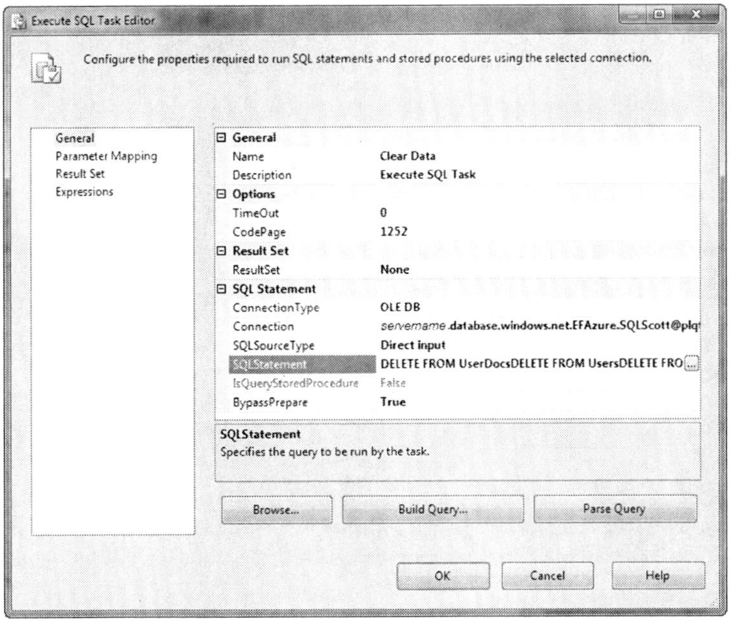

Figure 5-11. Execute SQL Task Editor

11. Back on the Control Flow tab in the SSIS package designer, make sure the Clear Data task is highlighted. Notice the green arrow coming from the bottom of the Clear Data task: click anywhere on this green arrow, and drag it to the first data flow task. Doing so creates a connection from the Clear Data task to the first data flow task, signifying the flow of execution. You can see an example of this in Figure 5-14.When the Clear Data task has completed executing, the first data flow task will then execute.

12. Let's add logic to the first data flow task. Double-click the linked data flow task (or right-click and select Edit). Doing so takes you to the Data Flow tab.

13. Drag an OLE DB Source task and an OLE DB Destination task to the Data Flow designer surface. This is where the actions of pulling data from the source database (the local DB) and copying it to the destination database (SQL Azure) take place.

14. Right-click the OLE DB Source task, and click Edit. Doing so opens the OLE DB Source Editor, where you define a connection to your local database, such as the connection shown in Figure 5-10. You already have a connection to the SQL Azure database, but you need to create a connection to your local database that your tasks use to copy the data.

15. On the OLE DB Source Editor task, you see the connection to the SQL Azure database. Click the New button to open the Configure OLE DB Connection Manager dialog. Click New again to open the Connection Manager dialog you saw in Figure 5-10.

16. In this dialog, enter the information to connect to your local copy of the TechBio database.

17. Test the connection, and then click OK in the Connection Manager dialog.

18. Click OK in the Configure OLE DB Connection Manager dialog.

19. Back in the OLE DB Source Editor, click the Table/View drop-down, select the Docs table, and then click OK.

20. As you did for the control flow task, drag the green arrow from the OLE DB Source task to the OLE DB Destination task.

21. Double-click the OLE DB Source task to edit the task properties, which is where the data is going: the SQL Azure database. Because you've already created a connection to the SQL Azure database, you can use that connection. In the OLE DB Destination Editor, select the SQL Azure connection, and then select the Docs table from the drop-down list of tables. Oops—you get the error shown in Figure 5-12.

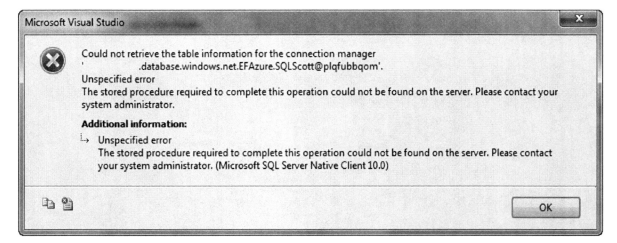

Figure 5-12. OLE DB connection error

This is interesting, because you didn't get this error when configuring the Execute SQL task. The difference is that the two Connection Manager dialogs don't operate quite the same way. The Connection Manager dialog for the Execute SQL task let you type in the table name, whereas the Connection Manager dialog for the OLE DB Destination task required you to select from the list. But when you expanded the list, you received the error shown in Figure 5-12.

The fix is to use an ADO.NET destination instead of the OLE DB destination. To do this, continue as follows:

22. Delete the OLE DB Destination task, and drag an ADO.NET Destination task onto the surface.

23. Connect to the two tasks, and then double-click the ADO.NET Destination task to configure it.

24. In the ADO.NET Destination Editor dialog, click the New button to configure a new ADO.NET connection.

25. Walk through the same steps as in the previous two connection configurations. This time, you're able to type the database name in the Connection Manager dialog.

26. Click OK in the all the dialogs until you're back to the ADO.NET Destination Editor.

27. Before you click OK in this dialog, click Mappings at left, as shown in Figure 5-13. Doing so ensures that the source table columns are appropriately mapped to the destination table columns. Click OK in the ADO.NET Destination Editor

If you're new to SSIS, congratulations: you've just configured your first SSIS data flow. Your data flow should look like Figure 5-14—not very exciting, but useful nonetheless. If you aren't new to SSIS, you still deserve congratulations, because you've successfully configured a data flow to migrate data to the cloud.

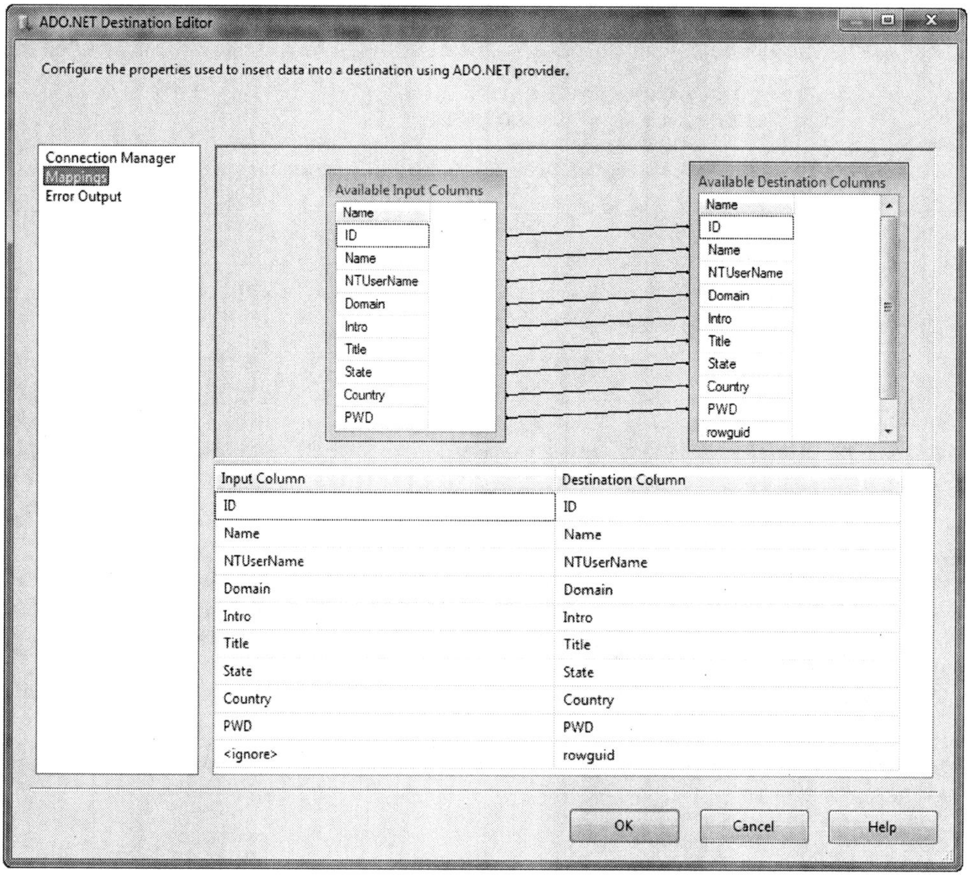

Figure 5-13. *ADO.NET Destination Editor with mappings*

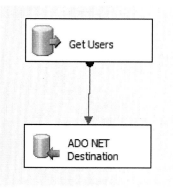

Figure 5-14. *Data flow*

Put down the root beer, though, because you aren't quite done. Continue with these steps:

28. Go back to the Control Flow tab, and connect the first data flow task to the second data flow task, and connect the second and third data flow tasks.

29. Double-click the second data flow task, and do the same thing you did for the first data flow beginning in step 12. You don't need to re-create the connections, but in the Source and Destination Editors for the second data flow, select the Users table.

30. Repeat the process for the third data flow task, this time selecting the UserDocs table.

When you're finished, your control flow task should look like Figure 5-15. The tasks aren't green (yet), but the flow should be similar.

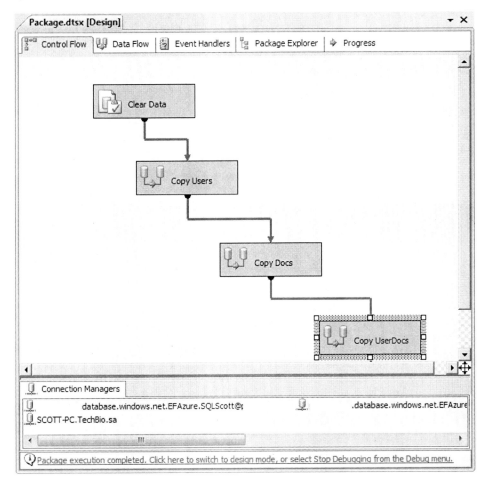

Figure 5-15. Successful execution of an SSIS package

Executing Your Migration Package

You're now ready to test your SSIS package. In Visual Studio, click the green arrow on the toolbar to begin package execution. Execution starts at the Clear Data task—which, as you recall, deletes all the data from the UserDocs, Users, and Docs tables. Execution next goes to the first data flow, which queries data from the local Docs table (source) and copies it to the TechBio database in the Docs table in SQL Azure (destination). Execution then goes the second and third data flow tasks.

When execution is complete, all the tasks are green, as shown in Figure 5-15, letting you know that they executed successfully. Any tasks that are yellow are currently executing. Red tasks are bad: that means an error occurred during the execution of the task, regardless of whether the task was in the control flow or data flow, and execution stops.

If your tasks are all green, you can go back to your root beer. Otherwise, the best place to start debugging is the Output window. All output, including errors, is written to this window. You can find errors easily by looking for any line that starts with Error: toward the end of the list.

Errors you receive may be SSIS specific or SQL Azure specific. For example, did you define your connections correctly? Microsoft makes testing connections very simple, and this doesn't mean the Test Connection button. The Source Editors dialog—regardless if whether it's an OLE DB or ADO.NET Editor—includes a Preview button that provides a small preview of your data, up to 200 rows. This ensures that at least your source connection works correctly.

Verifying the Migration

When you have everything working and executing smoothly, in Visual Studio click the blue square button on the toolbar to stop execution. Go back to SSMS, and query the three tables in your SQL Azure instance to verify that data indeed copied successfully. As shown in Figure 5-16, you should see roughly 100 rows in the Users table, two rows in the Docs table, and two rows in the UserDocs table.

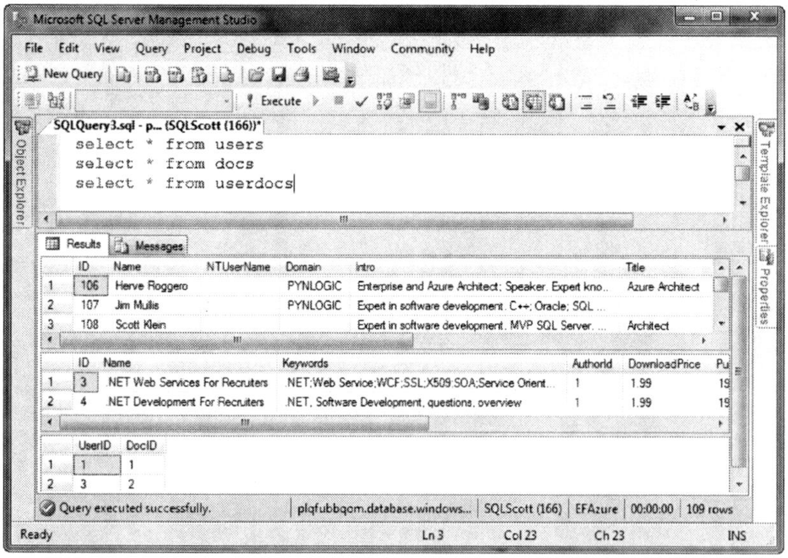

Figure 5-16. *Viewing migrated data in SSMS*

Other Cases to Consider

This example was simple; the source and destination tables were mirrors of each other, including column names and data types. This made data migration easy. However, in some cases the source and destination tables differ in column names and data types. There are tasks that help with this, such as the Derived Column, Data Conversion, and Lookup tasks. If you're using these tasks and are getting errors, start by looking at these tasks to make sure they aren't the source of data-truncation or data-conversion errors.

Again, this section isn't intended to be an SSIS primer. Great books about SSIS are available that focus on beginner topics all the way to advanced topics. Brian Knight is a SQL Server MVP who has written numerous books on SSIS; his books are highly recommended if you're looking for SSIS information and instruction.So far we have talked about SSIS and the SQL Server Generate and Publish Scripts wizard which both offer viable options for migrating your data, but with little differences. For example, SSIS doesn't migrate schema while the Scripts wizard does. Let's talk about the third tool, Bcp, which also provides a method for migrating data to SQL Azure.

Bcp

The bcp utility provides bulk copying of data between instances of Microsoft SQL Server. This utility is installed with SQL Server and requires no knowledge or understanding of T-SQL syntax. If you aren't familiar with the bcp utility, don't confuse or associate its functionality with that of the Import/Export Wizard in SQL Server. Although the bcp documentation refers to what bcp does as a "bulk copy," be aware that you can't bcp data from a source into a destination with a single statement. You must first bcp the data out of the source; then, you can bcp the data in to the destination.

▪ **Note** The bcp utility is very flexible and powerful, and you can apply a lot of options to it. This section doesn't go into the entire range of bcp options or dive deep into the many uses of the utility. You can find that information in the SQL Server Books Online or on the Microsoft MSDN web site at `http://msdn.microsoft.com/en-us/library/ms162802.aspx`.

This section describe show to use the bcp utility to export data from a local database and import the data into your SQL Azure database. It also discusses some things you should watch out for when using the bcp utility for SQL Azure.

Invoking BCP

The bcp utility has no GUI; it's a command prompt–driven utility. But don't let that intimidate you, especially given what you're using it for. It's very flexible and can seem a bit overwhelming, but it's quite simple. The basic syntax for the bcp utility is as follows:

`bcp table direction filename -servername -username -password`

where:

- *table* is the source or destination table based on the direction parameter.

- *direction* is in or out, depending on whether you're copying data into the database or out of the database.

- *filename* is the filename you're copying data to or from.

- *servername* is the name of the server you're copying data to or from.

- *username* is the username used to connect to either the local or SQL Azure database.

- *password* is the password associated with the username.

Let's get started by exporting the data from your source database.

Exporting the Data

Begin by copying data out of your local SQL instance. Open a command prompt, and type the command shown in Figure 5-17. Enter your own values for the server name, the target directory, and the username and password for your local server. (The password is blanked out in Figure 5-17.)

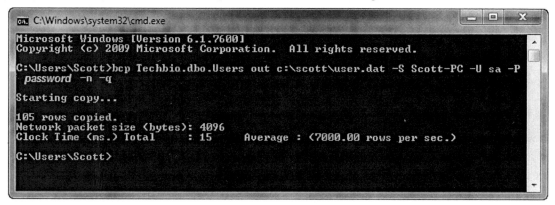

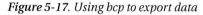

Figure 5-17. Using bcp to export data

Notice that in this example you're using the out keyword for the direction parameter. That's because you're copying data *out* of SQL Server.

The -n parameter performs the bulk-copy operation using the native database data types of the data. The -q parameter executes the SET QUOTED_IDENTIFIERS ON statement in the connection between the bcp utility and your SQL Server instance.

After you type in the command, press the Enter key to execute the bcp utility. In mere milliseconds, 105 rows are exported and copied to the user.dat file. Now, do the same for the Docs and UserDocs tables.

Importing the Data

The next step is to copy the data into the cloud—specifically, to your SQL Azure TechBio database. The syntax for copying *into* a database is very similar to the syntax for copying data *out*. You use the in keyword and specify the server name and credentials for your SQL Azure database, as shown in Figure 5-18.

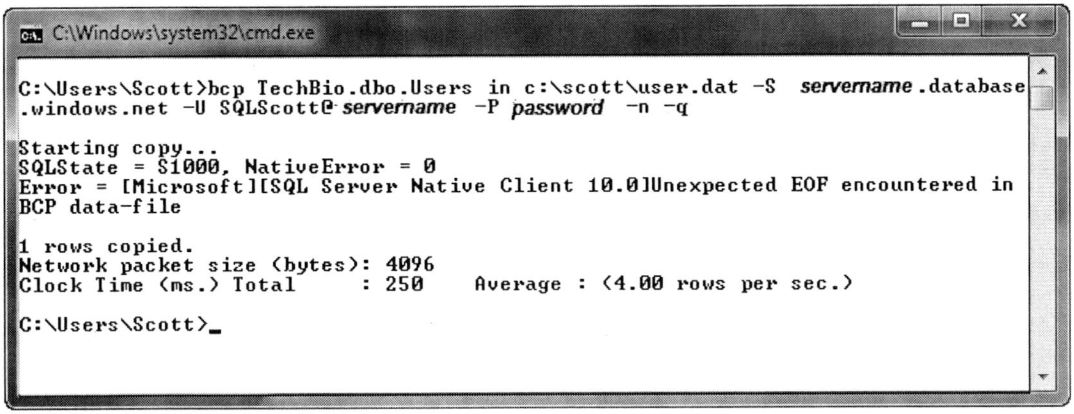

Figure 5-18. Uniqueidentifier data type error during bcp import

After you type in the command, press Enter to execute the bcp utility. Only one row is copied over, and then an error is generated, stating that an unexpected end-of-file (EOF) was encountered. This error isn't specific to SQL Azure; the bcp utility has issues with columns of the uniqueidentifier data type. You can find posts and blogs all over the Internet about this problem.

The solution is to execute the following T-SQL against the Users table in your SQL Azure database:
```
alter table users
drop column rowguid
```
The cool thing is that you don't need to re-export the data. You can re-execute the bcp import command. Do that, as shown in Figure 5-19, and all 105 rows are imported. Then, use the same syntax to import the Docs and UserDocs data.

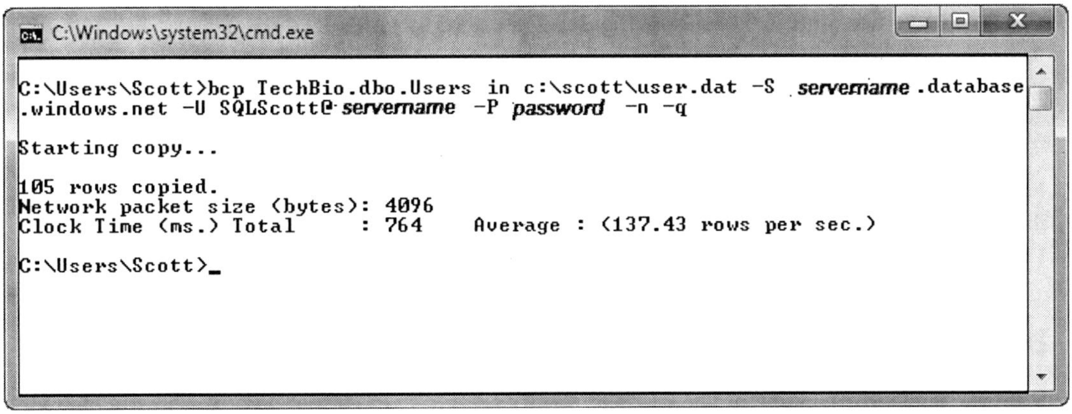

Figure 5-19. Successful bcp import

Don't forget to put the rowguid column back on the Users table. You can do this by using the same syntax as before:

```
ALTER TABLE Users
ADD rowguid uniqeidentifier
```

Next, let's make this a little simpler and put the export and import together, so you aren't running the statements one at a time.

Putting the Export and Import Together

You can put the export and import processes together into a single file to make them easier to use. To do so, open Notepad, and type in the following, replacing the italicized information with the appropriate information for your environment:

```
bcp Techbio.dbo.Users out c:\scott\user.dat -S Scott-PC -U sa -P Password -n -q
bcp Techbio.dbo.Docs out c:\scott\docs.dat -S Scott-PC -U sa -P Password -n -q
bcp Techbio.dbo.UserDocs out c:\scott\userdoc.dat -S Scott-PC -U sa -P Password -n -q

bcp Techbio.dbo.Users in c:\scott\user.dat -S servername.database.windows.net
-U SQLScott@ servername -P #ackThis -n -q
bcp Techbio.dbo.docs in c:\scott\docs.dat -S servername.database.windows.net
-U SQLScott@ servername -P #ackThis -n -q
bcp Techbio.dbo.userdocs in c:\scott\userdoc.dat -S servername.database.windows.net
-U SQLScott@ servername -P #ackThis -n -q
```

Save the file as AzureBCP.cmd, and navigate to its location. Double-click the file to execute it. A command window appears, showing the results of the bcp commands that export and import the data.

As stated earlier, SQL Server BOL is full of information about how to use the bcp utility. This section is a brief introductory look at how to use this utility to move data from your local SQL Server instance to SQL Azure. The bcp utility is bulk-copy method of moving data. It lacks SSIS's ability to convert data from one data type to another, and SSIS's workflow components. But if all you're interested in is moving data from one table to a similar destination table, bcp is your best friend.

SQL AZURE MIGRATION WIZARD

The tools discussed so far in the chapter are provided by Microsoft. However, a standout third-party utility is available, which was built specifically for migrating data to SQL Azure. That utility is the SQL Azure Migration Wizard, and it deserves some well-earned attention.

The goal of the SQL Azure Migration Wizard is to help you migrate your local SQL Server 2005/2008 databases into SQL Azure. This utility is wizard driven, making it very easy to use. It walks you step by step through all that is required, so migration is simple and nearly seamless.

You can find the SQL Azure Migration Wizard on CodePlex at http://sqlazuremw.codeplex.com/.

Note that although this nifty utility migrates both 2005 and 2008 databases, it requires SQL Server 2008 R2 to run.

SQL Azure Backup Strategies

Your data is in the cloud, but it really doesn't stop there. Much of the functionality that DBAs have at their fingertips when dealing with local data stores doesn't exist in the cloud yet. The operative word in that sentence is *yet*. At the time of this writing, SU4 was recently released, and it supports Database Copy functionality.

Database Copy enables you to copy your database to make a new database on the same SQL Azure server. Alternative, you can copy to a different SQL Azure server in the same subregion or data center. This functionality is much needed, but at the same time it has some shortcomings; some can be worked around, but others will require future service updates.

Copying a Database

The Database Copy feature allows you to create a single copy of a source database. You do so by adding a new argument to the CREATE DATABASE statement: AS COPY OF. As a refresher, the syntax for CREATE DATABASE is as follows:

```
CREATE DATABASE MyDatabase (MAXSIZE= 10 GB, EDITION= 'Business')
```

To create a copy of a source database, the syntax now becomes

```
CREATE DATABASE MyDatabase AS COPY OF [source_server_name].source_database_name]
```

Thus, if you want to create a copy of your TechBio database, the syntax is

```
CREATE DATABASE TechBio2 AS COPY OF servername.TechBio
```

Figure 5-20 shows the execution of the previous statement. The interesting thing to note is the message in the Messages window. When you execute the CREATE DATABASE statement with the AS COPY OF argument, you immediately get the "Command(s) completed successfully" message. Does this mean the copy finished that quickly? No. This message means the copy has *started*. You can also see in Figure 5-20 that the TechBio2 database is already listed in the list of databases; however, that doesn't mean the database copy has completed.

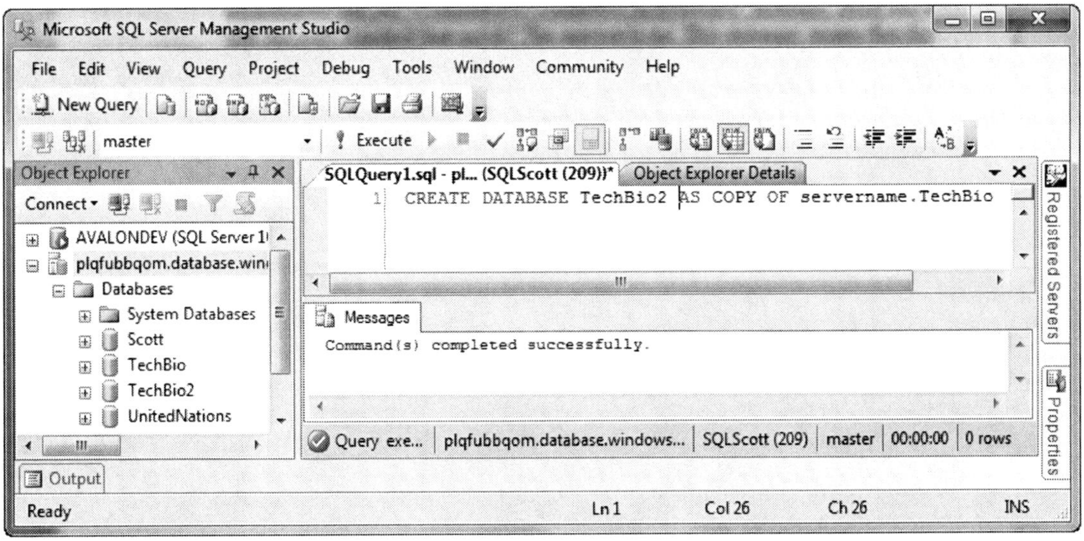

Figure 5-20. Copying a database

Knowing When a Copy Is Complete

The question then becomes, how do you know the copy is finished? The answer is that Microsoft created a new data management view (DMV) to return the details of the database copy operation. This DMV is called sys.dm_database_copies, and it returns a great deal of information about the status of the database copy, such as when the database copy process started and completed, the percentage of bytes that have been copied, error codes, and more. In addition, Microsoft modified the state and state_desc columns in the sys.databases table to provide detailed information on the status of the new database.

Figure 5-21 was generated by deleting the TechBio2 database and creating it again. This time, a statement looks at the sys.dm_database_copies DMV and checks the status of the copy. You can see the statement highlighted in Figure 5-21. You can also see results in the figure from the query against the DMV. The TechBio database was tiny to begin with, so the copy takes only a few seconds, if that.

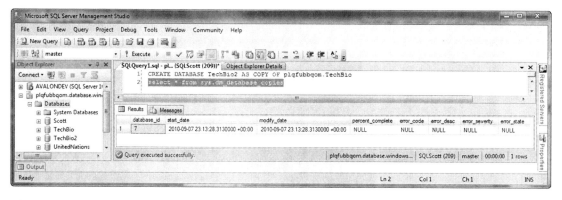

Figure 5-21. *Checking the database copy status*

Automating a Database Copy

You can schedule a database copy via an on-premises SQL Agent job and an SSIS package (as discussed earlier in this chapter). The job can be scheduled like a normal on-premises SQL job, as long as the connection information for the Execute SQL task points to the SQL Azure database.

Although this may not be the most favorable solution, it's certainly an option, and it does provide the scheduling capabilities you're looking for. The key for this solution is to first delete the copy database before you re-create it.

Maintaining a Backup History

The Database Copy functionality lets you create an instant backup of your database, but it doesn't provide a way to create a backup history. In other words, you can't append to the backup and create multiple days' worth of backups. You do have several options, however.

If all you care about is backing up the current day's data, you can delete the current backup copy and re-copy the database. This is a viable option and doesn't require a lot of maintenance.

If, on the other hand, you want a backup history, doing so is a bit more tricky. Many, if not most, companies like to keep a week's worth of backups. These companies back up their databases each night and keep seven days' worth of backups so they have the option to restore past the previous night's backup. To do this with the Database Copy functionality, you must create seven copies of the source database—you have seven backup copy databases.

This strategy works, but keep in mind that you're billed for those additional seven databases. The key here is that if you're using SQL Azure, a look at your backup plan is critical.

What does Microsoft have coming in future Service Updates? The company is working very hard on adding and improving SQL Azure backup and restore functionality. Microsoft wants to hear from you—your feedback is important. Talks of database cloning and continuous backups have surfaced; keep your fingers crossed that this functionality and more will appear in the near future.

Conclusion

In this chapter we discussed the several different migration options when migrating your database schema and associated data to SQL Azure. From our discussion we learned that there are pros and cons to each; for example the SQL Server script generation wizard will script the schema as well as the data, but SSIS and the Bcp utility does not. We also learned that if you use SQL Server 2008 R2 you have the option for scripting for SQL Azure which scripts the objects ready for execution in the SQL Azure environment.

We also discussed the SQL Azure Copy feature, which allows you to make a copy of your SQL Azure database for backup purposes.

With your database in SQL Azure, we can now focus on how to program applications for SQL Azure, which we will discuss in Chapter 6.

CHAPTER 6

■ ■ ■

Programming with SQL Azure

The chapters previous to this one have laid the foundation for the rest of the book. You've seen an overview of SQL Azure, learned about cloud computing design options, and walked through setting up your Azure account. You've read about SQL Azure security, including security compliance and encryption topics; and you spent the last chapter learning about data migration (how to get your data into the cloud) and backup strategies—the types of things a DBA likes to hear.

Starting with this chapter, the rest of the book focuses on developing with Azure. This chapter looks at using various Microsoft technologies to program against SQL Azure , including ODBC, ADO.NET, LINQ, and others. This chapter also discusses development considerations as you start to design and build new applications to work with SQL Azure or consider moving existing applications to SQL Azure.

You should begin getting the picture that SQL Azure really isn't *that* much different than your local SQL instances. The last chapter talked at length about some of the T-SQL differences in SQL Azure but also said that Microsoft is continually adding features and functionality; so, the differences gap closes at a very rapid pace (which has made writing this book a fun challenge, but that's another story). The key to developing applications isn't pointing your application to your cloud version of the database, but rather your approach to developing the application and design considerations for accessing your cloud database. Moving a database to the cloud and pointing your application to that instance can have disastrous results, such as degraded application performance and unwanted (and undesired) monetary costs.

This chapter first focuses on application design approaches to get the most from SQL Azure application development. The rest of the chapter discusses various technologies for accessing your SQL Azure database, showing you how to use those technologies to connect to and retrieve data. You learn the right place to use each of the technologies, because there are many technologies to choose from. The end of this chapter provides a simple, best-practice discussion of testing locally before deploying remotely to ensure a successful SQL Azure application deployment.

Application Deployment Factors

As stated earlier, you could use the information from Chapter 5 to push your *entire* database to SQL Azure. But is that the right thing to do?

Chapter 2 discussed at length the design aspects of architecting and publishing applications for the cloud, including topics such as storage, high availability, security, and performance. Each of those aspects is important (especially performance) and should be discussed when you're considering moving applications to the cloud. In addition to security, performance is one of the primary items of concern that companies have about cloud computing. One of the last things a company wants to do is decide to take a critical application and move it to the cloud, only to find that it doesn't perform as well as the on-premises version of the app.

Don't get the idea that moving an on-premises application to the cloud automatically results in security issues and a loss of performance—that isn't the case. With planning and the right approach, you can achieve a very successful application deployment into the cloud. The purpose of this discussion, and of Chapter 2, is to get you to think and plan before you deploy, so you take the right approach. The question is, what is that right approach?

This discussion is really about two things. First, when deciding to move an application to the cloud, do you move the entire application (meaning, database and app) or just a portion? Second, regardless of whether you move all or a portion of the database, do you also move the application, or do you keep the application on-premises? Let's not forget that using SQL Azure doesn't mean you automatically have to move your application to the Azure platform. You can move your database to the cloud and still host your application on-premises. As with everything, you have options. Let's discuss the different ways of hosting your SQL Azure application.

On-Premise Application

On-premise means your application is hosted locally and not in Azure, but your database is in SQL Azure. Your application code uses client libraries to access one or more SQL Azure databases. Some companies are reluctant to put business logic or application-specific logic outside of their corporate data center, and the on-premise option provides the ability to house the data in the cloud while keeping the application logic local.

Although this is a viable option, limitations are associated with it. For example, only the following client libraries are supported:

- .NET Framework 3.5 SP1 Data Provider for SQL Server (System.Data.SqlClient) or later

- Entity Framework 3.5 SP1 or later

- SQL Server 2008 R2 Native Client ODBC driver

- SQL Server 2008 Native Client Driver (supported, but has less functionality)

- SQL Server 2008 Driver for PHP version 1.1 or later

If your application uses OLE DB, you have to change your application so use one of the client libraries listed here.

The biggest consideration related to keeping your application on-premise is the cost. Any time you move data between SQL Azure and your on-premise application, there is an associated cost (currently, $0.10 in and $0.15 out per GB, or more if your selected geolocation is Asia). If you're using Azure Storage, there is also the cost of using that storage (currently, $0.15 per GB stored per month). Again, this is per GB, so the cost is low. An example of an expensive pattern is synchronizing large amounts of data multiple times per day. But keep in mind that synching even a 50GB database costs only $5.

These costs and limitations shouldn't deter you from using an on-premise solution for your application. However, let's look at what an Azure-hosted solution provides.

Azure-Hosted Application

Azure-hosted means that your application code is hosted in Windows Azure and your database is in SQL Azure. Your application can still use the same client libraries to access the database or databases in SQL Azure. Most companies right now are taking existing ASP.NET applications and publishing them to Windows Azure and accessing SQL Azure. However, you aren't limited to just web apps: you can use a Windows desktop app or Silverlight app that uses the Entity Framework and the WCF (Windows

Communication Foundation) Data Services client to access SQL Azure as well. Again, you have plenty of options.

The benefit of using an Azure-hosted solution is the ability to minimize network latency of requests to the SQL Azure database. Just as important is the fact that you're cutting the costs of data movement between SQL Azure and the application. As long as your Windows Azure and SQL Azure are in the same subregion, bandwidth usage between SQL Azure and Windows Azure is free.

By putting both your application and database in Azure, you also get the benefit of more efficient transactions between your app and the database, because doing so minimizes the network latency between your application and the database.

But you incur the compute cost, which is currently $0.12 per hour. *Compute hours* is the time your application is deployed to Windows Azure. Even if your application isn't in a running state, you're being billed. Billing is per hour, and partial hours are billed as full hours. When developing and testing your application, you should remove the compute instances that aren't being used. Thus, the key here is *to test locally before deploying remotely.*

Which to Choose?

The decision to move your application to the cloud versus keeping it local is entirely up to you and shouldn't be determined solely by what you read in the last two sections. The decision isn't that cut-and-dried. You need to look at several other factors, such as costs, data traffic, and bandwidth, and then base your decision of the analysis of this information. For example, it may not be a sound decision for a small company with little web traffic to host an application in Azure, due to the compute costs. However, that same company can keep its database in Azure while keeping the application on-premise because the data-transfer costs are minimal, yet gain the benefits of SQL Azure (failover, and so on).

In many companies, the initial goal isn't an all-or-nothing approach. The companies spend some time looking at their databases and applications, decide what functionality makes sense to put in the cloud, and test functionality on that. They test for performance foremost, to ensure that when deployed to Azure in production, performance is in the same ballpark. The thought is to keep the important things up front to ensure a successful Azure deployment. Roll your application out in pieces, if necessary, and test locally prior to deployment.

Whether you deploy all or part of your database and application is for you to decide. Chapter 2 discussed the issue at length, and this chapter doesn't rehash it except to say that before you make a decision, you should look at all the facts.

Connecting to SQL Azure

Developing applications that work with SQL Azure isn't rocket science, but it requires knowing what to expect and what functionality you have to work with. You read earlier that not all client libraries work with SQL Azure and saw the libraries that are supported. Chapter 5 also spent some time discussing what T-SQL functionality exists in SQL Azure. Even as this book is being written, the list of supported features changes as Microsoft continues to add functionality. This chapter now focuses on a client application's perspective.

This section looks at using several technologies to connect to and query a SQL Azure database, including ADO.NET, ODBC, and WCF Data Services. You read at length earlier about taking the right approach to move to the Azure platform. You must consider many things, including the following:

- SQL Azure is only available via TCP port 1433.

- SQL Azure doesn't currently support OLE DB.

- SQL Azure only supports SQL Server authentication. Windows Authentication isn't supported.

- When connecting to SQL Azure, you must specify the target database in the connection string. Otherwise, you're connecting to the *master* database.

- Distributed transactions (transactions that affect multiple resources, such as tables, or different databases via sharding) aren't supported in SQL Azure.

- You must ensure that your SQL Azure firewall is configured to accept connections.

- You must determine whether any embedded (in-line) T-SQL in your application is supported by SQL Azure.

- You must use the login name format `<login>@<server>` when connecting to SQL Azure, because some tools implement Tabular Data Stream (TDS) differently.

Most of the items in this list are self-explanatory, but let's talk about a couple of them. First, it's highly recommended that you read Appendix B, which discusses the T-SQL syntax that is and isn't supported. Also, if you have any inline or embedded T-SQL code, you need to go through your app and make sure the T-SQL meets the requirements listed in Appendix B. It also may behoove you look at the online help for supported T-SQL syntax, because of the gap between when this book is finished and when it's published (Microsoft may make some T-SQL changes in that time).

Second, although distributed transactions aren't supported, Chapter 10 discusses a technique called *sharding* that you can use to improve performance dramatically. Sharding is the concept of horizontally partitioning your data among several databases based on criteria (such as geolocation) and then using a technology such as the ADO.NET Task Parallel Library (TPL) to add parallelism and concurrency to your application.

Third, think carefully about OLE DB. SQL Azure currently doesn't support connecting via OLE DB, but supporting OLE DB is on Microsoft's radar. However, as you learned in Chapter 3, you can connect using OLE DB using SSIS. It isn't recommended, though, that you try to work in OLE DB—wait until it's fully supported.

Let's get to some coding. The next few sections show you how to connect to SQL Azure using different libraries such as ADO.NET, ODBC, the sqlcmd utility, and WCF Data Services to query SQL Azure.

ADO.NET

Microsoft makes it very easy to connect an application to SQL Azure by providing the necessary connection strings for both ADO.NET and ODBC, as shown in Figure 6-1. You can find the connection information on the SQL Azure Server Administration page by selecting a database and clicking the Connection Strings button.

Figure 6-1. Connection strings

Making the Connection

Let's first look at how to connect to an Azure database using ADO.NET. Fire up an instance of Visual Studio 2010, and create a new Windows Forms application. Then, follow these steps:

1. Place a button on Form1, and double-click the new button to view its click event.

2. Before you place any code in the click event, let's add a method to get a connection string. To demonstrate connecting to SQL Azure versus a local database, let's first connect to a local copy of the database. Then, you can change to connect to Azure. Below the click event, add a new method called GetConString that returns the connection string for your local instance of SQL Server. Here's the code to write:

```
string GetConString()
{
    return "Server=server;Database=TechBio;User ID=sa;Password=password;";
}
```

3. Go back to the button's click event, and add the following code. This code calls the GetConString method you previously added, returns the connection string, establishes and opens a connection to the local database, and then closes the connection:

```
private void button1_Click(object sender, EventArgs e)
{
    string connStr = GetConString();
    using (SqlConnection conn = new SqlConnection(connStr))
    {
        try
        {
            conn.Open();
            MessageBox.Show("Connection made.");
        }
        catch (SqlException ex)
        {
            MessageBox.Show(ex.Message.ToString());
        }
        finally
        {
            conn.Close();
        }
    }
}
```

4. Run the application, and click the button on the form. You should get a message box that says "Connection Made."

Now, let's change this simple application to connect to SQL Azure. Instead of returning the connection string to your local database, you want to return the ADO.NET connection string. Continue as follows:

5. On your SQL Azure Server Administration page, select the database you want to connect to.

6. Click the Connection Strings button, and click the Copy to Clipboard link for the ADO.NET connection string.

7. Back in your Visual Studio project, replace the local connection string in the GetConString method with the SQL Azure ADO.NET connection string, as shown in the following code. Be sure to enter your correct password into the connection string:

```
string GetConString()
{
    return "Server=tcp:servername.database.windows.net;Database=TechBio;
        UserID=SQLScott@servername;Password=password;
    Trusted_Connection=False;Encrypt=True;";
}
```

8. Before you run the application, make sure your Azure firewall settings are up to date (via the SQL Azure Server Administration page). Then, run the application, and click the button on the form. If everything is configured correctly, you should get a message box that says "Connection Made."

Granted, this is a very simple example, but it illustrates how easy it is to take an existing application and point it to SQL Azure. The caveat is what your application contains. As mentioned earlier, if you have any inline T-SQL, you at a minimum need to ensure that your inline T-SQL is supported by SQL Azure. The likelihood is that it is, but it's always safest to check and *test*.

Even though you've connected to SQL Azure, does that affect your data-access code? The next two sections discuss using a data reader and a dataset when connecting to SQL Azure.

Using a Data Reader

As you become more and more familiar with SQL Azure, you'll find that you don't need to make a lot of changes to your application code except possibly any inline T-SQL. The beauty of all this is that you're using a proven and trusted data-access technology, ADO.NET. Thus, nothing really changes. Let's modify the application and click event code to illustrate this. Follow these steps:

1. Add a new list box to the form.

2. In the click event, add the code in bold in the following snippet. This new code uses the SqlDataReader class to execute a simple SELECT command against the SQL Azure database and then iterate over the SqlDataReader to populate the list box:

```
private void button1_Click(object sender, EventArgs e)
{
    string connStr = GetConString();
    using (SqlConnection conn = new SqlConnection(connStr))
    {
        SqlCommand cmd = new SqlCommand("SELECT Name FROM Users", conn);
        conn.Open();
        SqlDataReader rdr = cmd.ExecuteReader();
        try
```

```
    {
        while (rdr.Read())
        {
            listBox1.Items.Add(rdr[0].ToString());
        }
        rdr.Close();
    }
    catch (SqlException ex)
    {
        MessageBox.Show(ex.Message.ToString());
    }
  }
}
```

3. Run the application, and click the button on the form. Within a few seconds, the list box populates with names from the Users table.

The key is that you can replace the connection string with your local connection string, and it still works. This is because you're using ADO.NET to handle the connection, and it doesn't care where the database is. Next, let's take this example one step further and look at how you use datasets.

Using a Dataset

In the last example, you found that there is no difference in using a SqlDataReader when querying a SQL Azure database. This example uses the SqlCommand class and the SqlDataAdapter to query SQL Azure and populate a dataset. Here are the steps:

1. In the button's click event, replace the existing code with the following:

```
using (SqlConnection conn = new SqlConnection(connStr))
{
    try
    {
        using (SqlCommand cmd = new SqlCommand())
        {
            conn.Open();
            SqlDataAdapter da = new SqlDataAdapter();
            cmd.CommandText = "SELECT Name FROM Users";
            cmd.Connection = conn;
            cmd.CommandType = CommandType.Text;
            da.SelectCommand = cmd;
            DataSet ds = new DataSet("Users");
            da.Fill(ds);
            listBox1.DataSource = ds.Tables[0];
            listBox1.DisplayMember = "Name";
        }
    }
    catch (SqlException ex)
    {
        MessageBox.Show(ex.Message.ToString());
    }
}
```

This code creates a new connection using the same connection information as the previous example, and then creates a new SqlCommand instance. The connection, text, and type of the SqlCommand are set and then executed using the instantiated SqlDataAdapter. A new dataset is created and filled from the SqlDataAdapter, which is then applied to the datasource property of the list box.

2. Run the application, and click the button on the form. Again, the list box is populated with the names from the Users table in the SQL Azure database. Again, you could change the connection string to point to your local database and the code would work fine.

So, when would code like this *not* work? Suppose your application had code such as the following, which creates a table without a clustered index:

```
using (SqlConnection conn = new SqlConnection(connStr))
{
    try
    {
        using (SqlCommand cmd = new SqlCommand())
        {
            conn.Open();
            SqlDataAdapter da = new SqlDataAdapter();
            cmd.CommandText = "CREATE TABLE TestTable(ID int, Name varchar(20))";
            cmd.Connection = conn;
            cmd.ExecuteNonQuery();
            cmd.CommandText = "INSERT INTO TestTable (ID, Name)
VALUES (1, 'Scott'), (2, 'Herve')";
            int val = cmd.ExecuteNonQuery();
        }
    }
    catch (SqlException ex)
    {
        MessageBox.Show(ex.Message.ToString());
    }
}
```

Although this code is certainly valid and runs successfully against your local SQL Server instance, it doesn't work when executing against your SQL Azure database. Why? Go ahead and replace the code in the button's click event with this code, and run the application. The error you get in the message box states that SQL Azure tables without a clustered index aren't supported. If you step through the code, you find out that the table is indeed created, but the error comes from trying to insert data into the table. You need to go through your application and look for these sorts of things, to ensure that the application will run successfully against SQL Azure.

We have discussed connecting with ADO.NET and the different options we have with ADO.NET, so let's move on to the other connection option, ODBC.

ODBC

There is nothing earth-shattering or truly groundbreaking here, but let's walk though an example to see how ODBC connections work and illustrate that your ODBC classes still work as you're used to. Follow these steps:

1. Do this the proper way and create an enumeration to handle the type of connection you're using.

2. Modify the GetConString method as shown in the following snippet to take a parameter. The parameter lets you specify the connection type so you can return the correct type of connection string (either ADO.NET or ODBC). Be sure to use your correct password and server name with the correct server. If the value of ADO_NET is passed into this method, the ADO.NET connection string is returned; otherwise the ODBC connection string is returned:

```
enum ConnType
{
    ADO_NET = 1,
    ODBC = 2
}
string GetConString(ConnType connType)
{
    if (connType == ConnType.ADO_NET)
        return "Server=tcp:servername.database.windows.net;Database=TechBio;
            User ID=SQLScott@servername;Password=password;
            Trusted_Connection=False;Encrypt=True;";
    else
        return "Driver={SQL Server Native Client
10.0};Server=tcp:servername.database.windows.net;
                    Database=TechBio;Uid=SQLScott@servername;Pwd=password;Encrypt=yes;";
}
```

3. Place a second button on the form, along with a DataGridView. In its click event, add the following code. This code is just like the code from the ADO.NET example, but it uses the Odbc data classes versus the Sql data classes. For clarity, change the Text property of this new button to "ODBC" so you know the difference between this button and the first button. Notice in the code that the value "ODBC" is passed in the GetConString method, returning the ODBC connection string:

```
string connStr = GetConString(ConnType.ODBC);

using (OdbcConnection conn = new OdbcConnection(connStr))
{
    try
    {
        conn.Open();
        OdbcDataAdapter da = new OdbcDataAdapter();
        OdbcCommand cmd = new OdbcCommand("SELECT Name FROM Users", conn);
        cmd.CommandType = CommandType.Text;
        da.SelectCommand = cmd;
        DataSet ds = new DataSet("Users");
        da.Fill(ds);
        listBox1.DataSource = ds.Tables[0];
        dataGridView1.DataSource = ds.Tables[0];
        listBox1.DisplayMember = "Name";

    }
    catch (OdbcException ex)
    {
        MessageBox.Show(ex.Message.ToString());
```

```
        }
}
```

4. Run the project, and click the ODBC button. As in the previous example, the list box populates with the names from the Users table. The grid also populates with the same set of names (see Figure 6-2).

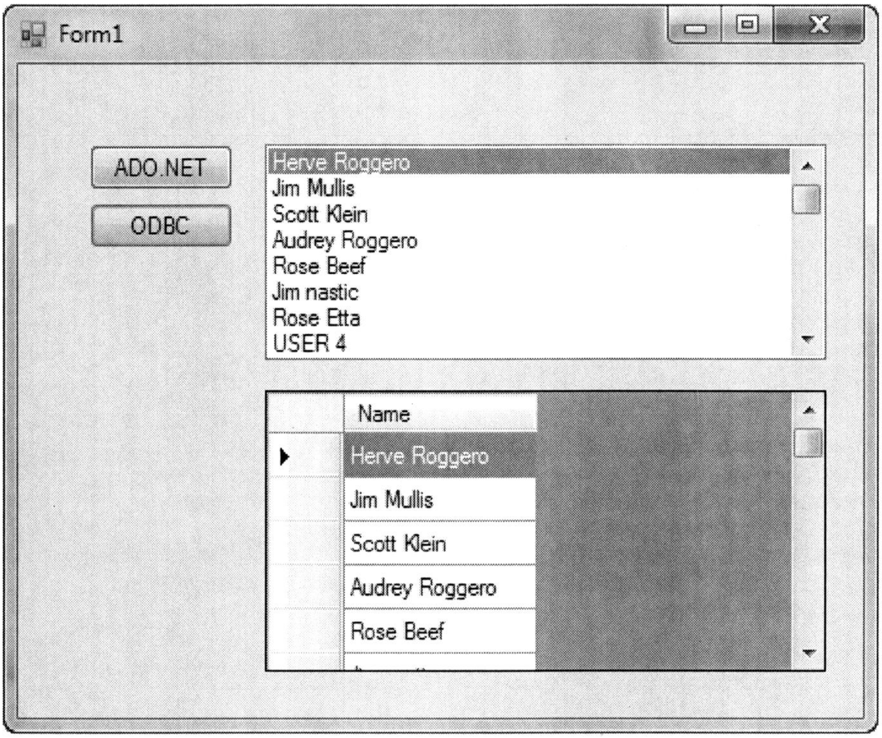

Figure 6-2. Finished form with data

From these examples, you can see that connecting to and querying SQL Azure is no different from connecting to a local instance of SQL Server. The end of this chapter discusses some guidelines and best practices to help you prepare for your move to SQL Azure.

So far we have discussed connecting with ADO.NET and ODBC along with the different options we have with each, so let's continue the discussion and talk about using the SqlCmd utility.

Sqlcmd

If you've worked with SQL Server for any length of time, chances are you've worked with the sqlcmd utility. This utility lets you enter and execute T-SQL statements and other objects via a command prompt. You can also use the sqlcmd utility via the Query Editor in sqlcmd mode, in a Windows script file, or via a SQL Server Agent job.

This section discusses how to use the sqlcmd utility to connect to a SQL Azure database and execute queries against that database. This section assumes that you have some familiarity with sqlcmd. This utility has many options, or parameters, but this section only discusses those necessary to connect to SQL Azure.

■ **Note** SQL Azure doesn't support the -z or -Z option for changing user passwords. You need to use ALTER LOGIN after connecting to the master database in order to change a password.

To use the sqlcmd utility, you first open a command prompt. At the command prompt, you need to provide the options and values necessary to connect to the SQL Azure database. As a minimum, the command syntax is the following:

```
sqlcmd -U login -P password -S server -d database
```

The parameters are nearly self-explanatory, but here they are, just in case:

- -U is the user login ID.

- -P is the user-specified password. Passwords are case sensitive.

- -S specifies the instance of SQL Server to which to connect.

Optionally, you can provide a database name via the -d parameter. Thus, the sqlcmd syntax looks something like the following:

```
Sqlcmd -U providerlogin@Server -P ProviderPassword -S ProviderServer -d database
```

Let's put this syntax to use. Follow these steps:

1. At the command prompt, use the sqlcmd syntax and type in your connection information, as shown in Figure 6-3. (In the figure, the server name and password are hidden.) Press Enter.

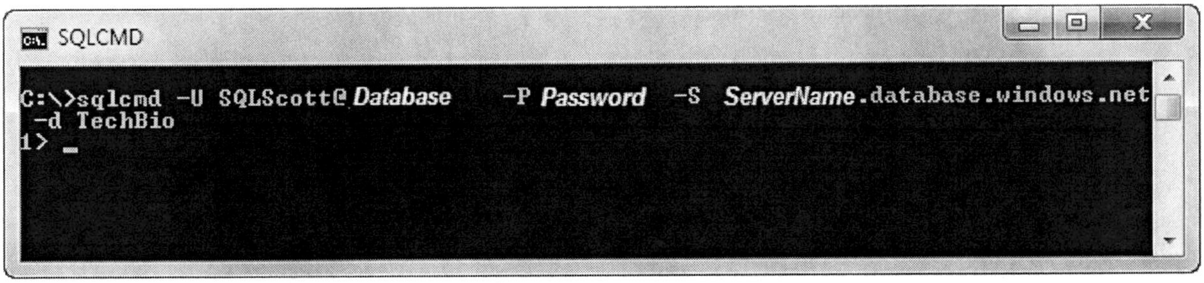

Figure 6-3. Connecting via sqlcmd

2. When the sqlcmd utility connects, you're presented with the sqlcmd prompt 1>, at which point you can begin typing in and executing T-SQL commands. The command to execute any T-SQL statement is GO. For example, in Figure 6-4, the following SELECT statement is entered and executed:

```
SELECT Name FROM Users
```

3. Press the Enter key on line 1> to create a new line. Pressing Enter executes the SELECT query. Type GO on line 2> and press Enter, to execute all statements since the last GO statement (see Figure 6-4). Figure 6-5 shows the results of the sqlcmd query entered. As you can see, executing a query isn't difficult.

Figure 6-4. *Executing a SELECT*

```
SQLCMD
C:\>sqlcmd -U SQLScott@           -P         -S          .database.windows.net
  -d TechBio
1> SELECT Name FROM Users
2> GO
Name
------------------------------
Herve Roggero
Jim Mullis
Scott Klein
Audrey Roggero
Rose Beef
Jim nastic
Rose Etta
USER 4
USER 5
USER 6
USER 7
USER 8
USER 9
USER 10
USER 11
USER 12
USER 13
USER 14
USER 15
USER 16
USER 17
USER 18
USER 19
USER 20
USER 21
USER 22
USER 23
USER 24
USER 25
USER 26
USER 27
USER 28
USER 29
USER 30
USER 31
USER 32
USER 33
```

Figure 6-5. *Sqlcmd query results*

Let's work through another example in which you create a table and add data. Here are the steps:

1. After the previous query is finished, you're back at the 1> prompt. Type in the statement shown in Figure 6-6.

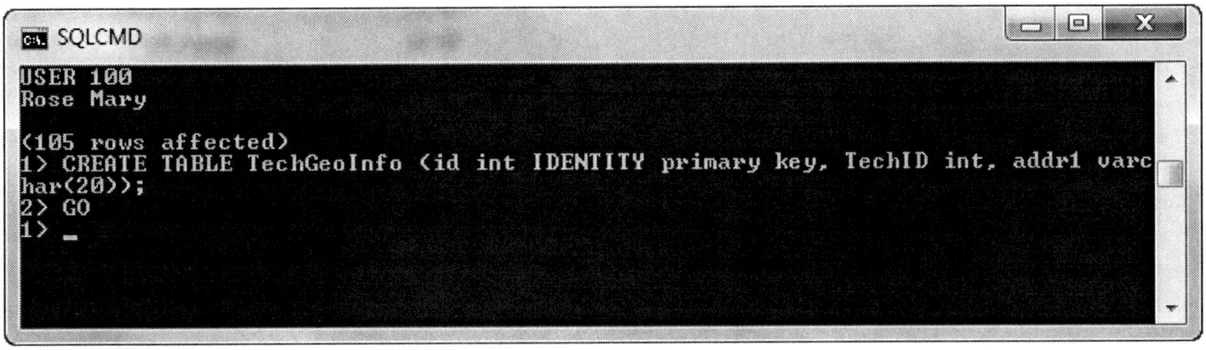

```
USER 100
Rose Mary

(105 rows affected)
1> CREATE TABLE TechGeoInfo (id int IDENTITY primary key, TechID int, addr1 varc
har(20));
2> GO
1> _
```

Figure 6-6. Creating a table

2. Press Enter, type GO on line 2>, and press Enter again, to execute the CREATE statement.

3. When the T-SQL command that you execute is the type that doesn't return data, the sqlcmd utility doesn't give you back a message but takes you to the 1> prompt. However, you can verify that a statement executed successfully by going into SQL Server Management Studio (SSMS), connecting to your SQL Azure instance, and expanding the Tables node of your chosen database. Figure 6-7 shows the results from doing that—you can see that the table was indeed created.

The table you created is called TechGeoInfo, and it has three columns: an ID column that is the primary key (clustered index), a TechID column, and an address column. The table is simple, but it's good enough to demonstrate functionality.

▪ **Note** You know from earlier in the chapter that the id column must be a primary key clustered index, or you won't be able to add data to the table.

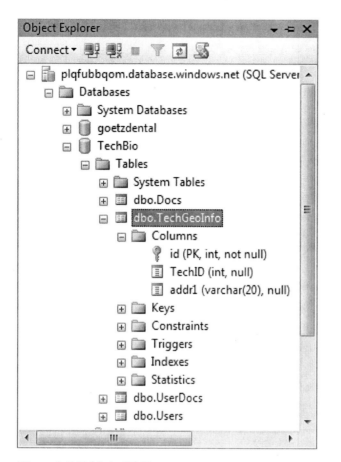

Figure 6-7. *Table in SSMS*

4. Add some data to the table by going back to the command window and typing in the INSERT statements shown in Figure 6-8. The great thing about the sqlcmd utility is that you can enter in as many commands as you want and not execute them until you type GO. Here you use two INSERT statements that add two records the table you created in the previous step.

5. Type GO on line 3>, and press Enter. Although the sqlcmd utility tells you 1 rows affected, you can query this new table in SSMS and see the two new rows that were added, as shown in Figure 6-9.

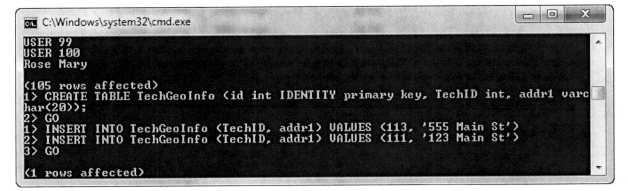

Figure 6-8. Inserting rows via sqlcmd

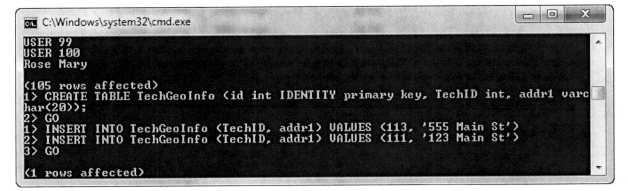

Figure 6-9. Viewing results via SSMS

As you can see, using the sqlcmd utility is straightforward. Just remember that it doesn't work with SQL Azure if you're trying to use heap tables. All tables must have a primary key. Also, as mentioned earlier, the -z and -Z parameters don't work.

This section has discussed the different mechanisms for connecting and querying SQL Azure, including examples for ADO.NET, ODBC, and SqlCmd. You can see that it quite similar to the way you currently connect to and query an on-premise database. However, with an overall industry push to an SOA architecture, let's take the discussion to the next level and discuss using services, specifically WCF Data Services, to connect to our Azure database.

WCF Data Services

WCF Data Services, formerly known as ADO.NET Data Services, enables the creation and consumption of OData services. OData, the Open Data Protocol, is a new data-sharing standard that allows for greater sharing of data between different systems. Before it was called WCF Data Services, ADO.NET Data Services was one of the very first Microsoft technologies to support OData with Visual Studio 2008 SP1. Microsoft has broadened its support of OData in products such as SQL Server 2008 R2, Windows Azure Storage, and others. This section discusses how to use WCF Data Services to connect to and query your SQL Azure database.

Creating a Data Service

First you need to create a data service. Follow these steps:

1. Create a new ASP.NET web application, and call it WCFDataServiceWebApp. (You can host data services a number of different environments but this example uses a web app.)

2. The next step in creating a data service on top of a relational database is to define a model used to drive your data service tier. The best way to do that is to use the ADO.NET Entity Framework, which allows you to expose your entity model as a data service. And to do that, you need to add a new item to your web project. Right-click the web project, and select New Item. In the Add New Item dialog, select Data from the Categories list, and then select ADO.NET Entity Data Model from the Templates list. Give the model the name TechBioModel.edmx, and click OK.

3. In the first step of the Data Model Wizard, select the Generate From Database option, and click Next.

4. The next step is Choose Your Data Connection. Click the New Connection button, and create a connection to your SQL Azure database. Save the entity connection settings as TechBioEntities, and then click Next.

5. The next step of the wizard is the Choose Your Database Objects page. Select all the tables. Note the option that is new to ADO.NET Entity Framework version 4.0, which pluralizes or singularizes generated objects names. If you leave this option checked, it comes into play later. Leave it checked, and click Finish.

6. The Entity Framework looks at all the tables you selected and creates a conceptual model on top of the storage schema that you can soon expose as a data service. In Visual Studio, you should see the Entity Framework Model Designer with a graphical representation of the tables, called *entities*, and their relationships. Close the Model Designer—you don't need it for this example.

7. What you need to do now is create the data service on top of your data model. In Solution Explorer right-click the web application and select Add, then select New Item. In the Add New Item dialog, select the Web category, then scroll down the list of templates and select the WCF Data Service template. Enter a name of TechBioDataService the click Add, as shown in Figure 6-10.

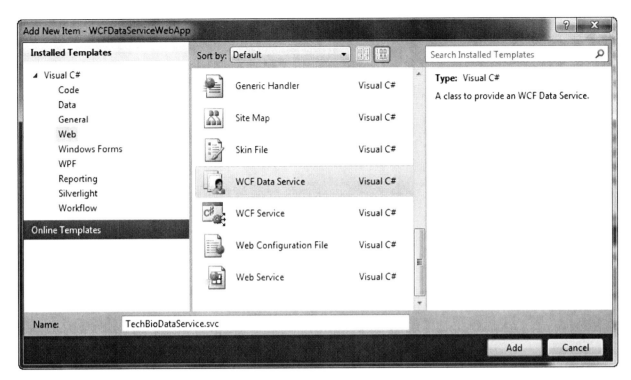

Figure 6-10. Adding a WCF Data Service to the Solution

When the ADO.NET Data Service is added to your project, the associated .cs file will automatically be displayed in the IDE. As you can see the ADO.NET Data Service template has generated for you the beginnings of your data service.

Connecting the Service to the Model

Now you need to wire up your data service to your data model so that the service knows where to get its data. You know where to do this because as you can see in the code it tells you where to enter that information. Thus, change the line:

```
public class TechBioDataService : DataService< /* TODO: put your data source
class name here */ >
```

To:

```
public class TechBioDataService : DataService< TechBioEntities >
```

Wiring up your data service to the model is as simple as that. Believe it or not, you're ready to test your service. However, let's finish what you need to do on this page. By default, the WCF Data Service is secured. The WCF Data Service needs to be told explicitly which data you want to see. The instructions in the code tell you this, as you can see in code in the InitializeService method. Some examples are even provided in the comments to help you out.

For your example, you don't want to restrict anything so you really want to unlock all the entities and explicitly define access rights to the entity sets. You do this by adding the code below to the

InitializeService method. The code below sets the access rule for the specified entities to All, providing authorization to read, write, delete, and update data for the specified entity set:

```
// This method is called only once to initialize service-wide policies.
public static void InitializeService(DataServiceConfiguration config)
{
    // TODO: set rules to indicate which entity sets and service operations are visible,
updatable, etc.
    // Examples:
    config.SetEntitySetAccessRule("Docs", EntitySetRights.All);
    config.SetEntitySetAccessRule("UserDocs", EntitySetRights.All);
    config.SetEntitySetAccessRule("Users", EntitySetRights.All);
    config.SetEntitySetAccessRule("TechGeoInfo", EntitySetRights.All);
    config.DataServiceBehavior.MaxProtocolVersion = DataServiceProtocolVersion.V2;
}
```

If you don't feel like specifying each entity one by one, you can optionally specify all the entities with a single line, as follows:

```
config.SetEntitySetAccessRule("*", EntitySetRights.All);
```

The above line assumes that you want to specify the same rights to all the entities. Not recommended, but will do for this example. In a production environment you want to more specific with what rights you specify for each entity.

There are other EntitySetRights options, such as AllRead, AllWrite, None, ReadSingle, and WriteAppend. You won't cover them all here but you can read about them here: http://msdn.microsoft.com/en-us/library/system.data.services.entitysetrights.aspx

So far, you've created your Web application, added your data model, and added your WCF Data Service. Right now your Solution Explorer should look like Figure 6-11.

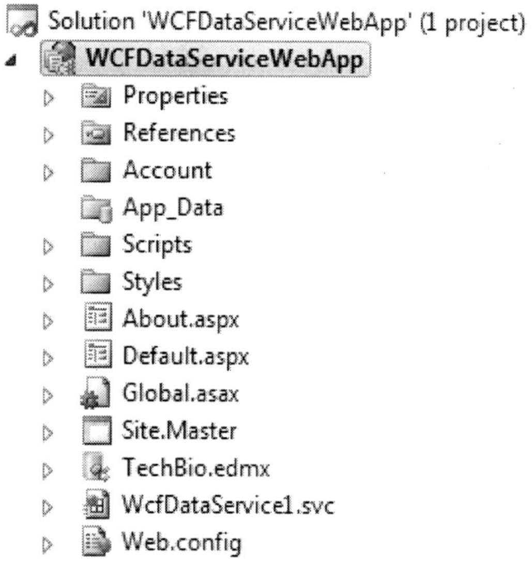

Figure 6-11. Solution Explorer

Creating the Client Application

The next step is to add the client application. In Solution Explorer right click the solution and select Add->New Project. In the Add New Project Dialog, select the Cloud project types then select Windows Azure Cloud Service, providing a name of TechBioSite, as shown in Figure 6-12.

Figure 6-12. Adding an Azure Cloud Service

Click OK on the Add New Project dialog.

Next, in the New Cloud Service Project dialog, select ASP.NET Web Role to add it to the Cloud Service Solution pane, leaving the default name of WebRole1, then click OK.

Next, right click the Web Role project in Solution Explorer and select Add Service Reference from the context menu. This will bring up the Add Service Reference dialog shown in Figure 6-13.

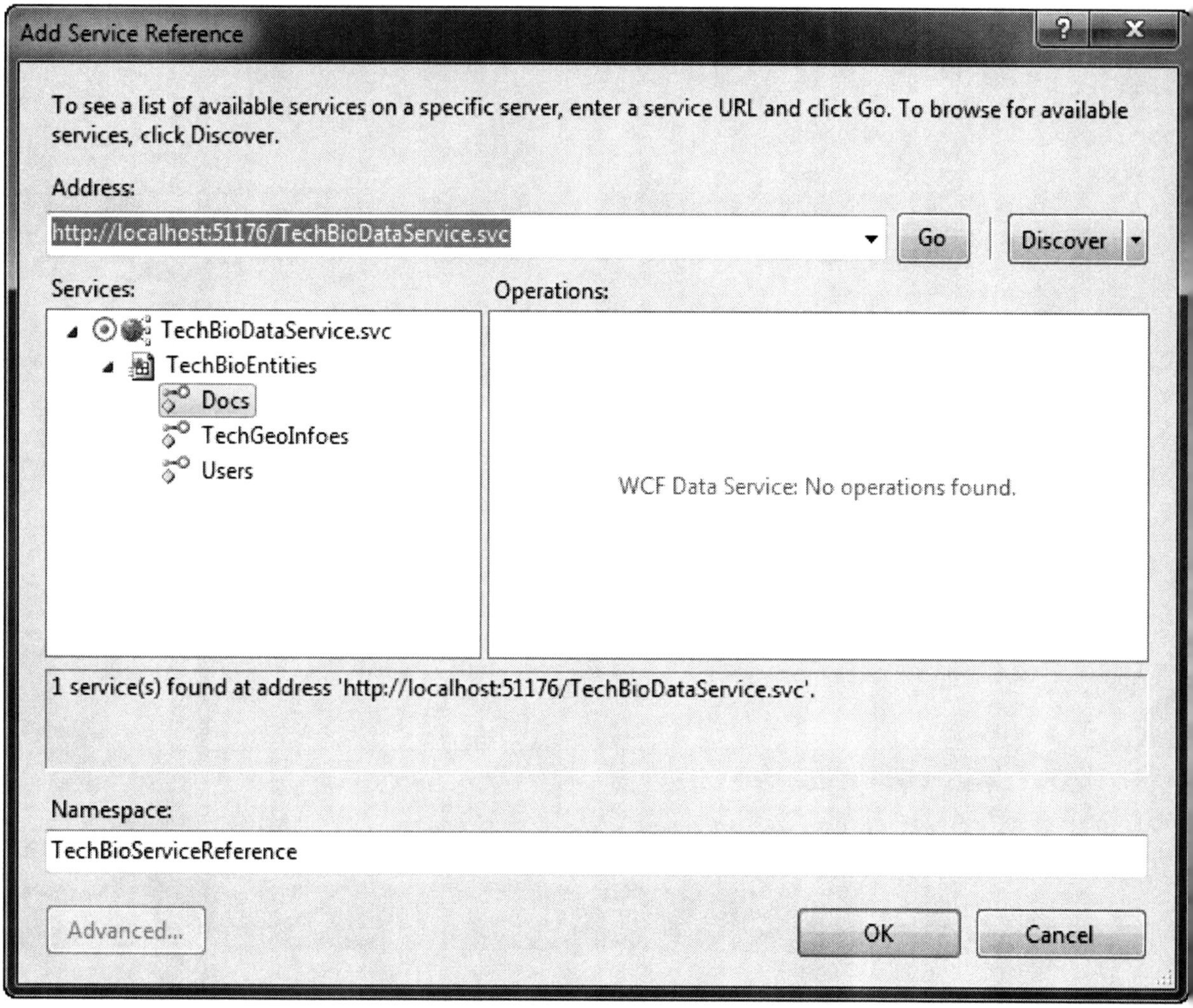

Figure 6-13. *Adding a Service Reference*

In the Add Service Reference click the Discover button, which will interrogate your solution for existing services and display them in the Services list. As you can see from Figure 6-12, the discovery function did in fact find your TechBioDataServices service in your Web application project. The discovery also provides your local URI for the service as well as the Entities that are exposed by the service. Give the service a namespace name of TechBioServiceReference and click OK.

At this point your Solution Explorer will have your TechBioSite Cloud Service project, your WCFDataServiceWebApp project and your web role. You should see those items as they're shown in Figure 6-14.

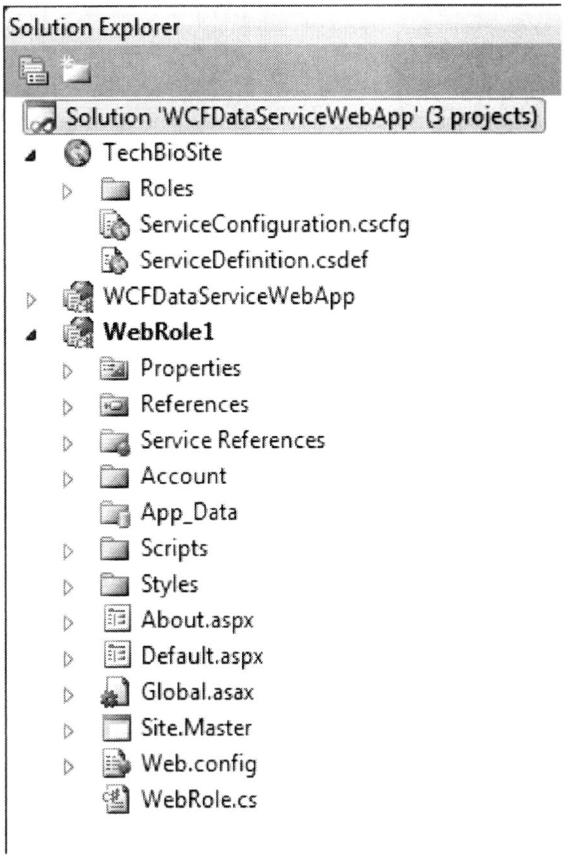

Figure 6-14. *Projects in Solution Explorer*

Creating the User Interface

You're almost done. You need a user interface in which to display the data you query via the data service, so open up the Default.aspx in the Azure Web Role project and select the Source tab. Replace the code that you see with the following code which defines a list box, label, and combo box:

```
<%@ Page Title="Home Page" Language="C#" AutoEventWireup="true"
    CodeBehind="Default.aspx.cs" Inherits="WebRole1._Default" %>

<html xmlns="http://www.w3.org/1999/xhtml">
<head runat="server">
    <title></title>
</head>
<body>
    <form id="form1" runat="server">
        <div>
            <asp:ListBox ID="docsList" runat="server"
```

```
                    OnSelectedIndexChanged="docsList_SelectedIndexChanged"
                    AutoPostBack="true">
            </asp:ListBox>
            <br />
            <br />
            <asp:Label ID="infoLabel" runat="server"></asp:Label>
            <br />
            <br />
            <asp:DropDownList ID="authorList" runat="server">
            </asp:DropDownList>
        </div>
    </form>
</body>
</html>
```

The last thing you need to do is add the events that are defined in the code above, specifically the docsList_SelectedIndexChanged event. Click the Design tab for the Default.aspx page and double click the list box, which will create the docsList_SelectedIndexChanged event. However, before you put code in this event, you need to put some code in the Page_Load event as well as define a few variables. First, add the following using statements:

```
using System.Data.Services.Client;
using WebRole1.TechBioServiceReference;
```

Next, add the following declarations. These define the DataServiceContext and URI to the data service. You can get the URL from the Add Service Reference box shown in Figure 6-13:

```
private TechBioEntities context;
private Uri svcUri = new Uri("http://localhost:51176/TechBioDataService.svc");
```

Next, add the following code to the Page_Load event. This instantiates the data service context, and loads the list box with available documents and the combo box with available users:

```
context = new TechBioEntities(svcUri);

DataServiceQuery<Doc> docs = context.Docs;
DataServiceQuery<User> users = context.Users;

foreach (Doc d in docs)
{
    docsList.Items.Add(new ListItem(d.Name, d.ID.ToString()));
}

foreach (User u in users)
{
    authorList.Items.Add(new ListItem(u.Name, u.ID.ToString()));
}
```

Finally, add the following code to the docsList_SelectedIndexChanged event. This code queries the docs table to get the document information for the selected doc and displays the associated document description and price in the label, then selects the author (userid) for the selected document. By the way, the query you see below is LINQ to Entities, a LINQ (Language-Integrated Query) query that enables developers to write queries using LINQ syntax against an Entity Framework conceptual model:

```
var docInfo = (from d in context.Docs
            where d.ID == Convert.ToInt32(docsList.SelectedItem.Value)
            select d).FirstOrDefault();
```

```
infoLabel.Text = string.Concat("Desc: ", docInfo.Descr, "    ", "Price: ",
docInfo.PurchasePrice.ToString());

authorList.SelectedIndex = docInfo.AuthorId;
```

Running the Application

You're ready to run your application! Make sure that the Web Role project is the startup project by right clicking the Web Role project and selecting Set as Startup Project from the context menu. Go ahead and press F5 to build and run the project. When the web page in Figure 6-15 comes up, the list box will be populated with the list of documents from the Docs table. Scroll through the list and select a document which will then populate the label with the appropriate description and price, as well as select the associated author in the combo box.

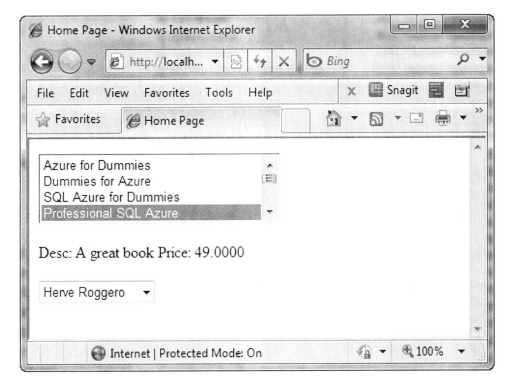

Figure 6-15. Running Application

Congratulations, you've successfully built a WCF Data Service that connects to, and queries, a SQL Azure database. While this was a fairly simple example, it should be enough to provide you with a solid foundation on which to start building and architecting data services for the cloud.

Record Navigation in WCF Data Services

Before you finish this chapter, let's talk a few more minutes about the WCF Data Service you built and how you can use that to navigate through records. Record navigation is one of the things that really gets me excited about WCF Data Services. Let's dive right in.

If your project is still running, stop the project and open the Solution Explorer and navigate to the data service. For simplicity, you'll do this right from the solution. Right mouse click the data service and select View in Browser. The service will fire up and what you see is a REST (Representational State Transfer) based service on top of your relational database, a mere XML representation of the service and the entities exposed via the service, shown in Figure 6-16. You see the entities listed because you set the entity set rights to ALL. If you were to go back to the code a few pages back where you set the entity set rights, and comment those lines out, you would not see the entities listed (Docs, TechGeoInfoes, and Users).

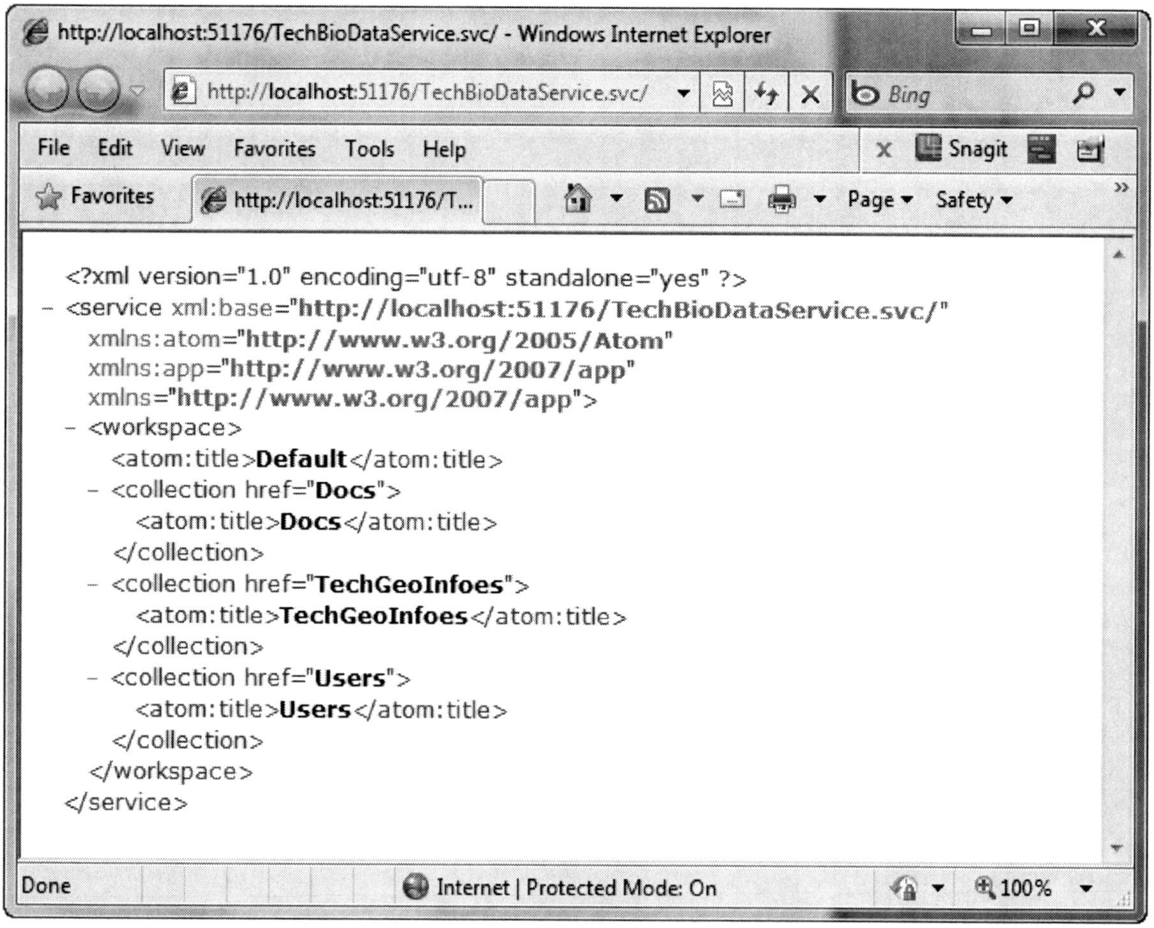

Figure 6-16. Viewing the WCF Data Service via REST

The question though, is how do you view the data that you really want to see. The answer is simple. Specify an entity at the end of your URI, and you'll see data for that entity. For example, specify the following URI to see data on the Users entity:

`http://localhost:51176/TechBioDataService.svc/Users`

Take care to get the case correct. Entity names are case sensitive. Specify users instead of Users, and you'll get a "The webpage cannot be found" error message.

■ **Tip** Take time out now to mistype an entity name and see the resulting message. That way you'll more readily recognize the problem when you make same mistake inadvertently. Sooner or later, you all make that mistake.

Disabling Internet Explorer's Feed Reading View

At this point you either get an XML representation of the data in the Users table, or the web page shown in Figure 6-17. If it's the latter, then you need to go turn off the feed reading view in Internet Explorer IE . That is because IE thinks that the data coming back is the type you would get in an RSS feed. You can see in the message that the browser thinks you're trying to view an RSS feed.

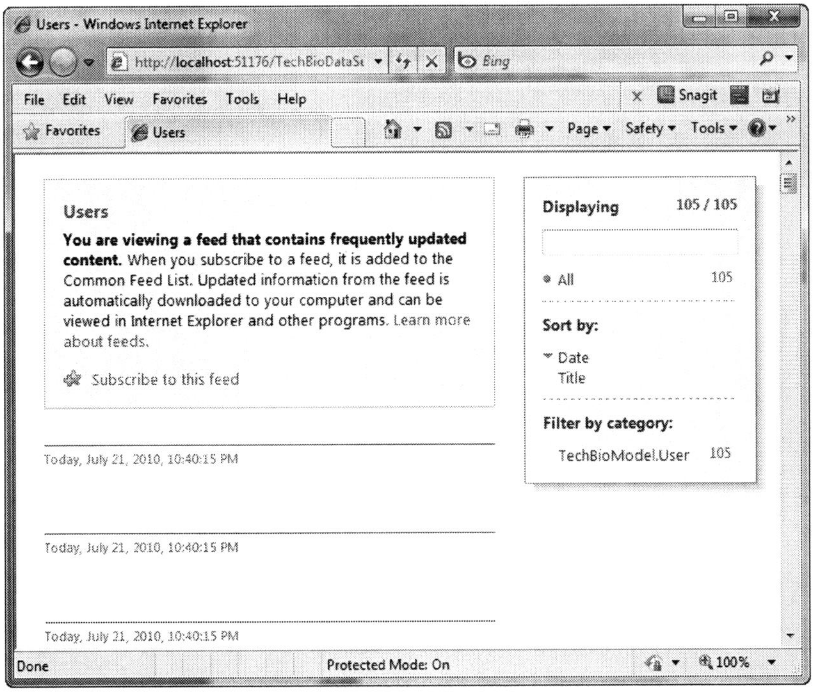

Figure 6-17. RSS Feed Page

To fix the RSS feed issue you need to turn off this feature in Internet Explorer. With IE open, from the Tools menu select Options which open the Internet Options dialog. This dialog has a number of tabs along the top which you might be familiar with. Select the Content tab and on that tab click the Settings button under Feeds and Web Slices.

Clicking the Settings button will display the Settings dialog, and on this dialog you need to uncheck the Turn on feed reading view checkbox, shown in Figure 6-18. Click OK on this dialog and the Internet Options dialog.

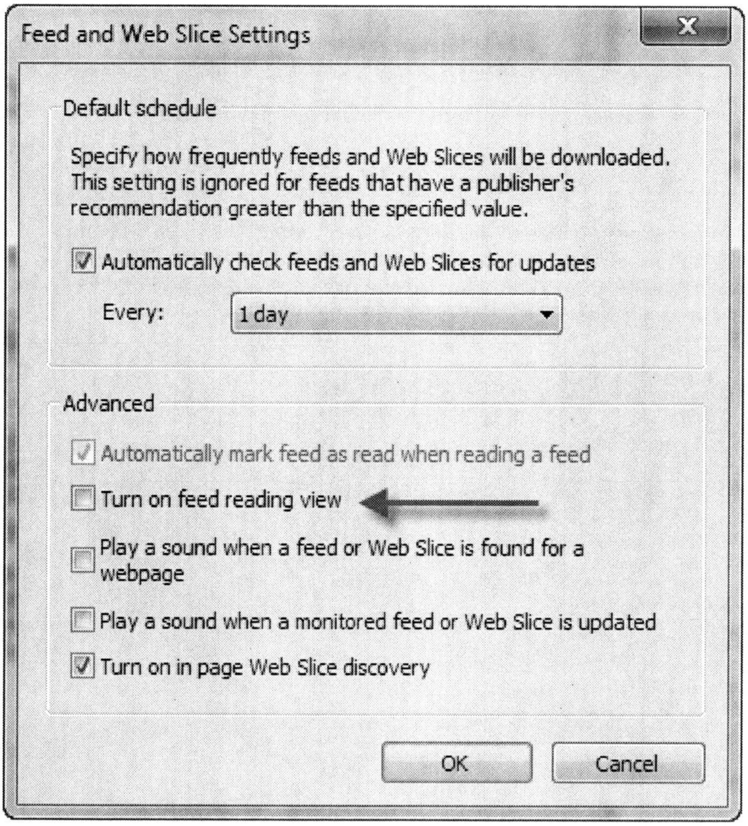

Figure 6-18. Disabling Feed Viewing

Viewing the Final Results

Back on your web page, press F5 to refresh the page. What you should get back now is a collection of Users, shown in Figure 6-19, by querying the underlying database for the Users.

However, you aren't done yet because there is still so much more you can do here. For example, the page you're currently looking at displays all the Users, but what if you want to return a specific user?

Looking at the data you can see that the each record contains the id of the specific row, and you can use that to your advantage by including that in your URI. For this example let's use ID 113. Modify the

URI by appending the number 113 to the end of the URI enclosed in parenthesis, as shown in Figure 6-20.

By loading the URI which includes the id of a specific record, I can now drill down further and return just the record I am looking for. This is just like applying a WHERE clause to a T-SQL query, in this case WHERE ID = 113. In this case I have queried the underlying store for a specific user by passing the appropriate ID in the URI.

Additionally I can return a specific field by adding the field I want to the URI, such as:

http://localhost:51176/TechBioDataService.svc/Users(113)/Name

Specifying the specific field along with the id will return just the field you request. In the code snipped above, the value in the Name column for User ID 113 is returned, as shown in Figure 6-21.

You can also use this same methodology to navigate between tables. For example, you could do the following to return documents for a specific User ID:

http://localhost:51176/TechBioDataService.svc/Users(113)/Docs

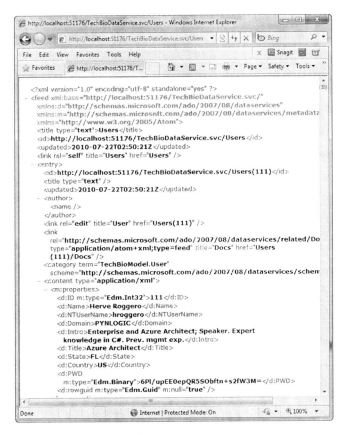

Figure 6-19. Viewing All Users

Figure 6-20. Viewing a Specific User

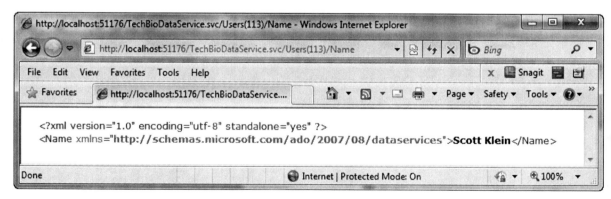

Figure 6-21. Viewing the Name of a Specific Users

While this information isn't critical to connect to SQL Azure it's good information to have so you know how REST services work and can benefit from its functionality in your application. While this chapter did not go deep into the Entity Framework or REST technology, there are plenty of good books by APress or information on MSDN about this technology. I highly recommend that you explore these technologies further to enhance your SQL Azure applications.

Azure Programming Considerations

To wrap up this chapter, let's spend a few minutes talking about some things you should consider when developing applications for the cloud. You spend a large portion of this chapter discussing how to connect to SQL Azure, but even before you start coding the very first thing you should consider is your connection. First and foremost, secure your connection string from injection attacks and man-in-the-middle attacks. The .NET Framework provides a simple class in which to create and manage the contents of connection strings used by the SqlConnection class. This class is called the SqlConnectionStringBuilder class.

The following example illustrates how to use this class. I first define four static variables to hold the username, password, database name and server:

```
private static string userName = "SQLScott@server";
private static string userPassword = password;
private static string dataSource = "tcp:server.database.windows.net";
private static string dbName = "TechBio";
```

I then modify my GetConString method to use the SqlConnectionStringBuilder class to dynamically build my connection string:

```
string GetConString(int connType)
{
    if (connType == 1)
        SqlConnectionStringBuilder connstr = new SqlConnectionStringBuilder();
        connstr.DataSource = dataSource;
        connstr.InitialCatalog = dbName;
        connstr.Encrypt = true;
        connstr.TrustServerCertificate = false;
        connstr.UserID = userName;
        connstr.Password = userPassword;
        return connstr.ToString();
    ...
}
```

Thus, consider the following when connecting to a SQL Azure database.

- Use the SqlConnectionStringBuilder class to avoid injection attacks.

- Encrypt your connection. Set the Encrypt parameter to True and the TrustServerCertificate to False to ensure a properly encrypted connection to avoid any man-in-the-middle attacks.

- Use MARS (Multiple Active Results Sets) whenever possible to lessen the trips to the database.

Lastly, let's discuss some connection constraints. You discussed these previously briefly but in bears repeating them because you're discussing SQL Azure connections. The idea is that Azure is handling the connections, and because multiple resources will more than likely using the same server as you, the last thing Microsoft want is for you to hog all the resources and bring the server to its knees. Thus, your connection can, and probably will, be closed automatically if your connection meets any of the following criteria:

- Long running queries and Long running single transactions - If your query takes a long time to execute (right now the time is set at 30 seconds) then Azure will kill your connection. Equally, if you have a single transaction

- Idle Connections - Play nice with others and close your connections. Don't leave them hanging open.

- Excessive resource usage - This should go without saying. Because you share the resources with others, don't hog all the resources. Again, play nice.

- Failover because of server failures - This one is obvious. If the server fails, so will your connection. But when your application reconnects, you'll automatically connect to one of the failover databases.

You have control over the first three items, you don't have control over the last item. Items one and three you referenced at the beginning of the chapter. The bottom line is to test locally before deploying remotely. This is a must, an absolute must. Spend some time looking at your queries and their execution plans to ensure they will execute efficiently and timely. Don't deploy to the cloud until you're satisfied that your database will play nice with the others.

Conclusion

We began the chapter with a discussion surrounding the different factors for deploying your application, such as keeping your application on-premise or hosting your application in Azure. We also covered application deployment from the database side, providing some ideas and concepts around things to consider when moving your database to the cloud, such as considering how much of your data to move.

We then discussed the different methods different programming approaches for connecting to and querying a SQL Azure database, providing examples for each method including ADO.NET and ODBC.

Lastly, we discussed accessing your SQL Azure database through WCF Data Services. With the strong emphasis on SOA architecture not only from Microsoft, the discussion on WCF Data Services provided a solid foundation for providing a services layer for your SQL Azure database. This information provides a great introduction into the next chapter, which discusses OData, a standardized method for querying and updating data over the web.

■ ■ ■

CHAPTER 7

OData with SQL Azure

Technical authors typically write books because they're excited about the technology about which they're writing and want to share their excitement with the readers. As the authors work through the chapters, they get to illustrate the exciting ways in which to use the technology and apply it in real-world scenarios. Occasionally, they get to work on a chapter where the technology is so cool that they don't look forward to the chapter ending.

This is one of those chapters. It's about OData, a platform-independent protocol for querying and updating data. Using OData, you can get at your data even from a mobile phone.

How cool is it to hook up a Windows Mobile 7 phone using OData to a SQL Azure database to view your data, with almost the greatest of ease? Very cool. By the time you get to the end of this chapter, we hope you agree.

You may be wondering what OData is, and how it and Windows Mobile relates to SQL Azure. This chapter answers those questions, among others, by discussing the OData protocol, what it is and why it exists, and how it relates to SQL Azure. You also learn how to use OData to query your SQL Azure database and then build applications (such as a Windows Mobile phone application) in which to display data from your Azure database via OData.

Services are a critical and fundamental part of application development today, and even more so in the applications of tomorrow. This is why technologies such as WCF Data Services and OData are covered in this book, with OData covered specifically in this chapter as it relates to SQL Azure. OData continues to be a widely accepted protocol used in many applications and environments that use web technologies such as HTTP. Let's dive in to OData.

OData Overview

OData stands for Open Data protocol. It's a REST-based web protocol for querying and updating data completely independent of the platform or source. OData accomplishes this by utilizing and enhancing existing web technologies such as HTTP, JavaScript Object Notation (JSON), and the Atom Publishing Protocol (AtomPub). Through OData, you can gain access to a multitude of different applications and services from a variety of sources including relational databases, file systems, and even content-management systems.

The OData protocol came about from experiences implementing AtomPub clients and servers in an assortment of products over the past few years. OData relies on URIs for resource identification, which provides consistent interoperation with the Web, committing to an HTTP-based and uniform interface for interacting with the different sources. OData is committed to the fundamental web principles; this gives OData its great ability to integrate and interoperate with a plethora of services, clients, tools, and servers.

It doesn't matter if you have a basic set of reference data or are architecting an enterprise-size web application: OData facilitates the exposure of your data and associated logic as OData feeds, thus making the data available to be consumed by any OData-aware consumers such as business intelligence tools and products as well as developer tools and libraries.

OData Producers

An OData *producer* is a service or application that exposes its data using the OData protocol. For example, you can deduce that because this book—and, specifically, this chapter—pertains to SQL Azure and OData, SQL Azure can expose data as OData. But so can SQL Server Reporting Services and SharePoint 2010, among other applications. Later in this chapter, you walk through how to expose an OData service on your SQL Azure database.

Many public (or *live*) OData services have been made available, which anyone can consume in an application. For example, Stack Overflow, NerdDinner, and even Netflix have partnered with Microsoft to create an OData API. You can view a complete list of such OData producers, or services, at `www.odata.org/producers`.

■ **Note** Let's take a quick look at Netflix's OData service. Open your web browser, and navigate to `http://OData.netflix.com/Catalog`. The examples in this chapter used Internet Explorer 7.0 or greater. Using Firefox or Chrome might yield different results.

In the browser, you see a list of the categories by which you can browse or search for a movie offered by Netflix, as shown in Figure 7-1. Now, if you didn't skip reading Chapter 6, you probably look at Figure 7-1 and think, "This looks a lot like WCF Data Services." That is correct, because, as stated earlier, OData facilitates the exposure of your data and associated logic as OData *feeds*, making it much easier via a standardized method to consume data regardless of the source or consuming application.

Thus, in Figure 7-1 you can see the categories via which you can search Netflix movie catalog. For example, you can see the different endpoints of the API through which to find a movie, such as Titles, People, Languages, and Genres.

As you learned in Chapter 6, you can begin navigating through the vast Netflix catalog by entering your query as a URI. For example, let's look at all the different genres offered by Netflix. The URI is `http://OData.netflix.com/Catalog/Genres`

You're given a list of genres, each of which is in an `<entry>` element with the name of the genre in the `<Name>` element in the feed, shown in Figure 7-2.

Figure 7-1. Netflix catalog

Figure 7-2. Netflix genres

Figure 7-2 shows the Comedy genre. Additional information lets you know what you need to add to the URI to drill down into more detail. For example, look at the `<id>` element. If you copy the value of that element into your browser, you see the detailed information for that genre.

Continuing the Comedy example, let's return all the titles in the Comedy genre. To do that, you need to append the /Titles filter to the end of the URI:

`http://OData.netflix.com/Catalog/Genres('Comedy')/Titles`

The Netflix OData service returns all the information for the movies in the Comedy genre. Figure 7-3 shows one of the movies returned from the service, displayed in the browser.

Figure 7-3. *Viewing Netflix titles*

At this point you're just scratching the surface—you can go much further. Although this chapter isn't intended to be a complete OData tutorial, here are some basic examples of queries you can execute:

- To count how many movies Netflix has in its Comedy genre, the URI is
  `http://netflix.cloudapp.net/Catalog/Genres('Comedy')/Titles/$count?$filter=Type%20eq%20'Movie'.`

  Your browser displays a number, and as of this writing, it's 4642.

- To list all the comedies made in the 1980s, the URI is
  `http://OData.netflix.com/Catalog/Genres('Comedy')/Titles?$filter=ReleaseYear%20le%201989%20and%20ReleaseYear%20ge%201980.`

- To see all the movies Brad Pitt has acted in, the URI is
  http://OData.netflix.com/Catalog/People?$filter=Name%20eq%20'Brad%20Pitt'&
  $expand=TitlesActedIn.

The key to knowing what to add to the URL to apply additional filters is in the information returned by the service. For example, let's modify the previous example as follows:
http://OData.netflix.com/Catalog/People?$filter=Name%20eq%20'Brad%20Pitt'

On the resulting page, several <link> elements tell you what additional filters you can apply to your URI:
<link rel="http://schemas.microsoft.com/ado/2007/08/dataservices/related/Awards"...
<link rel="http://schemas.microsoft.com/ado/2007/08/dataservices/related/TitlesActedIn"...
<link rel="http://schemas.microsoft.com/ado/2007/08/dataservices/related/TitlesDirected"...

These links let you know the information by which you can filter the data.

OData Consumers

An OData *consumer* is an application that consumes data exposed via the OData protocol. An application that consumes OData can range from a simple web browser (as you've just seen) to an enterprise custom application. The follow is a list of the consumers that support the OData protocol:

- **Browsers.** Most modern browsers allow you to browse OData services and Atom-based feeds.

- **OData Explorer.** A Silverlight application that allows you to browse OData services.

- **Excel 2010.** Via PowerPivot for Excel 2010. This is a plug-in to Excel that has OData support.

- **LINQPad.** A tool for building interactive OData queries.

- **Client libraries.** Programming libraries such as .NET, PHP, Java, and Windows Phone 7 that make it easy to consume OData services.

- **Sesame (an OData browser).** A browser built by Fabrice Marguerie specifically for browsing OData.

- **OData Helper for webMatrix.** Along with ASP.NET, let's you retrieve and update data from any service that exposes its data via the OData protocol.

There are several more supported client libraries. You can find a complete list of consumers at www.odata.org/consumers.

OK, enough about OData. If you want to learn more, the OData home page is www.OData.org/home.

You should spend some time reading up on OData and start playing with some of the services provided by the listed producers. When people began getting into web services and WCF services, there was an obvious learning curve involved in understanding and implementing these technologies. Not so much with OData—it has the great benefit of using existing technologies to build on, so understanding and implementing OData is much faster and simpler.

Enabling OData on an Azure Database

When you first look at OData and its interoperation with SQL Azure, you may think you're in for a lengthy process and a ton of reading. Wrong. Enabling OData is simple and takes no time at all. This section spends a couple of pages walking you through the process of enabling OData on your SQL Azure database.

Up until now, you've done most of your work through the SQL Azure Portal at http://sql.azure.com. But as you read about enabling OData and other topics such as SQL Azure Sync Services in Chapter 11, you use Microsoft SQL Azure Labs at http://sqlazurelabs.com. SQL Azure Labs, as the front page says, is a place where you can access early previews of Azure products and enhancements to SQL Azure. So, this is where you begin your venture into several topics such as OData and Azure Sync Services.

Getting Started at SQL Azure Labs

Browse to SQL Azure Labs. Then, follow these steps:

1. On the home page, you see a list at left of things Microsoft is working on. Click the SQL Azure OData Services tab, which first asks you to log in using a Windows Live account.

2. When you've logged in, you're presented with the window shown in Figure 7-4: a summary of OData and, more important the first step of configuring your SQL Azure OData Service. The Create a New Server link on the right takes you to the SQL Azure home page where you can sign up for an Azure account, and so on. Because you've already done that, you skip that link. In the Connection Information section, enter your complete server name plus your username and password, and then click Connect.

Figure 7-4. Configure OData Service Connection Information section

▥ **Note** One of the tabs you see in Figure 7-4 is Project Houston, which is discussed in Appendix A.

3. After your information is validated, a Database Information section appears on the page. Select the database on which you want to enable OData, and select the Enable OData check box. At this point you may think you're done, but not quite. When you click the Enable OData check box, a User Mapping section appears on the page, as shown in Figure 7-5.

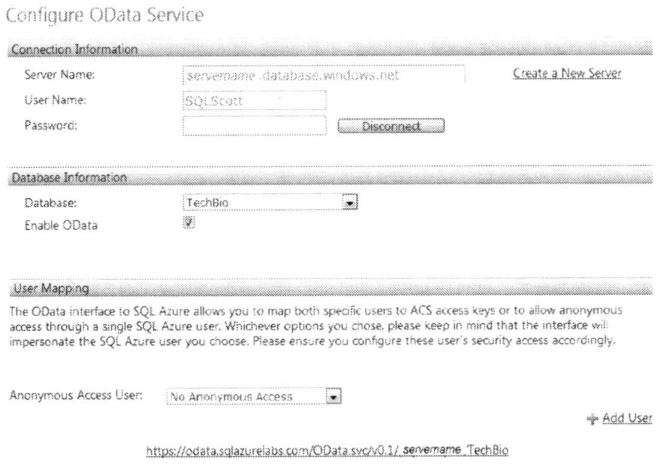

Configure OData Service

Connection Information

Server Name:	*servername* .database.windows.net	Create a New Server
User Name:	SQLScott	
Password:		Disconnect

Database Information

Database:	TechBio
Enable OData	☑

User Mapping

The OData interface to SQL Azure allows you to map both specific users to ACS access keys or to allow anonymous access through a single SQL Azure user. Whichever options you chose, please keep in mind that the interface will impersonate the SQL Azure user you choose. Please ensure you configure these user's security access accordingly.

Anonymous Access User: No Anonymous Access   ▼

➕ Add User

https://odata.sqlazurelabs.com/OData.svc/v0.1/ *servername* .TechBio

Figure 7-5. Configure OData Service Database Information section

As the User Mapping section explains, you can map specific users to the Access Control Service (ACS) keys or allow anonymous access to your SQL Azure database via OData through a single SQL Azure account. Now that we have our data exposed via a REST interface it is through the User Mapping that we control access to our SQL Azure data.

The Anonymous Access User drop-down defaults to No Anonymous Access, but you can also choose to map and connect via dbo, as shown in Figure 7-6. This chapter talks about anonymous access shortly. Selecting the dbo option allows you to connect using the database dbo account, basically as administrator. In a moment you learn the correct way to connect to the OData service.

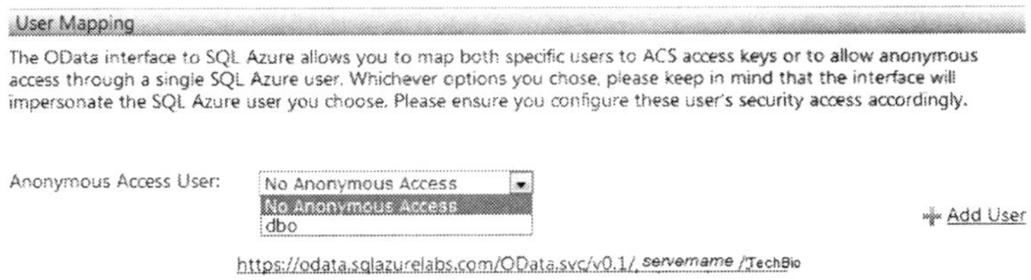

User Mapping

The OData interface to SQL Azure allows you to map both specific users to ACS access keys or to allow anonymous access through a single SQL Azure user. Whichever options you chose, please keep in mind that the interface will impersonate the SQL Azure user you choose. Please ensure you configure these user's security access accordingly.

Anonymous Access User: No Anonymous Access   ▼
                         No Anonymous Access
                         dbo

➕ Add User

https://odata.sqlazurelabs.com/OData.svc/v0.1/ *servername* /TechBio

Figure 7-6. Configure OData Service User Mapping section

Notice also that this section provides a URI link that you can use to browse your SQL Azure data in a web browser. How nice is that? Highlight it and copy and paste it into something like Notepad; you use that link in several places later in the chapter, and having it handy will make things much easier. Also in this section is a link to add a user to your list (discussed shortly).

For the sake of this example, select dbo. You have now OData-enabled your SQL Azure database. Before you proceed, let's spend a few minutes discussing in more detail anonymous access and the ACS and how it applies to SQL Azure.

Understanding Anonymous Access

Anonymous access means that authentication isn't needed between the HTTP client and SQL Azure OData Service. Keep in mind, however, that there is no such thing as anonymous access to SQL Azure. If you want to allow anonymous access, you must specify a SQL Azure user that the SQL Azure OData Service can use to access SQL Azure. Figure 7-7 shows how you do that.

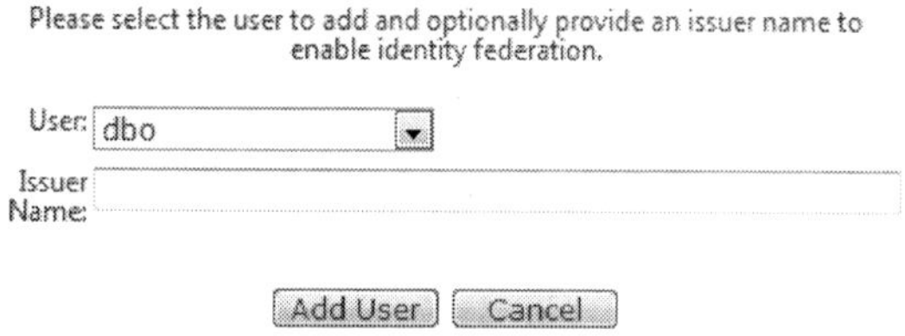

Please select the user to add and optionally provide an issuer name to enable identity federation.

User: dbo

Issuer Name:

Add User   Cancel

Figure 7-7. Adding an OData user

The SQL Azure OData Service access has the same restriction as the SQL Azure user. Therefore, if the SQL Azure user being used in SQL Azure OData Service anonymous access has read-only permissions to the SQL Azure database, SQL Azure OData Service can only read the data in the database.

Depending on the requirements of the application, you may consider creating a read-only user for your SQL Azure database. The syntax to do that is as follows:

```
EXEC sp_addrolemember 'db_datareader', username
```

Let's talk a moment about ACS and how that applies to SQL Azure.

Understanding the Access Control Service

ACS is part of the Windows Azure AppFabric. It's a hosted service that provides federated authentication and rules-driven, claims-based authorization for REST based web services, allowing these web services to rely on ACS for simple username/password scenarios.

In the Community Technology Preview (CTP) of SQL Azure OData Service, it's necessary for you to sign up for the AppFabric and create a service namespace to be used with the SQL Azure OData Service. This allows a single user to access SQL Azure OData Service through the Windows Azure AppFabric Access Control. This user must have the same user id as the database user.

Implementing Security Best Practices

Now that you know a little about security regarding SQL Azure OData, you need to be familiar with a few best practices surrounding SQL Azure OData Service:

- Always create a new SQL Azure user instead of allowing anonymous access to SQL Azure OData Service.

- Never use your SQL Azure Administrator username to access SQL Azure OData Service.

- Don't allow the SQL Azure user that is used by SQL Azure OData Service to have write access to SQL Azure OData Service through anonymous access.

The problem you run into by not creating a new user is that you then allow anyone to read from and write to your database. You also have no way to control how much data or what type of data they write.

But with all of that said, because SQL Azure OData is currently in CTP, it's easier to test with anonymous access than with a read-only SQL Azure user. But when out of CTP, you should build your client to use anything other than anonymous access. The browser doesn't support simple web token authentication natively, and this is required for SQL Azure OData Service via ACS. Thus, in production, don't use anonymous access.

Viewing OData-Enabled SQL Azure Data

It's time to view the fruits of your labors (not that it was a lot of hard work). You first briefly view your data in the browser, just as you did the Netflix data, to prove that you can indeed consume the data via OData. You then use a third-party app to view the data in a more pleasant-looking format. Then, you build your own little application to consume the data.

Open your browser, and type in the following URL. Be sure to enter the appropriate server name for your SQL Azure database: `https://odata.sqlazurelabs.com/OData.svc/v0.1/`*servername*`/TechBio`. By now, what you see in Figure 7-8 should look familiar. These are the same REST-based results you saw earlier in this chapter as well as in Chapter 6, except that in this example you're looking at the list of tables, or entities, that the SQL Azure OData service is providing from the TechBio database. Listed are the Users and Docs tables, as well as several other tables that pertain to SQL Azure Data Sync Service (discussed in Chapter 11).

As in previous example, you can navigate into the different entities to look at specific data. For example, in Figure 7-9 the URL is modified slightly to look at a specific user in the Users table.

The key is that in this example, your SQL Azure database is your OData producer, and your browser is the OData consumer. Those two alone allow you to easily navigate through the data, applying different filters

You should now have a good understanding of OData. But let's take a quick look at one of the OData consumers listed earlier, to give you an idea of the possibilities you have to consume an OData feed.

Figure 7-8. TechBio OData feed

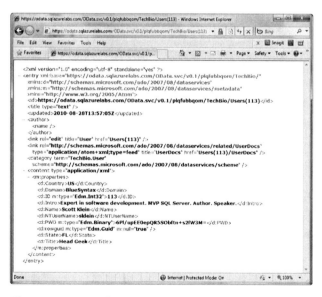

Figure 7-9. Query for a specific user in TechBio

Viewing Data through an OData Consumer

Earlier, the chapter listed several existing OData consumers that you can use today to view data exposed via your SQL Azure OData-enabled database. This section takes a quick look at one of them: the web-based Silverlight OData Explorer. In your browser, navigate to the following URL: www.silverlight.net/content/samples/ODataexplorer/.

When the page first loads, you're presented with what you see in Figure 7-10: a dialog asking you to name your workspace and provide the URI to your OData service. The workspace name can be any name, such as TechBioTest. After you've entered this information, click OK.

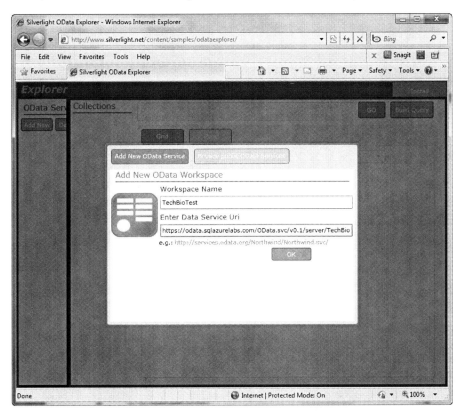

Figure 7-10. Add New OData Workspace dialog

The OData Explorer lists your OData service namespace at left, along with the list of collections it found. As you click the individual collections, the data is displayed in a grid, as shown in Figure 7-11.

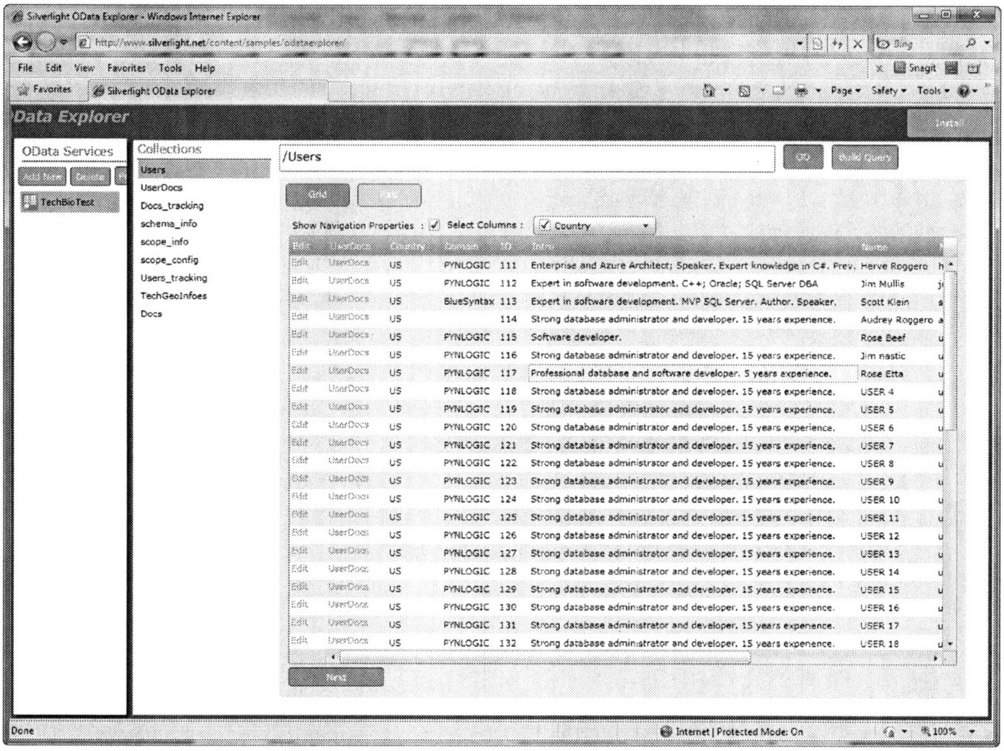

Figure 7-11. OData Explorer

This page also allows you to edit the data of each record via an Edit link on each row in the grid (if the SQL Azure user selected in the User Mapping section in Figure 7-5 is write-enabled). You can also view related data via links on each row (determined by examining relationships). You can navigate to specific data via the text box at the top of the form (just as you did in the browser examples), or you can build your own query via the Build Query button.

This section doesn't explore all the functionality of the application, but it does show what can be done to view data exposed via an OData service. Frankly, this is a nice application, and it should give you an idea of what you can do.

If you have some time, look at the other OData consumers. But just as important, let's move on to the next section, in which you build your own OData consumers.

Building Two OData Consumer Applications

The rest of this chapter focuses on building two applications that consume the OData service that you just enabled on your SQL Azure database. The first one is very simple, to whet your appetite and show you the basics. The second is the cool one. (But don't skip the first one!)

Simple Demo App

For this first example, create a Windows Forms Application project. The name of the project and language don't matter. When your project is created, follow these steps:

1. Drop a list box and a button on the form.

2. In Solution Explorer, right-click the References node, and select Add Service Reference from the context menu.

3. When the Add Service Reference dialog appears, you need the URI you copied from Figure 7-6. Paste it into the Address field, and click the Go button. After several seconds the available services and associated endpoints appear in the Services section of the form, as shown in Figure 7-12.

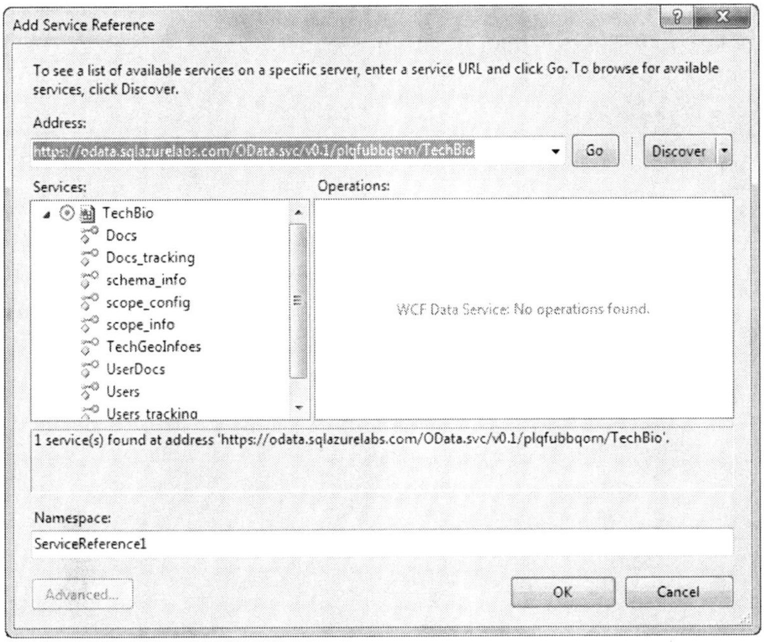

Figure 7-12. Adding the OData service reference

4. Leave the Namespace name as is, and click OK. A new Service Reference node appears in Solution Explorer, which lists the service you just added.

5. In the code behind the form, add the following using statements:

```
using System.Data.Services;
using System.Data.Services.Client;
```

6. In the declaration section, add the following two lines of code. The first line declares your context variable, which references the newly added service; the second line defines the URI that accesses the OData service:

```
private ServiceReference1.TechBio context;
private const string svcUri =
"https://OData.sqlazurelabs.com/OData.svc/v0.1/servername/TechBio";
```

7.   In the button's click event, add the following code:

```
context = new ServiceReference1.TechBio(new Uri(svcUri));

var userQuery = from u in context.Users
                select u;

foreach (var u in userQuery)
{
    listBox1.Items.Add(u.Name);
}
```

8.   Run the application. When the form displays, click the button. After a few seconds, the list box populates with usernames, as shown in Figure 7-13.

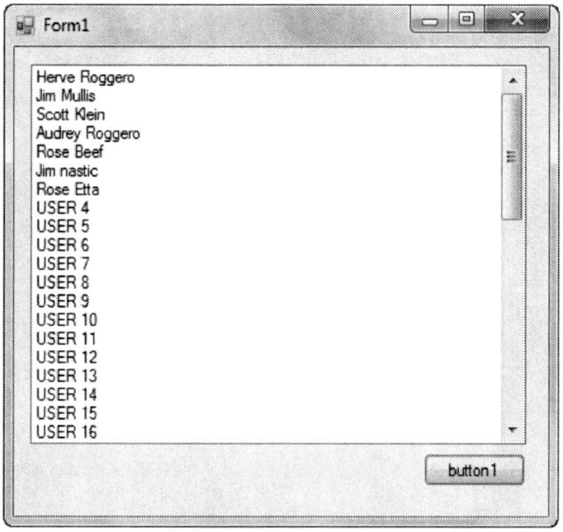

Figure 7-13. Form displaying data via the OData service

Very simple, but a good foundation to build on. This example gives you an idea of how you can consume on OData service via a .NET application. But you're probably tired of waiting, so let's move on to the really cool example: the Windows Phone application.

Windows Mobile 7 Application

Let's build something cool (not that you haven't done that prior to this point). In this example, you create a new application that consumes the same OData service that you consumed in the last example, but this time you use a Windows Phone 7 application to consume the service.

For this example, you need to download and install a couple of things. First is the OData Client Library for Windows Phone 7 Series CTP, which is available at www.microsoft.com/downloads/details.aspx?FamilyID=b251b247-70ca-4887-bab6-dccdec192f8d&displaylang=en. The install extracts several files to a directory that you specify.

The second item to download is the Windows Phone Developer Tools, which installs the Visual Studio Windows Phone application templates and associated components that provide integrated Visual Studio design and testing of Windows Phone 7 phone applications. The Windows Phone Developer Tools is available at http://developer.windowsphone.com/windows-phone-7/. To download the tools, click the Download the Developer Tools! link.

When the installs are finished, follow these steps:

1. Start a new instance of Visual Studio 2010, and create a new project. In the New Project dialog, select the Silverlight for Windows Phone template (which was installed as part of the Windows Phone Developer Tools), and then select Windows Phone Application, as shown in Figure 7-14. The project name isn't important, but feel free to give it a meaningful name such as WP7ODataApp.

Figure 7-14. Creating a Windows Phone Project

2. Before you can start coding and consuming the OData service, you need to do a couple of things. First, the OData Client Library installation extracted a file called System.Data.Services.Client.dll. In Solution Explorer, right-click the References node, and select Add Reference. In the Add Reference dialog, browse to the directory where you extracted the DLL file, and add that file to your references.

3. Next, you need to create a service proxy class that your OData service will use. Open a command prompt, and navigate to the following folder: C:\Windows\Microsoft.Net\Framework\v4.0.30319\.

4. Enter the following command:

```
datasvcutil.exe /uri:https://odata.sqlazurelabs.com/OData.svc/v0.1/servername/↩
TechBio /out:C:\directory\TechBio.cs /Version:2.0 /DataServiceCollection
```

DataSvcUtil is a command-line tool provided by WCF Data Services that consumes an OData feed and generates the client data service class or classes that are needed to access a data service in a .NET client application. In this above, where you see bolded and italicized text, be sure to enter your SQL Azure server and the directory in which you want to save the proxy class.

5. Press the Enter key to generate the proxy class. Figure 7-15 shows the results.

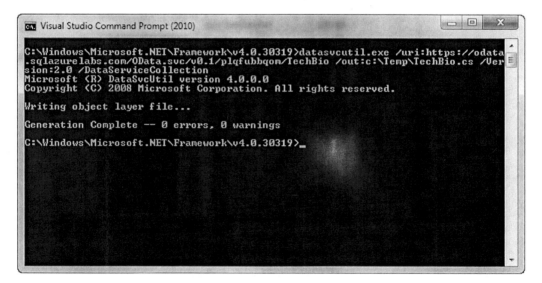

Figure 7-15. Creating the proxy class

If no errors are generated, you're set to go. The next step is to include this file in your project:

6. Right-click the project name in Solution Explorer, and select Add →Existing Item from the context menu. Navigate to the directory where you create the proxy class, and add the proxy class to your project.

7. Add a new class to the project. This class will be used to create the connection to the OData service, define and execute the query against the OData service, and load the Docs collection that will bind to the UI. For this example, name the new class TechBioModel.

When you've added all the components discussed, your Solution Explorer should look like Figure 7-16. You're ready to start adding some code.

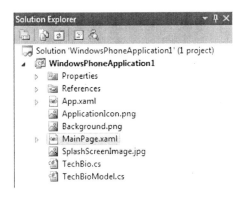

Figure 7-16. Solution Explorer

8. Open the TechBioModel class, and add the following namespaces. These namespaces provide additional functionality needed to query your OData source and work with collections. For example, the System.Collections.ObjectModel namespace contain classes that can be used as collections in the object model of a reusable library. The System.Data.Services.Client namespace represents the Silverlight client library that your application uses to access the data service:

```
using System.Linq;
using System.ComponentModel;
using System.Collections.Generic;
using System.Diagnostics;
using System.Text;
using System.Windows.Data;
using TechBioModel;
using System.Data.Services.Client;
using System.Collections.ObjectModel;
```

9. Add the following code to the TechBioModel class. This class calls out to your OData service. First, you initialize a new TechBio object (the object you created via the DataSvcUtil and added to your project) using the URI to your OData service. Then, you execute a LINQ query and populate your Docs DataServiceCollection which is used to bind to the list box on the phone's user interface. In this example, the query asks for all the document data from the Docs table (Entity) where the AuthorID is 113:

```
public MainViewModel()
{
```

```
        LoadData();
    }

    void LoadData()
    {
        TechBio context = new TechBio(new Uri("https://odata.sqlazurelabs.com/↩
OData.svc/v0.1/plqfubbqom/TechBio"));

        var qry = from u in context.Docs
                    where u.AuthorId == 113
                    select u;

        var dsQry = (DataServiceQuery<Doc>)qry;

        dsQry.BeginExecute(r =>
        {
            try
            {
                var result = dsQry.EndExecute(r);
                if (result != null)
                {
                    Deployment.Current.Dispatcher.BeginInvoke(() =>
                    {
                        Docs.Load(result);
                    });
                }
            }
            catch (Exception ex)
            {
                MessageBox.Show(ex.Message.ToString());
            }
        }, null);

    }

    DataServiceCollection<Doc> _docs = new DataServiceCollection<Doc>();

    public DataServiceCollection<Doc> Docs
    {
        get
        {
            return _docs;
        }
        private set
        {
            _docs = value;
        }
    }
```

You're probably wondering why you use the Dispatcher for this call. You do so because the call isn't guaranteed to be on the UI thread. You need to use the Dispatcher to marshal the call to the UI thread.

   10.   In App.xaml.cs, add the following code to the App class:

```
private static TechBioModel viewModel = null;
public static TechBioModel ViewModel
{
    get
    {
        if (viewModel == null)
            viewModel = new TechBioModel();

        return viewModel;
    }
}
```

11. Right-click MainPage.xaml in Solution Explorer, and select View Code. Add the following code below the MainPage constructor:

```
protected override void OnNavigatedTo(System.Windows.Navigation.NavigationEventArgs e)
{
    base.OnNavigatedTo(e);

    if (DataContext == null)
        DataContext = App.ViewModel;

}
```

12. Set the ItemSource property of the list box on the phone UI as shown in Figure 7-17. This binds the list box to the Docs DataServiceCollection so that when the collection is populated, the list box displays the data.

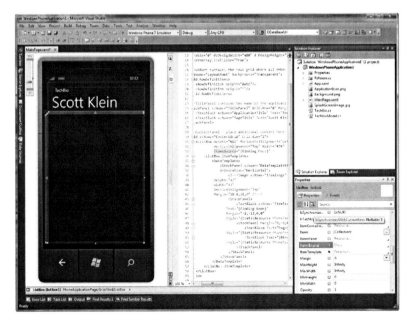

Figure 7-17. Setting the ItemSource property

13. Press F5 to run the project. The Windows Mobile 7 Phone emulator appears, and initially it has a blank screen. But if you look in the status bar at lower-left in Visual Studio, you see that Visual Studio is connecting to the Windows Phone 7 emulator and then deploying the application to the phone. After several seconds, you should see the phone populate with the list of books for Scott Klein, as shown in Figure 7-18.

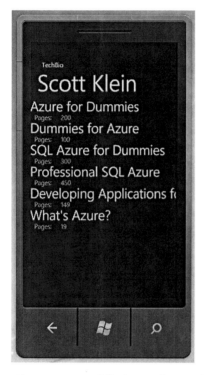

Figure 7-18. Book listing on the Windows Mobile Phone 7 via OData

Now that you've completed this example, you should agree that this is really cool. Getting data on your mobile device has never been easier.

Conclusion

This chapter discussed several topics surrounding OData and SQL Azure. OData is an open protocol for sharing data, providing a way to increase the shared value of data and enabling applications to use a broader set of data. By enabling SQL Azure to expose its data via the OData protocol, myriads of applications can take advantage by consuming that data easily and efficiently.

You saw several examples of OData consumers and producers and then walked through how to OData-enable your SQL Azure database. You then worked on a couple of examples of how to consume the data, specifically via a Windows Phone 7 application, to illustrate how a data consumer can interoperate with a data producer that is far more powerful than before.

In Chapter 8 we discuss how to use SQL Azure with SQL Server Reporting Services (SSRS) to provide reporting capabilities when your data is in SQL Azure.

■ ■ ■

Reporting Services with SQL Azure

Research for this chapter found that other than a few blog and forum posts, not much information is available regarding the use of SQL Server Reporting Services (SSRS) with SQL Azure. The goal of this chapter is to provide a brief overview and example of how to use SSRS and Report Designer to build reports for SQL Azure, to discuss ways you may be able to improve your SSRS experience with SQL Azure, and to look at ways to improve reporting performance.

The main question that comes up when working with reports and SQL Azure is primarily based on where the data for the report comes from. The answer to this question isn't cut and dried—as with everything else Azure, the answer is "it depends." For example, you may end up creating a report that draws on a mix of both on-premises data and SQL Azure data.

Not every report is the same or pulls the same data. You can easily have one report that pulls all of its data from an on-premises database, another report that is 100 percent SQL Azure, and a third report that pull data from both locations.

This chapter first illustrates how to connect a report to, and pull data from, a SQL Azure database using SQL Server 2008 R2 Report Services. You then modify the example to add a subreport to pull additional report data from your local instance. This chapter assumes that you're familiar with SQL Server Reporting Services and how to create and work with reports and subreports. Plenty of great books on SSRS are available if you need an introduction.

Let's get started.

Starting a SQL Azure–Based Report

When you're creating reports that access data from SQL Azure, the process is the same as creating reports that access local data, with one slight difference: the connection to the data. These examples use SQL Server 2008 R2. It comes with Visual Studio 2008 Business Intelligence Development Studio (BIDS), and that is what you use to create and deploy the reports. To create a report, follow these steps:

1. Open BIDS, and create a new Report Server Project. In Figure 8-1 the project is called AzureReports, but feel free to change the name. Click OK.

■ **Note** All the projects throughout this book have used Visual Studio 2010, which uses the .NET Framework 4.0. But because SQL Server 2008 R2 ships with Visual Studio 2008 BIDS, this example uses version 3.5 of the .NET Framework. So, don't be confused by what you see in this chapter's figures versus what you see in other chapters.

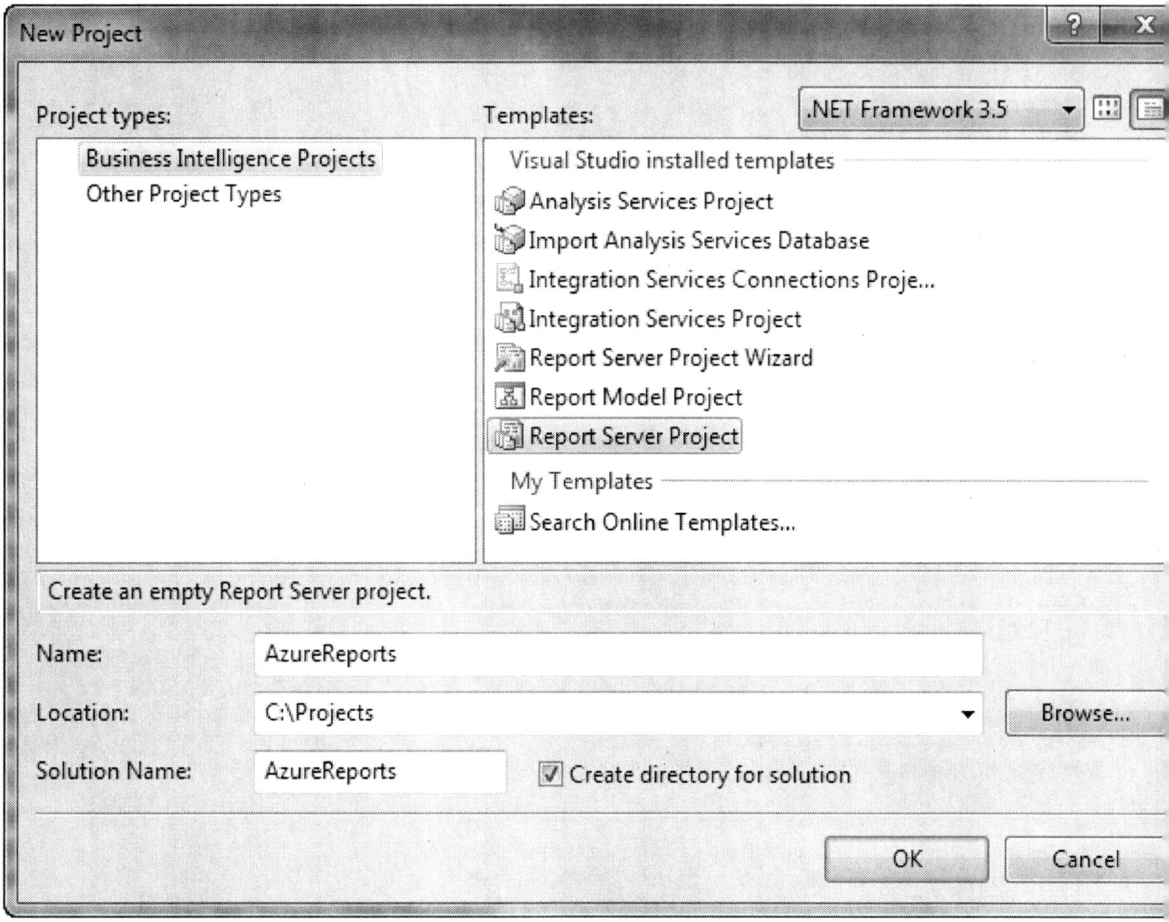

Figure 8-1. New Report Server Project

2. In Solution Explorer, right-click the solution, and select Add → New Item from the context menu.

3. In the Add New Item dialog, select the Report template, and name this report Documents, as shown in Figure 8-2. Click OK.

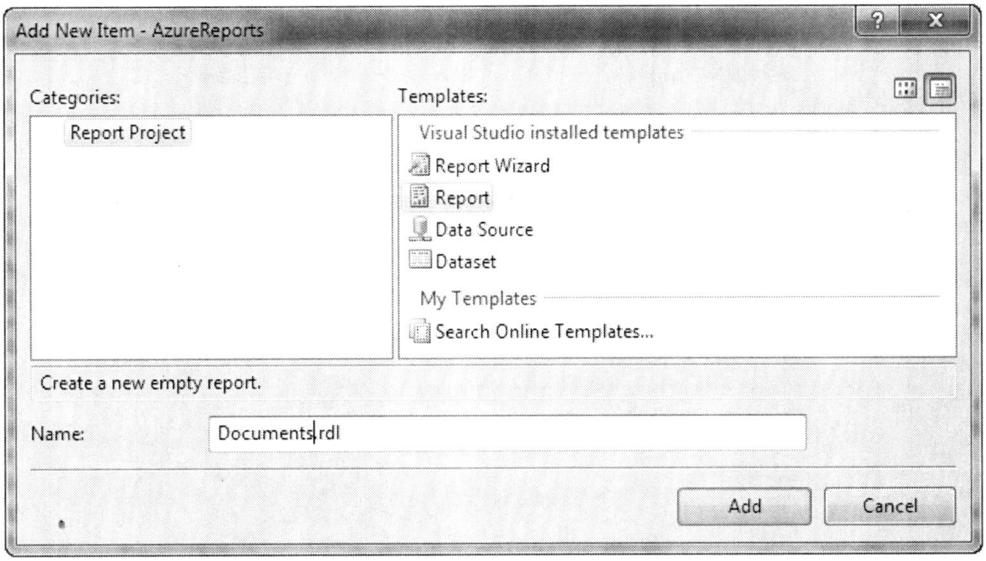

Figure 8-2. Adding a report

At this point, you're staring at a blank report, but you also see a new Report Data tab displayed in the Visual Studio IDE. Your task is to tell the report where to get its data from, and SQL Server 2008 R2 makes it very easy. Prior to SQL Server 2008 R2, you had a couple of data providers to choose from: ADO.NET (SqlClient) and OLE DB. However, R2 added a new SQL Azure–specific provider. You see this shortly.

Creating the SQL Azure Data Source

Continue with these steps:

1. In the Report Data window, right-click the Data Sources node, and select Add Data Source from the context menu, as shown in Figure 8-3.

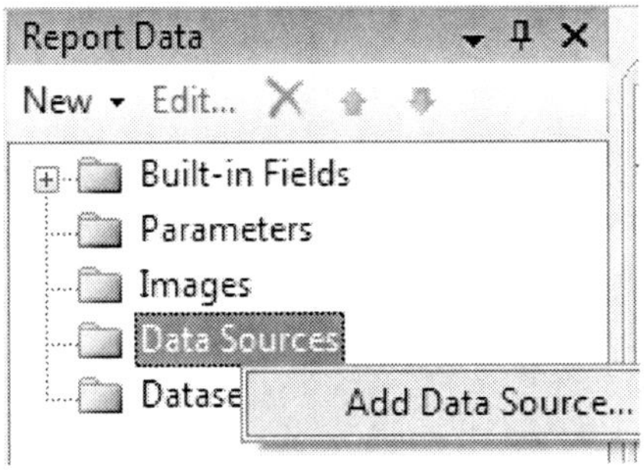

Figure 8-3. Adding a data source

2. In the Data Source Properties dialog, you define the type of connection and the connection properties. Select the "Embedded connection" option, and then click the Type down arrow. You read earlier that SQL Server 2008 R2 includes SQL Azure–specific providers, and this is where you find them. As shown in Figure 8-4, select the new data provider for SQL Azure called Microsoft SQL Azure (what else are you going to call it?).

When you select this provider, the Connection String text box defaults to
`Encrypt=True;TrustServerCertificate=False`

Although these two parameters and associated values are defaulted for you, it's recommended that you not change them. The `Encrypt` parameter indicates that SQL Server will use SSL encryption for all data sent between the server and client if the server has a cert installed. The `TrustServerCertificate` property tells the transport layer to use SSL to encrypt the channel and bypass walking the cert chain to validate trust. When both `Encrypt` and `TrustServerCertificate` are set to `True`, the encryption level specified *on the server* is used even if the value of the `Encrypt` parameter in this connection string is set to `False`.

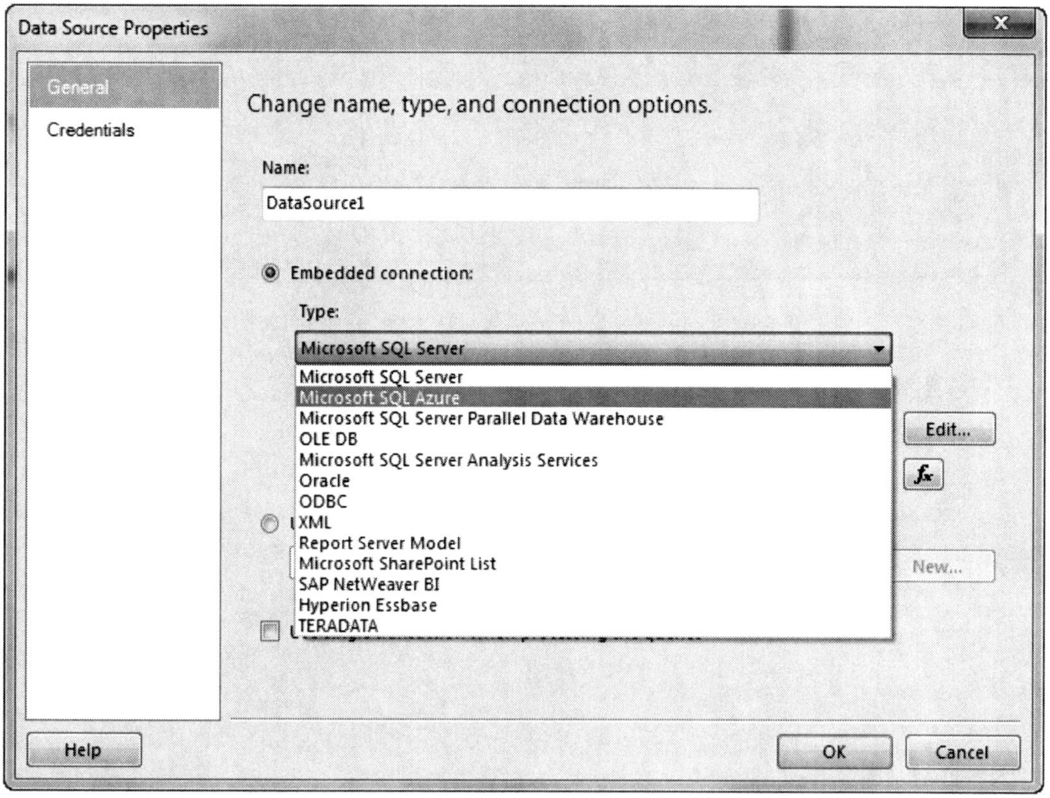

Figure 8-4. Data Source Properties dialog

However, even with this default string set, you still need to add the SQL Azure connection information, so continue as follows:

3. Click the Edit button to open the Connection Properties dialog, shown in Figure 8-5. Enter your SQL Azure database, username, and password. You should know by now that you can't use Windows Authentication with SQL Azure, so make sure you enter the SQL Azure account username and password.

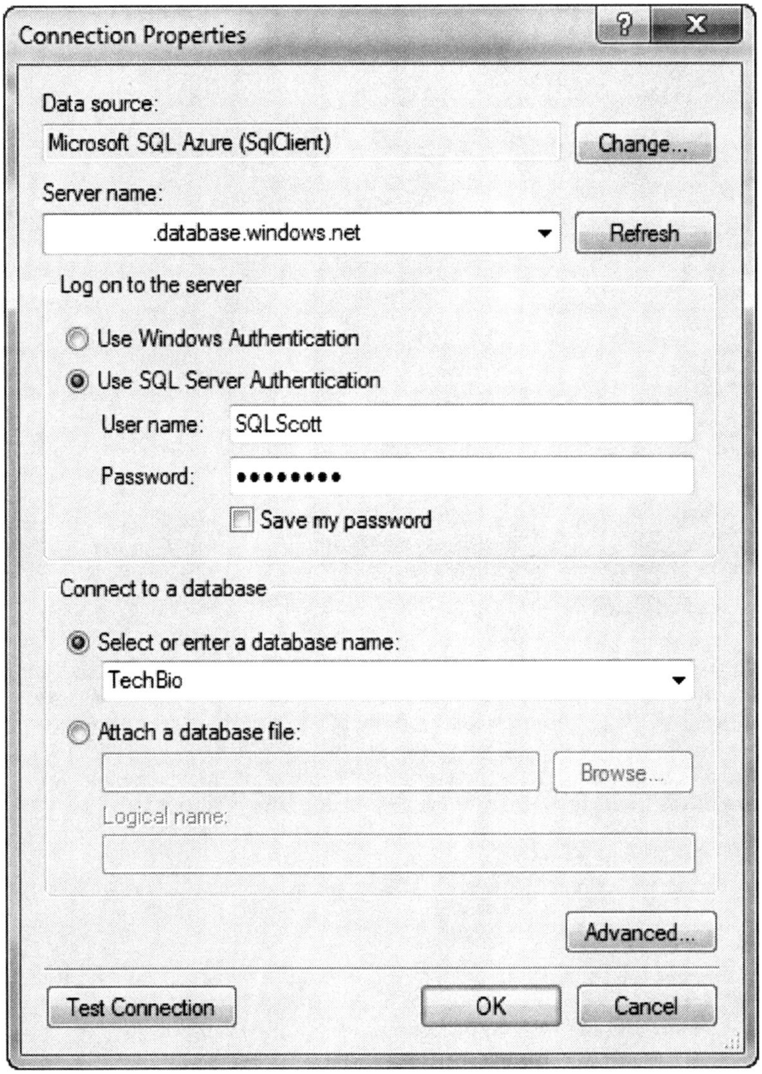

Figure 8-5. Connection Properties dialog

4. Select (or type in) the database you want to pull the data from, and then click Test Connection to ensure that all your settings are correct.

5. Click OK to close this dialog and take you back to the Data Source Properties dialog. It should now look like Figure 8-6, which shows the appropriate connection type and connection string.

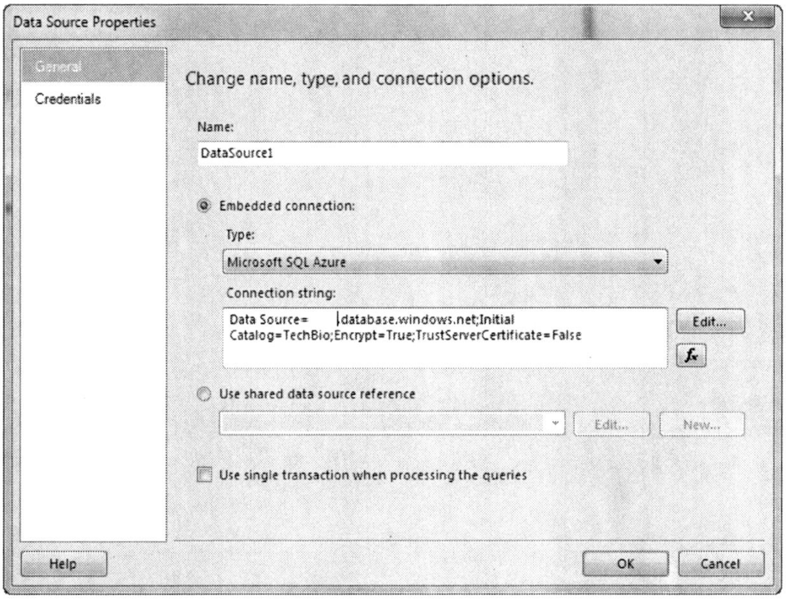

Figure 8-6. Completed Data Source Properties dialog

Granted, these steps are no different than those for connecting to a local database. But although the steps are the same, some of the key selection components are different, such as those in Figures 8-4 and 8-5, where you select the specific Microsoft SQL Azure provider and the SQL Azure–specific connection information.

Your data source definition also allows you to specify the credentials with which to connect to your data source. Selecting Credentials at left in the Data Source Properties dialog shows you four options.

- Windows Authentication (integrated security)
- Prompt for credentials
- Specify a user name and password
- Do not use credentials

Obviously, you need to use credentials, so not specifying credentials isn't the option you want. And integrated security isn't available with Azure, so that won't work either. You can either prompt for credentials or specify a username and password. The default value is to prompt for credentials; if you leave that setting, the report prompts you to enter a username and password every time you run the report. Continue as follows:

6. Best practice says that in a production environment, you should use integrated security. But because that isn't an option with SQL Azure, select the "Specify a user name and password" option, and enter the username and password of an account that has access to the appropriate database.

With your data source created, you now need to add a dataset for the report. For each data source, you can create one or more datasets. Each dataset specifies the fields from the data source that you would like to use in the report. The data set also contains, among other things, the query used to get the data and any query parameters to filter the data:

7. In the Report Data window, right-click the Datasets node, and select Add Dataset from the context menu. Doing so opens the Dataset Properties window, shown in Figure 8-7.

8. The Query page of the Dataset Properties window allows you to do two primary things: specify the data source on which this dataset is based, and specify the query type and associated query. For this example, base your dataset on the data source you created earlier. The query type is Text, meaning you type a T-SQL statement in the Query field. For this example, you want to return everything (all rows and columns) from the Users table, so enter the SELECT statement shown in Figure 8-7. The Name of the dataset defaults to DataSet1, which is fine for this example. Click OK.

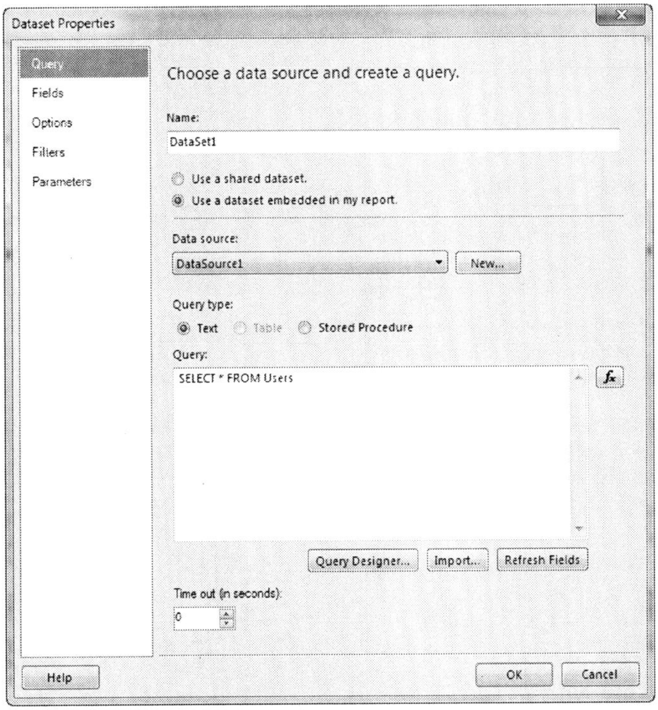

Figure 8-7. *Dataset Properties dialog*

There is nothing else you need to do for your dataset; you're ready to define and lay out your report.

Creating the Report Design

With your report in Design view, you can now start laying it out. In this example you don't do anything flashy or extensive, just something simple to demonstrate your connectivity to SQL Azure. Follow these steps:

1. From the Toolbox, drag a text box and table onto the Report Designer window. Move the text box to the top of the report: it's the report title. Change the text in the text box to `My First Azure SSRS Report`.

2. The table you placed on the report has three columns, but you need five. Right-click any of the existing columns, and select Insert Column → Right from the context menu to add an additional column. Add one more column for a total of five.

3. From the Report Data window, drag the Name, Intro, Title, State, and Country columns from the dataset to the columns in the table, as shown in Figure 8-8.

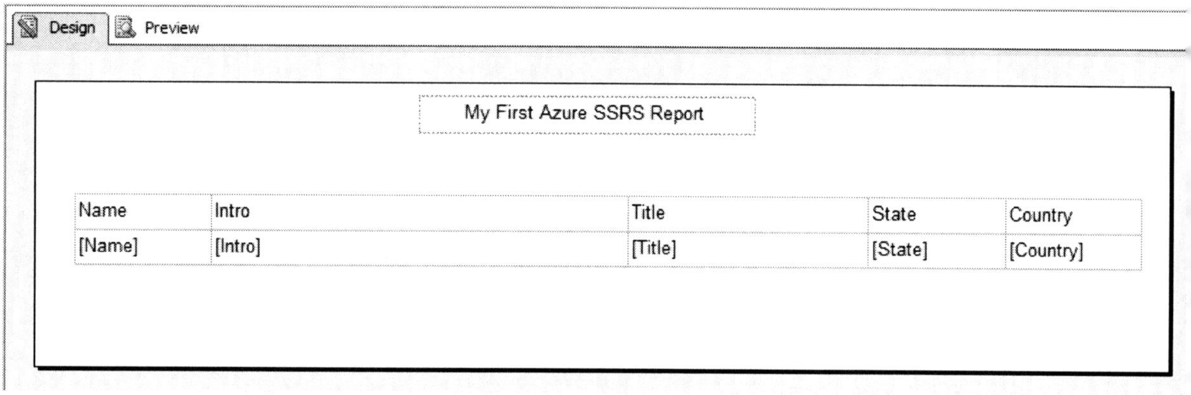

Figure 8-8. Report Design view

Your simple report is finished—it isn't complex or pretty, but it's functional. You're now ready to test the report: to do that, select the Preview tab. You see the result in Figure 8-9.

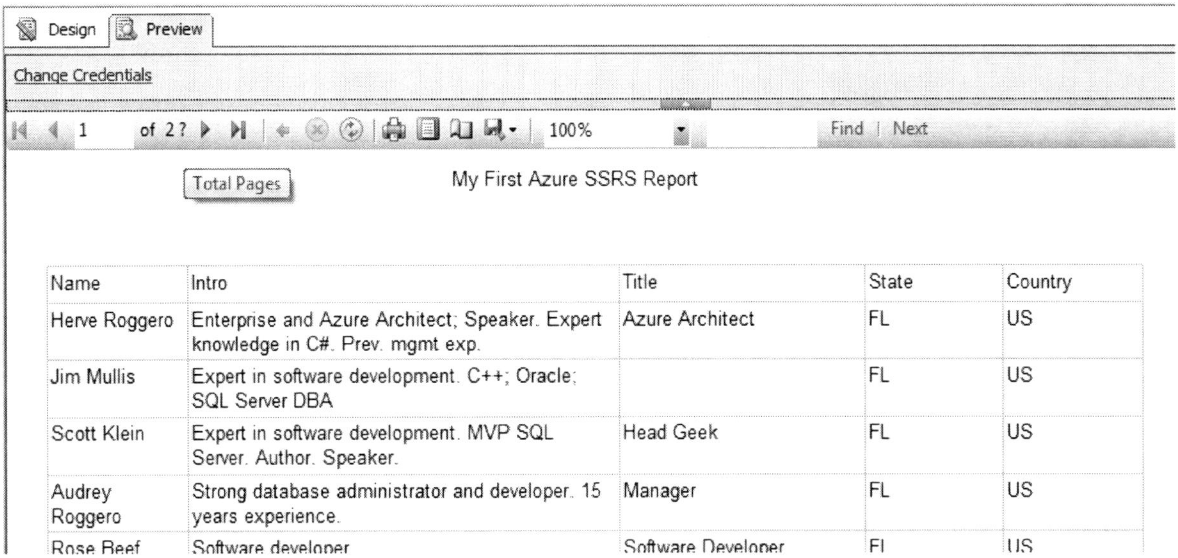

Figure 8-9. Report Preview view

Figure 8-9 shows the results of your labors, displaying the Name, Intro, Title, State, and Country data from the Users table in your SQL Azure database. If your report looks like this, congratulations are in order—you just created a report that queries a SQL Azure database.

Deploying the Report

Currently, you can't deploy a report to Azure, so all reports must be deployed locally. To deploy a report, follow these steps:

1. Right-click the report solution, and select Properties from the context menu.

2. In the Property Pages dialog, the only thing you need to enter is the TargetServerURL, shown in Figure 8-10. Notice also the name of the TargetReportFolder, which in this case is AzureReports—the name of your Visual Studio solution.

3. Right-click the solution in Solution Explorer, and select Deploy from the context menu.

4. When the report has deployed successfully, open your browser, and navigate to http://[machinename]/Reports. You should be presented with your SQL Server Reporting Services Home folder and the AzureReports folder. In the AzureReports folder is your newly created Documents report. To view the report, click the link for it.

You just walked through a simple example of creating a report that pulls data from SQL Azure. Let's modify it to add a subreport that pulls data from the on-premises database.

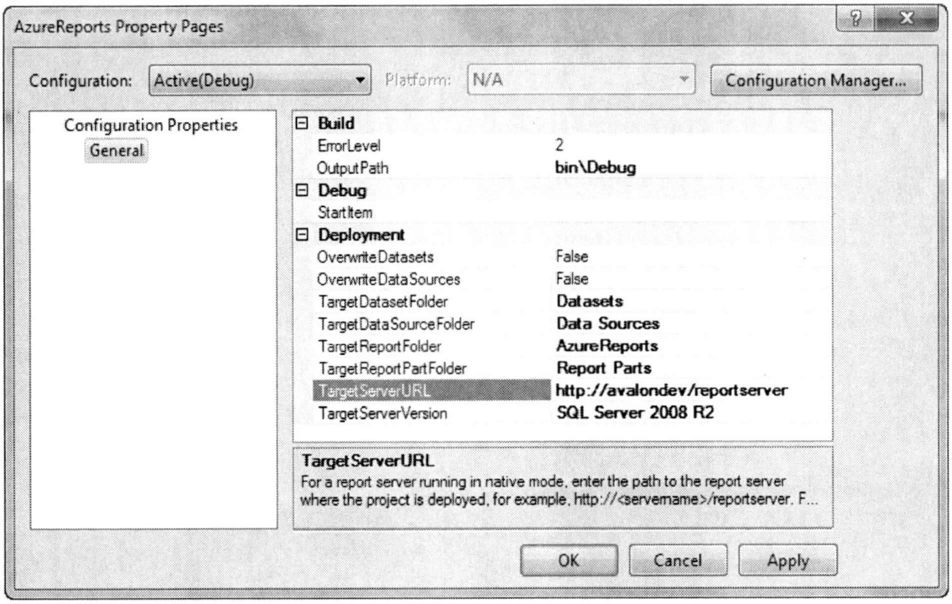

Figure 8-10. Solution Property Page

Creating a Subreport

Your report is called Documents, but it displays users—and that's why you're going to add a subreport. You want to display all documents for the related users (one user can have multiple documents). To do this, you need to create another report and, along with it, a new data source and dataset. This time, however, you want to pull the documents from your on-premises database. Thus, the users come from SQL Azure, and the related documents from your on-premises database. Follow these steps:

1. You need to create the subreport to display the documents. Using the steps outlined earlier in this chapter, create a new report and an associated data source and dataset. For this exercise, the name of this new report doesn't matter. The data source should be pointed to the local, on-premises copy of the database, and the dataset should be the same as the dataset for the Azure-based report.

2. With the new report open in Design mode, create a new data source that points to your local (on-premises) copy of the TechBio database. This new data source can use a different authentication method if you like, such as Windows Authentication (integrated security).

3. Create a new dataset based on this new data source. On the Query page in the Dataset Properties dialog, select the data source you just created, and use the Text query type. Enter the query shown in Figure 8-11: it pulls from the Docs table, and you need to apply a filter so that it gives you only the documents for the associated user. You want this to be dynamic, so your filter uses a parameter that you define shortly.

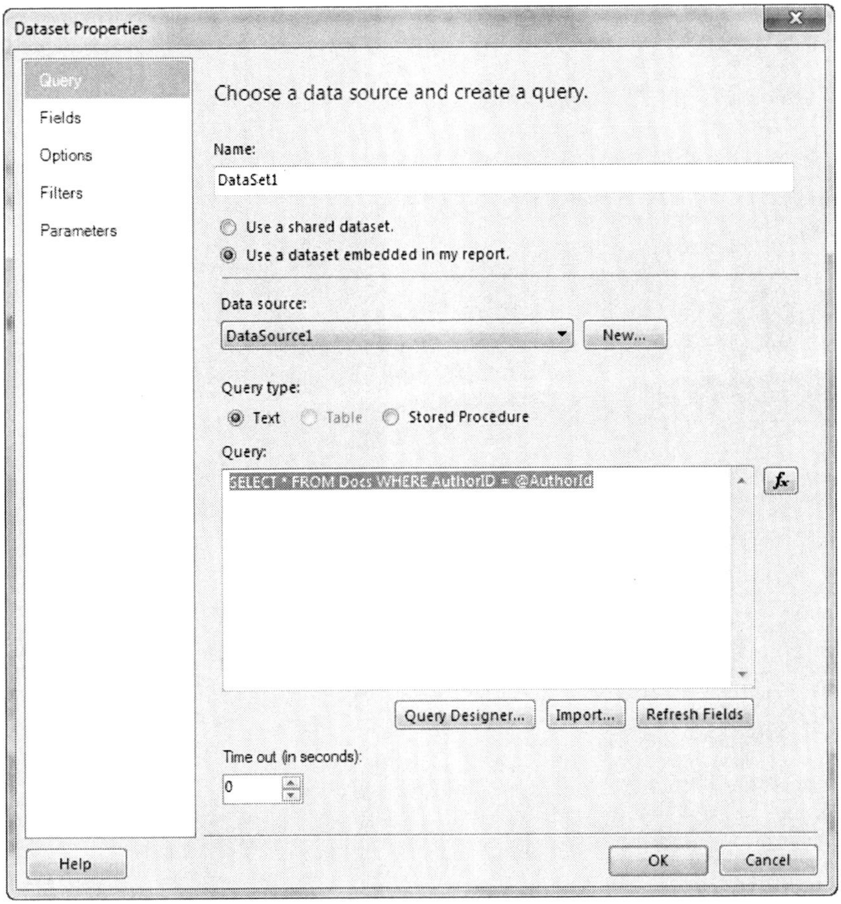

Figure 8-11. Dataset for the local database

4. Select the Parameters page of the Dataset Properties dialog (see Figure 8-12), and notice that the parameter was added for you when you used it in the query on the Query page. It's nice to see that SSRS automatically picks up this information.

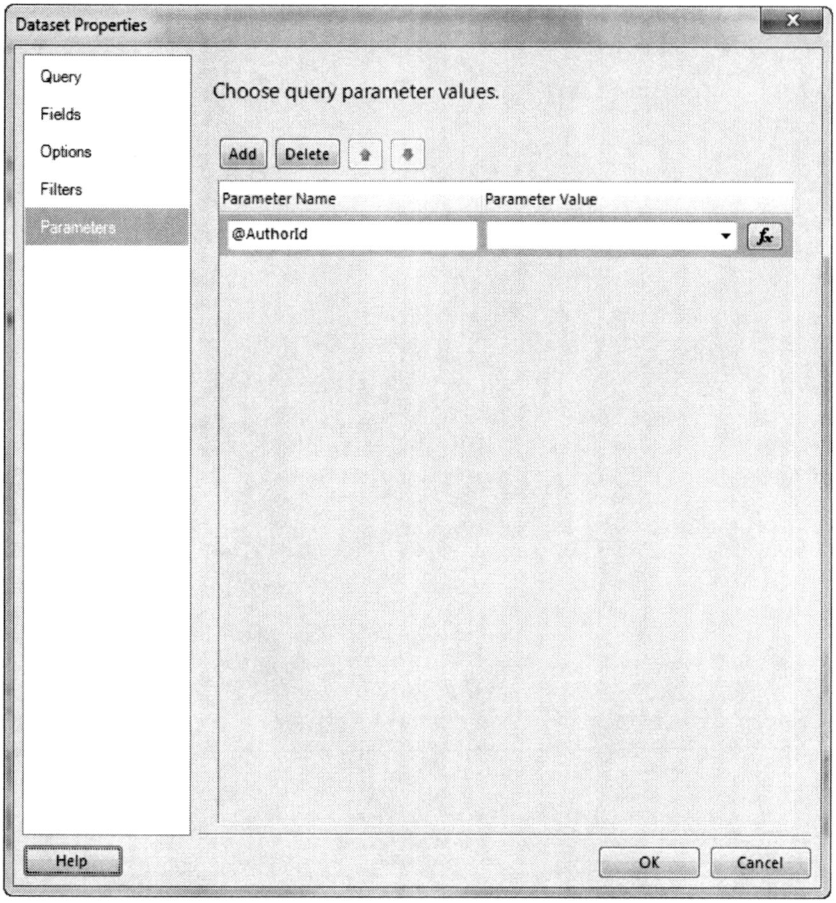

Figure 8-12. Parameters page

5. Your next step is to design your report. Back on the report, make sure the Design tab is selected, and drag a table onto the report. Again, the table has three columns by default, and you want to display five; so, add two more columns, and then center the table on the report.

6. From the Report Data window, drag Name, Descr, Pages, Download Price, and Purchase Price columns onto the table. When you're done, the report should look like Figure 8-13.

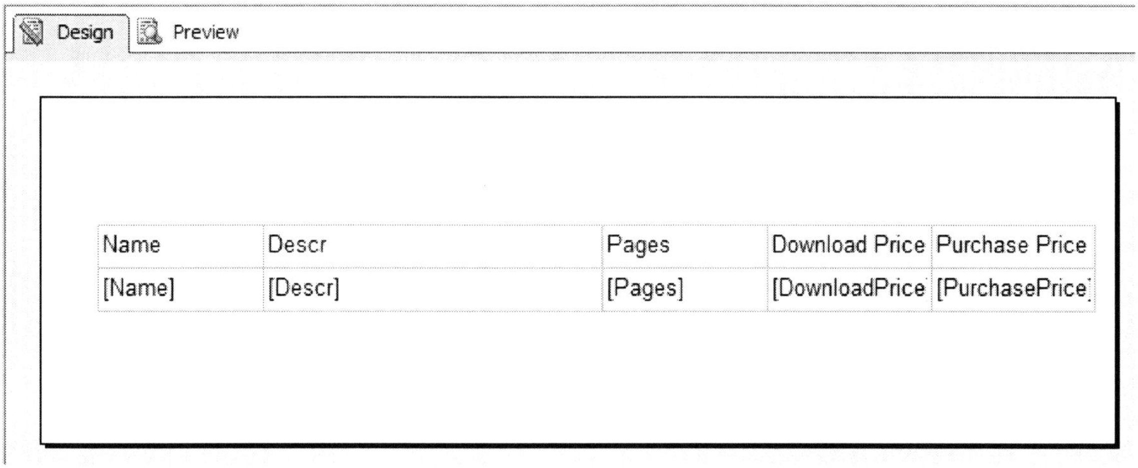

```
┌──────────────────────────────────────────────────────────────────────────┐
│ 🖳 Design  🔍 Preview                                                       │
├──────────────────────────────────────────────────────────────────────────┤
```

Name	Descr	Pages	Download Price	Purchase Price
[Name]	[Descr]	[Pages]	[DownloadPrice]	[PurchasePrice]

Figure 8-13. *Completed subreport*

7. Test the report by selecting the Preview tab. The report prompts you for an AuthorId value: type in a valid value (111 or 113 should work). The report should display the appropriate data for the id you entered.

Adding the Subreport to the Main Report

Now that you're confident that your subreport works, let's wire it up to the main report:

1. With the first report open (the Documents report), there are two ways you can add a subreport: you can either drag the report you've designated as a subreport from Solution Explorer onto the parent report, which automatically sets the appropriate properties of the subreport; or you can drag a SubReport control from the Toolbox onto the parent report and manually set the properties. How you choose to do it isn't important, as long as the appropriate properties are set; you access them by right-clicking the subreport and selecting Properties. In the Subreport Properties dialog, make sure the correct report is selected as the subreport.

2. Select the Parameters page, and add the parameter that is being passed from the parent report to the subreport—in this case, AuthorId.

3. You need to make a change to the parent report so your data is displayed correctly. Right now, the table lists all of the users. If you kept it that way, the report would list all the users and then list all the documents. Instead, you want it to list the users and associated documents, grouped by user. To do this, delete the table on the parent report and, from the Report Data window, drag the Name, Intro, and Title fields from the dataset onto the report, as shown in Figure 8-14. Now, when you run the report, it lists a user and that user's documents, as shown in Figure 8-15.

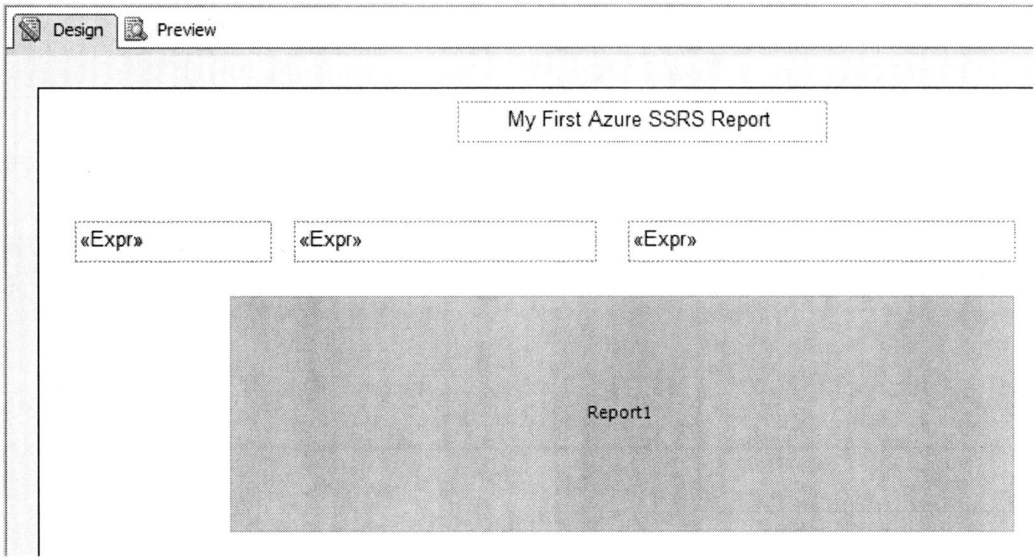

Figure 8-14. Modified master report

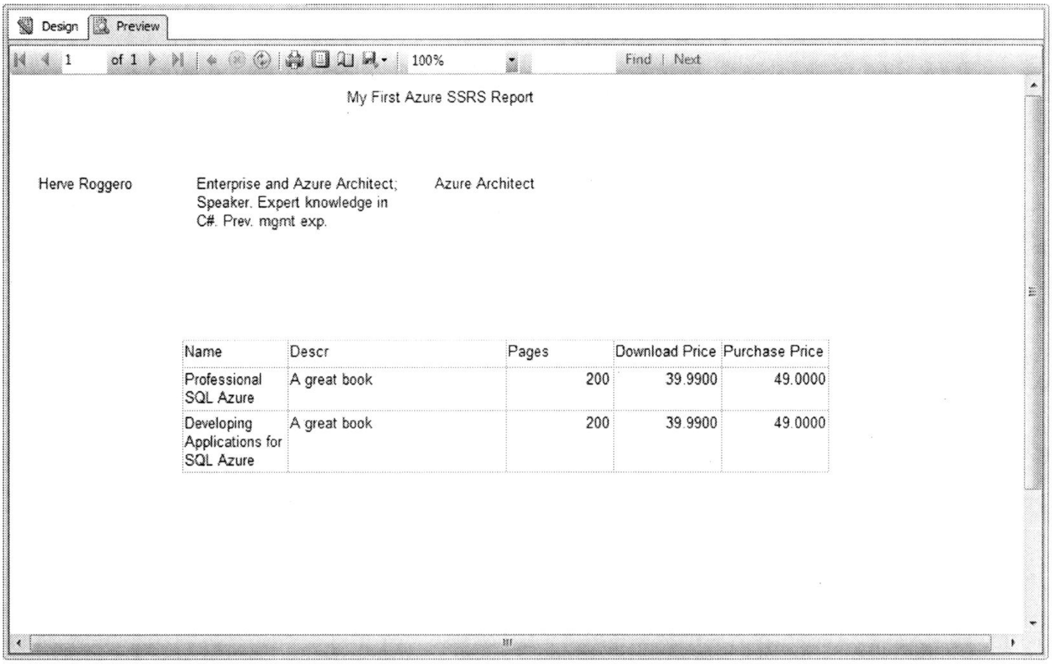

Figure 8-15. Finished report

Conclusion

In this chapter, you've seen how to create a SQL Server Reporting Services report that gets its data from SQL Azure. You've also seen how to create a hybrid report that pulls data from both SQL Azure on an on-premises database. Chapter 9 will discuss how to deploy an ASP.NET application in Windows Azure and how to connect to it SQL Azure.

■ ■ ■

Windows Azure and ASP.NET

This chapter walks you through the steps of creating a Windows Azure application and deploying it in the cloud. Whenever you see a reference to Windows Azure, it means you're building a web solution that can be deployed in the cloud. By now, you know you can't create WinForms applications in Windows Azure.

An application published in the Microsoft cloud is referred to as a *service*, even if it's a web site. So, you first create a new Windows Azure service to host the web site. Then, you create a simple ASP.NET application and publish it in the cloud.

Creating a Windows Azure Service

First, you need to set up a Windows Azure service in the cloud so you can deploy a Windows Azure application later. Each Windows Azure service created in the cloud is mapped to a virtual machine; however, you have no control over the virtual machine itself—you can only deploy your applications and configure certain parameters. Follow these steps:

1. Open Internet Explorer, and go to http://windows.azure.com. You're prompted to sign in with your Windows Live account.

2. When you've logged in, you see the Windows Azure project you created in Chapter 3. Click your project name; this gives you the list of Azure services you've created so far, as shown in Figure 9-1.

▓ **Note** This chapter assumes you've signed up for the Windows Azure service. Signing up for the service automatically creates a Windows Azure project in the cloud.

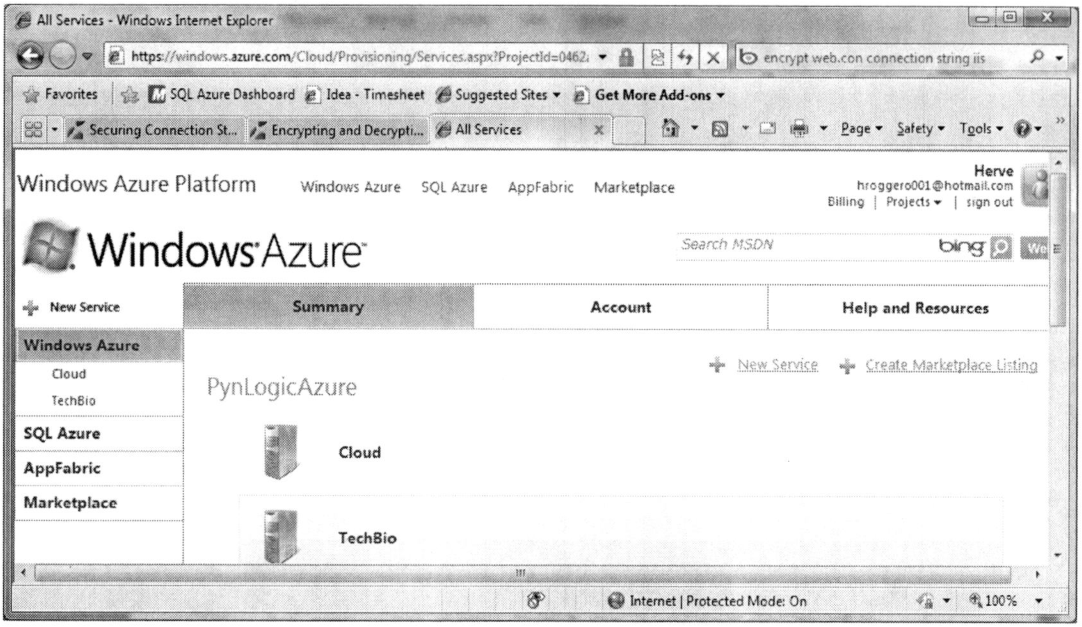

***Figure 9-1.** Windows Azure services summary page*

3. Click New Service to create your first Windows Azure service. Doing so brings up a page asking which kind of service you want to create:

4. **Storage Account**. Lets you store large amounts of data

5. **Hosted Services**. Lets you run services and web applications

6. Click Hosted Services. Another page opens, and you're prompted to enter a Service Label and a Service Description (see Figure 9-2). The Service Label must be unique across all existing services in the cloud. If the name you enter is already registered, a message says so. Click Next.

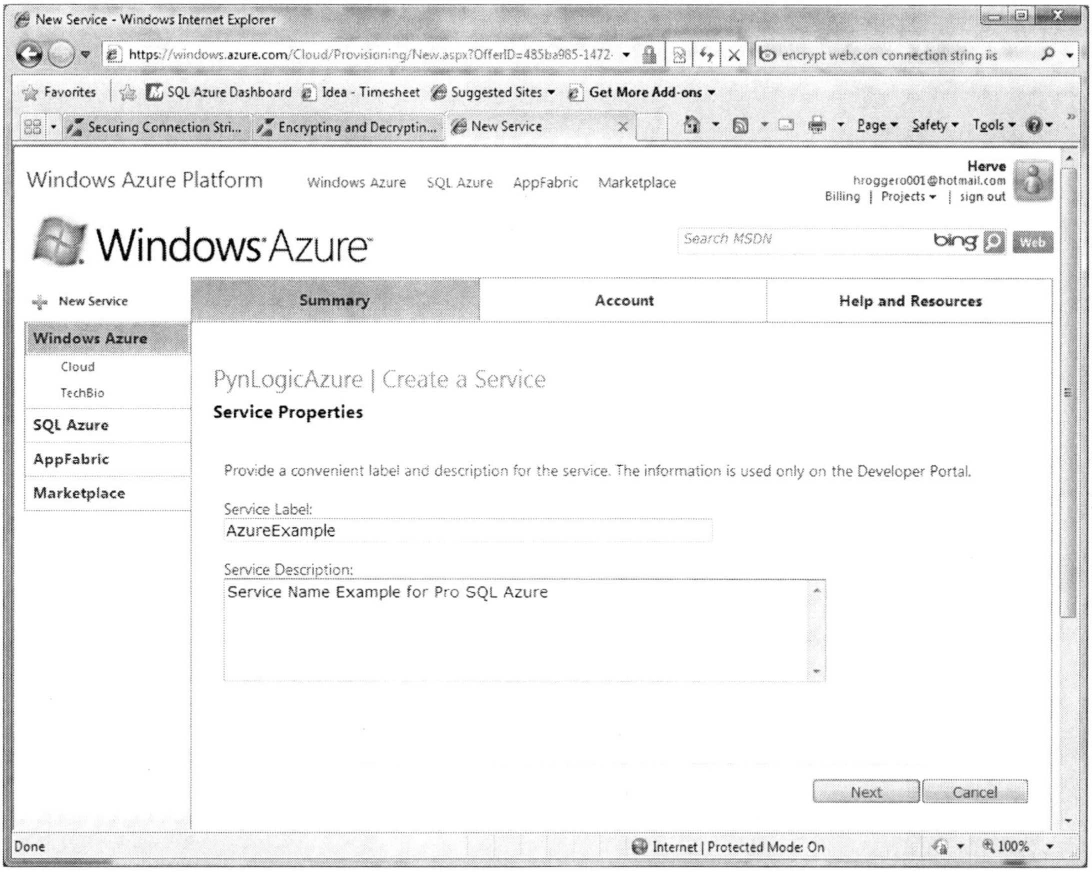

Figure 9-2. Creating a new Azure service

7. The configuration screen in Figure 9-3 allows you to select a unique service name to use for your URL. This URL is available on the public Internet and as such must be globally unique. You also need to select a Service Affinity option. Figure 9-3 shows that you're creating a new service to be made available through http://AzureExample.cloudapp.net and hosted in an existing affinity group that you created when creating your SQL Azure database. The affinity group is called USSouthGroup, and it's located in South Central US.

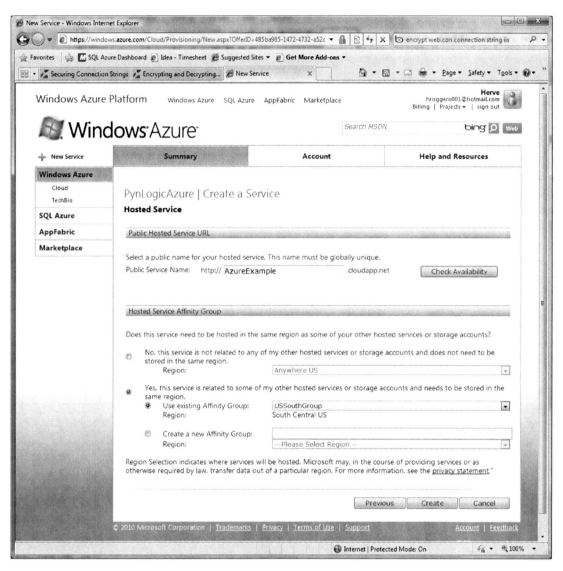

Figure 9-3. Windows Azure service configuration page

As mentioned in Chapter 1, creating an affinity group is very important for two reasons:

- **Price**. When a Windows Azure service connects to a SQL Azure database located in the same region, there are no additional charges when transferring data between the service and the database.

- **Failover**. If something happens and either the Windows Azure service or the SQL Azure database must failover to another region, all the services in the same affinity group are moved together if possible, keeping the performance and cost structure of the service consistent.

8. To make sure your service is created successfully, click Check Availability in the configuration window shown in Figure 9-3. A message is returned indicating whether the check was successful. If is the service name is available, click Create. When the service is created, you see a page similar to the one shown in Figure 9-4.

Figure 9-4. Windows Azure service management page

■ **Note** As long as no code is deployed on this service, you aren't charged. However, as soon as you deploy something, the clock starts ticking from a billing standpoint.

Creating a Windows Azure Project

Let's create a simple Windows Azure application in Visual Studio that displays a list of database users. The Windows Azure project is an ASP.NET application created with a special project template: Cloud.

Configuring Your Development Environment

You must first configure the Windows Azure Tools on your development environment to be able to develop a Windows Azure ASP.NET application. You must be running Windows Server 2008 or higher, or Windows Vista or higher. The Windows Azure Tools provide a runtime environment on your machine that allows you to develop and test a Windows Azure project. It basically runs a local cloud for development purposes. After it's installed, you see a new project type: Cloud. When creating your project in Visual Studio, you can select the Cloud project type; an option to install the Windows Azure Tools is available the first time you do so.

■ **Note** If you need to download the Windows Azure Tools, go to the Microsoft Download Center at www.microsoft.com/downloads/. Search for Azure Tools, and pick the version that applies best to your Visual Studio version. Make sure to download and install this extension.

Creating Your First Visual Studio Cloud Project

To create a Visual Studio cloud project, follow these steps:

1. Start Visual Studio in elevated mode (as an Administrator). To do so, right-click Microsoft Visual Studio 2008 or Microsoft Visual Studio 2010, and select "Run as administrator," as shown in Figure 9-5. Running as Administrator is required by the Windows Azure simulation tools that give you the ability to test your Azure solution locally.

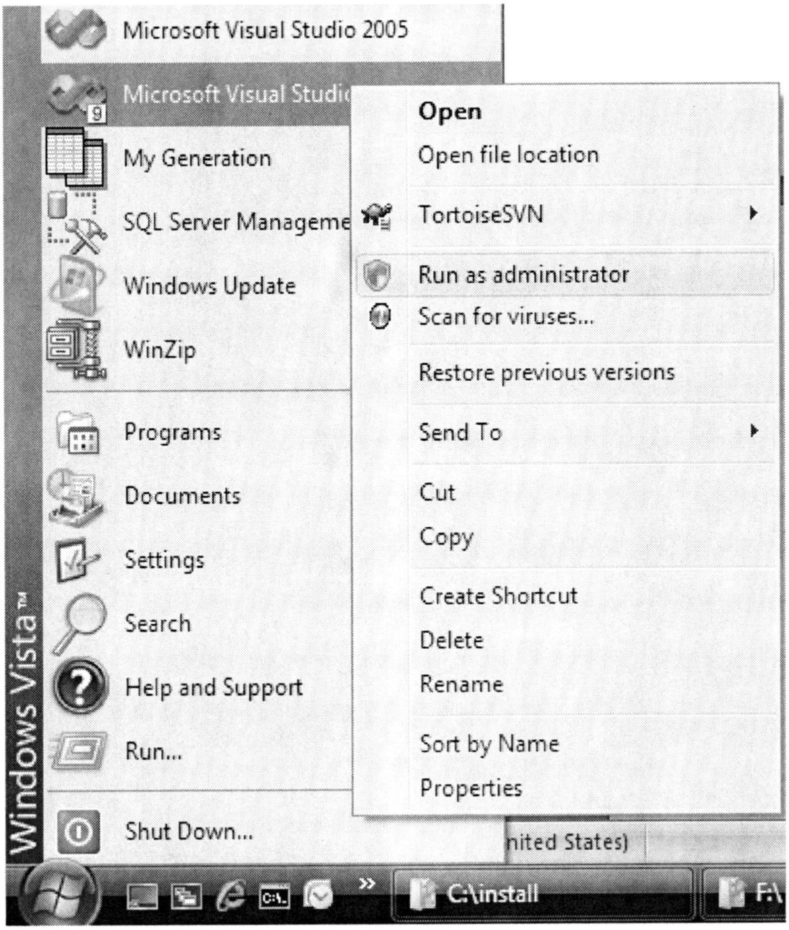

Figure 9-5. Start Visual Studio in elevated mode.

If you don't start Visual Studio in elevated mode, you're able to create the project but you can't run it. If you try, you get an error message telling you to restart Visual Studio, as shown in Figure 9-6.

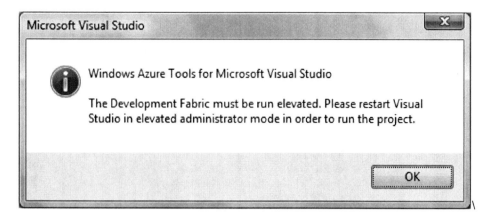

Figure 9-6. Error trying to run an Azure project when not in elevated mode

2. Choose File → New → New Project to bring up the window shown in Figure 9-7 for Visual Studio 2008 or Figure 9-8 for Visual Studio 2010. Select the Cloud project type (Cloud Service in Visual Studio 2010), and choose Windows Azure Cloud service.

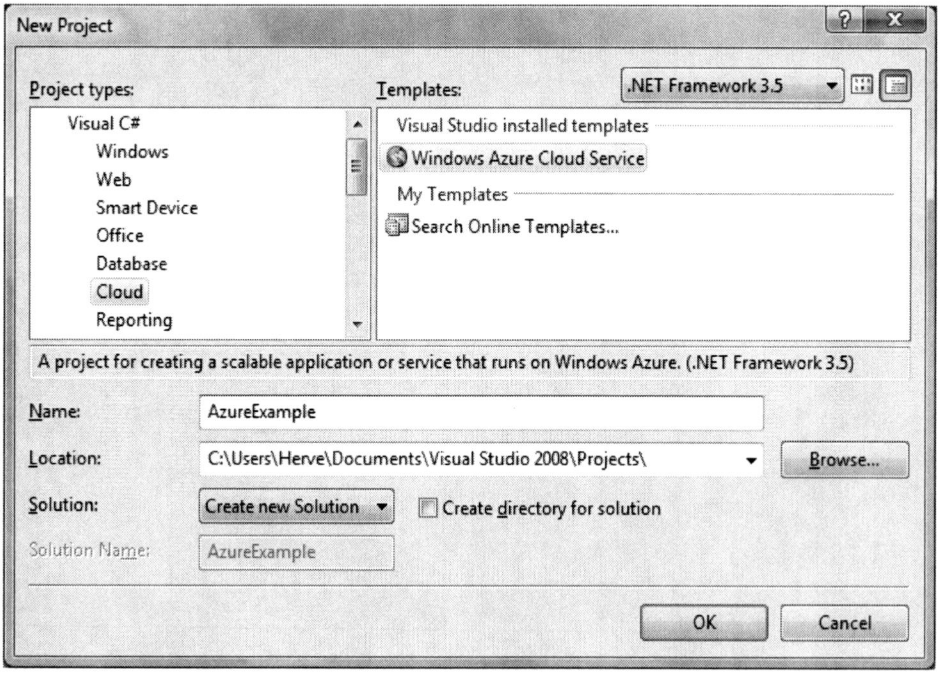

Figure 9-7. Cloud project type in Visual Studio 2008

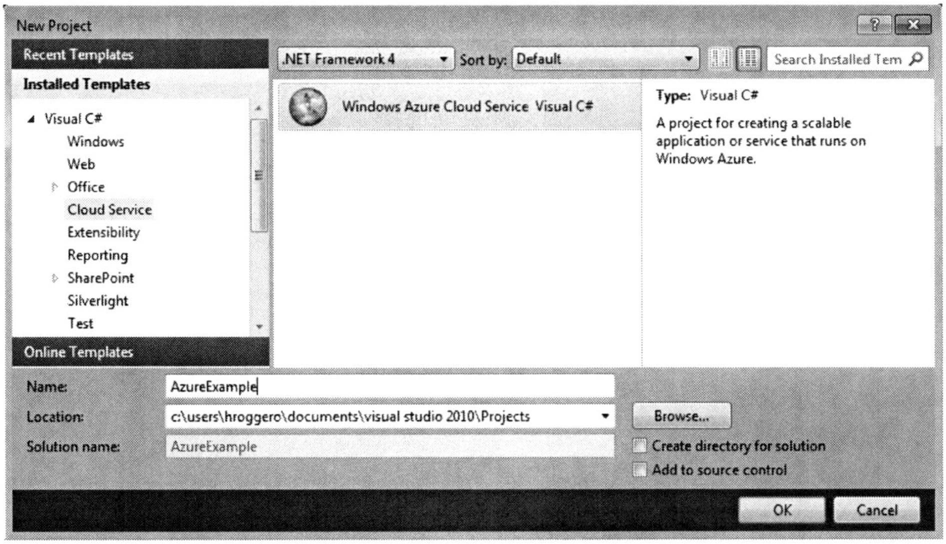

Figure 9-8. Cloud Service project type in Visual Studio 2010

3. Enter a name for your project, and click OK. A new screen comes up (see Figure 9-9) in which you can select a role for your application. The role of your ASP.NET application dictates its primary purpose and what you're able to do with the project. The following roles are available:

- **ASP.NET Web Role**. Lets you create a web site with ASP.NET.

- **ASP.NET MVC 2 Web Role**. Lets you create an MVC 2 web application (only available in Visual Studio 2010).

- **WCF Web Service Role**. Allows you to create a WCF service in Windows Azure.

- **Worker Role**. Equivalent to a background service in Windows Azure that has no user interface.

- **CGI Web Role**. Lets you create a web application using a technology other than ASP.NET, such as Python.

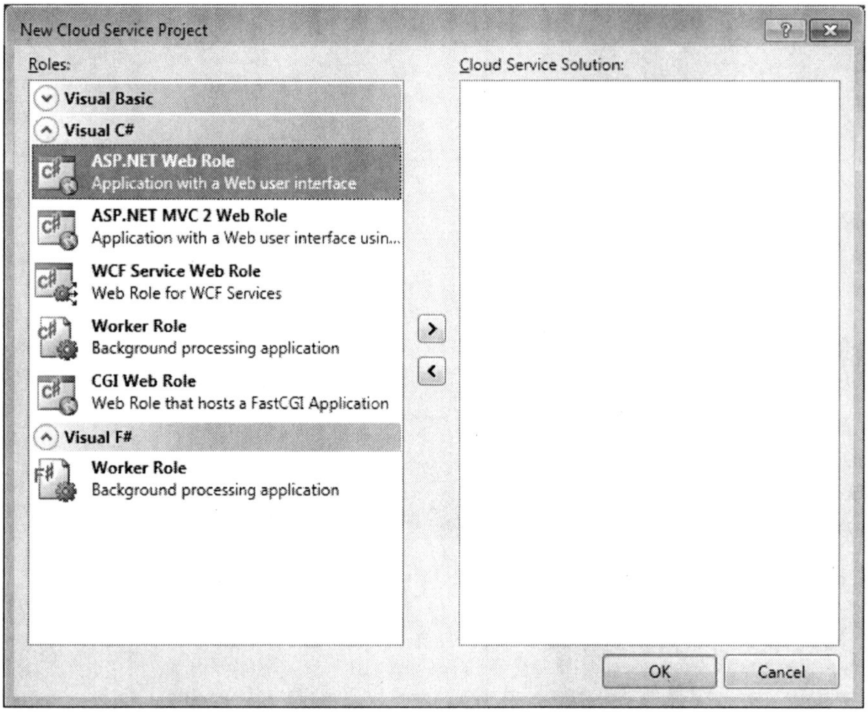

Figure 9-9. Role Types in Visual Studio 2010

4. For this example, select the first option (ASP.NET Web Role), and click the right arrow (⬛). Doing so adds a new ASP.NET web role in the list of services, named of WebRole1.

5. To change the name, select WebRole1 and press the F2 key or click the Edit link. To see the Edit link, place your mouse somewhere on the WebRole1 service list item: you see two icons come up on the right. The first one (with the pencil) allows you to edit the name, and the second lets you remove this web role (see Figure 9-10).

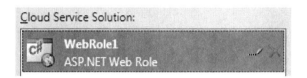

Figure 9-10. Editing the web role's name

6. Change the name to **wrAzureExample**, and press the Enter Key. Don't use AzureExample as the web role name, or there will be a conflict with the solution name provided earlier. The web role should now look like Figure 9-11.

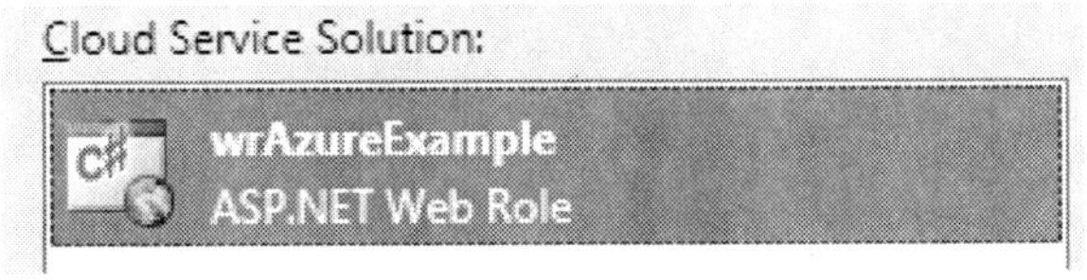

Figure 9-11. Web role name changed

7. Click OK.

At this point, you've created a new cloud solution. Solution Explorer looks a little different than it does for a typical ASP.NET project. Your cloud solution contains two projects: the AzureExample project and the wrAzureExample web role, which is itself a project, as shown in Figure 9-12. The AzureExample project contains configuration files that will be deployed later in Windows Azure.

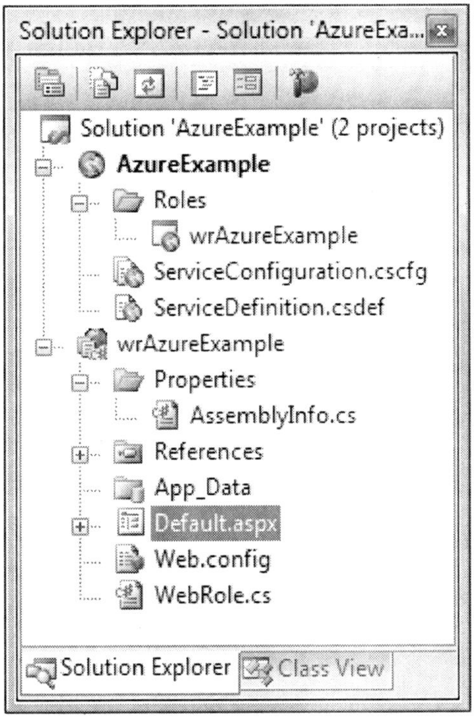

Figure 9-12. Project layout for the ASP.NET web role

■ **Note** At the time of this writing, Windows Azure supports .NET 3.5 SP1 and .NET 4.0.

Connecting a GridView to SQL Azure

Continue the example by following these steps:

1. Add a GridView control on the Default.aspx page, and connect it to a SQL Azure database. Although SqlDataSource is compatible with SQL Azure, it isn't possible to add a SqlDataSource and configure it with the built-in wizard; these steps next show you how to configure the SqlDataSource manually.

2. Open the Default.aspx page, and select Design view.

3. Drag a SqlDataSource from the Toolbox. Drag a GridView control on the page as well, and set its Data Source property to SqlDataSource1, as shown in Figure 9-13.

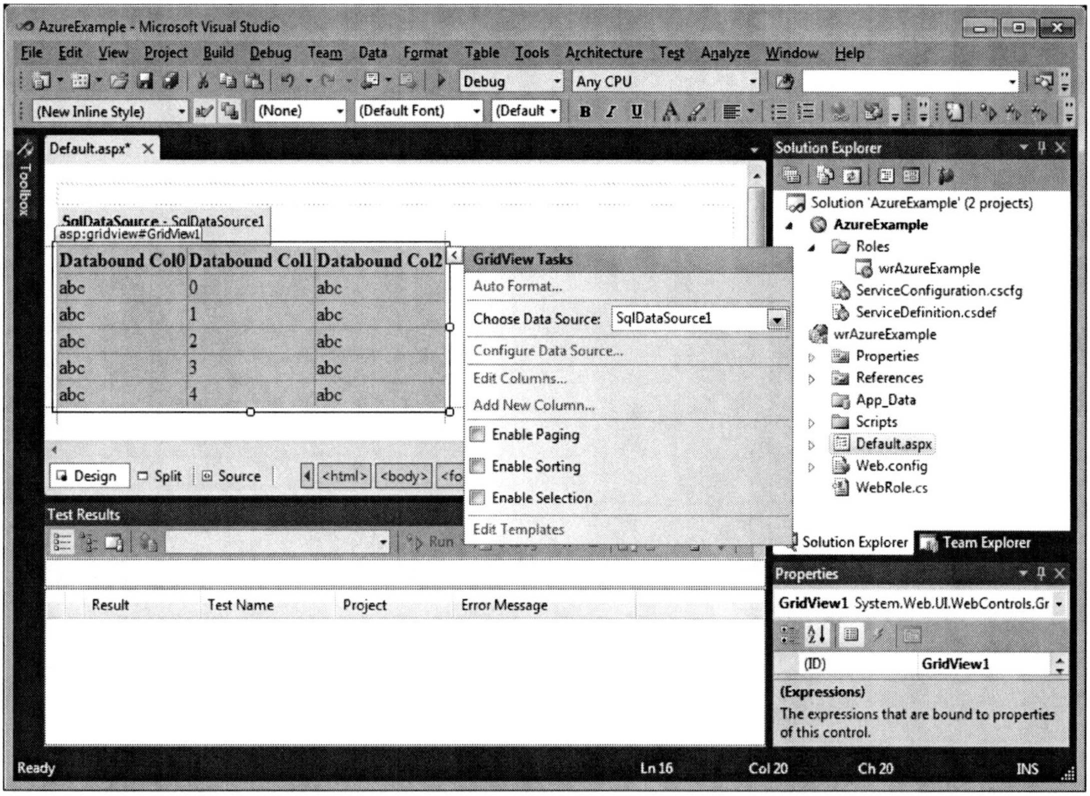

Figure 9-13. Changing the GridView's Data Source property

4. Open the web.config file, and enter your connection string. (Chapter 3 explains how to retrieve your connection string from the Azure Portal.) You need to add a connectionStrings node under the configuration node, as shown in the following example:

```
<connectionStrings>
    <add
        name="Connection1"
        providerName="System.Data.SqlClient"
        connectionString="Server=tcp:jt4y4mmglp.database.windows.net;
            Database=EnzoLog;User ID=test@jt4y4mmglp;
            Password=yourPasswordHere;
            Trusted_Connection=False;Encrypt=True;"/>
</connectionStrings>
```

■ **Note** Make sure to specify the user ID as *<user name>@<server name>*.

---

5. Go back to the Default.aspx page, and change the SqlDataSource settings as follows by adding the ConnectionString and the SelectCommand settings manually.

```
<asp:SqlDataSource ID="SqlDataSource1" runat="server"
    ConnectionString="<%$ ConnectionStrings:Connection1 %>"
    SelectCommand="SELECT uid, name FROM sys.sysusers ORDER BY 1" >
</asp:SqlDataSource>
```

Running the project should give you output similar to that shown in Figure 9-14.

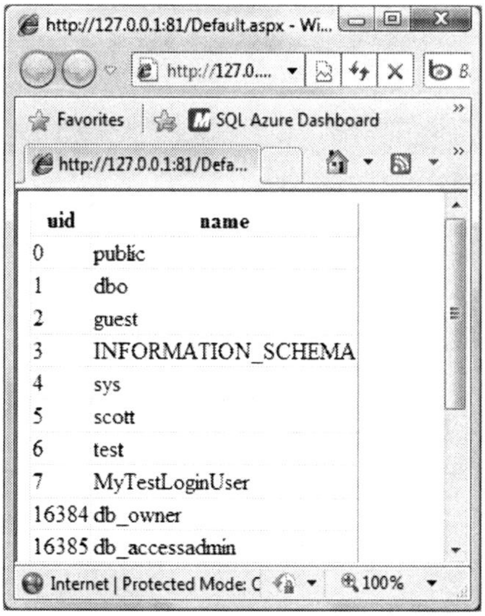

Figure 9-14. Running the solution locally and fetching data from SQL Azure

So far, you're running this project on the local machine. Although the Windows Azure Tools are required, this project doesn't use any of the Windows Azure storage options; it connects directly to a live SQL Azure database.

You could have created the same project as a regular ASP.NET application and obtained the same result. However, because you're about to deploy this project on Windows Azure, you must create a cloud project.

■ **Note** This chapter assumes you've configured the SQL Azure firewall correctly. Also, connecting from a Windows Azure service requires you to set the "Allow Microsoft Services access to this server" option in the firewall configuration. If you get a connection error stating that you aren't allowed to connect from a specific IP address, see Chapter 3 for detailed information about how to properly set up the SQL Azure firewall.

Deploying an ASP.NET Application in Windows Azure

You're almost there. In this section, you walk through the steps of deploying the ASP.NET application in the cloud:

1. You need to publish your project. Right-click AzureExample, and click Publish. This action, upon success, opens two windows:

   - **Windows Explorer.** This window contains the two files you need to deploy in Windows Azure. You need this window soon, so don't close it.

   - **Internet Explorer.** The Windows Azure Portal is automatically shown as well, because you need to deploy the binaries there. You may be prompted to sign in first.

2. When you've logged in, the Internet Explorer window shows you the home page for your Windows Azure projects. Click the Windows Azure project under which you previously created the AzureExample service.

3. You should see the page shown in Figure 9-1 at the beginning of this chapter. Click AzureExample, which should bring you to what you saw earlier in Figure 9-4.

4. On the right side of the browser page is a vertical bar with a left-pointing triangle. Click the triangle to open a split page with both Production and Staging sections, as shown in Figure 9-15. Deploying in staging creates a temporary service that you can use to test before promoting to the final public URL. This way, you can test that your application is working as desired before deploying it.

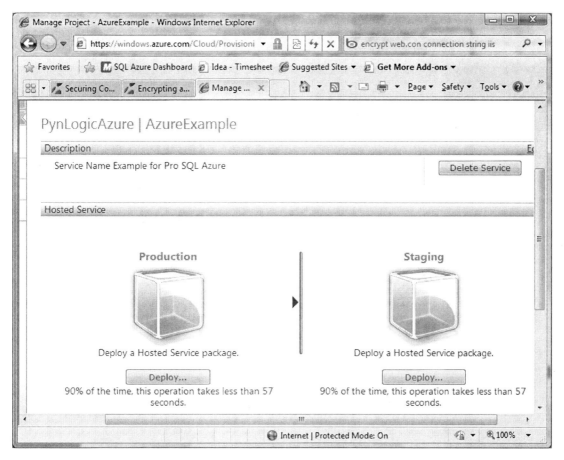

Figure 9-15. Viewing the production and staging environments

5.   Click the Deploy button under Staging. Doing so brings up a new page (see Figure 9-16) with the following fields:

- **Application Package**. This is the package that Visual Studio built for you. It's the file with extension `.cspkg` in the Windows Explorer window. Clicking Browse opens an Open form. You may find it easier to copy the entire path from the Windows Explorer window and paste it in the Open form. Select the package file, and click Open.

- **Configuration Settings**. This is the configuration file of your cloud service project with a `.cscfg` extension. Again, click Browse and select the configuration file from the Open form.

- **Operating System Settings**. This section allows you to configure the specific version of the operating system you're using for this service. Leaving Upgrade Method set to Automatic ensures that you get the latest security patches and

.NET upgrades automatically. You can also choose Manual and select the desired system.

- **Service Deployment Name**. Under Service Deployment Name, you need to enter a label for your service. Type **TEST001**, for example.

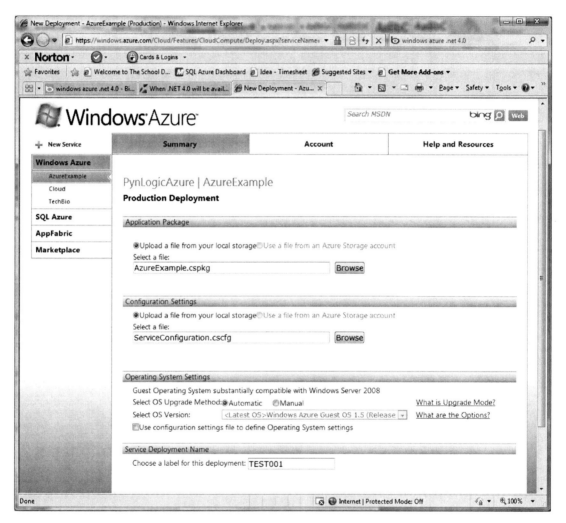

Figure 9-16. Windows Azure first-time deployment page

6. When the information provided looks like Figure 9-16, click Deploy. Doing so first copies the appropriate files to the cloud and creates the virtual machine in which your project will be deployed (see Figure 9-17). After it's deployed, your service isn't be running just yet; however, you start incurring charges immediately.

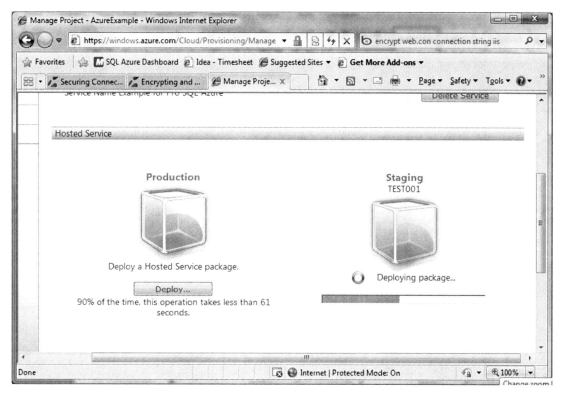

Figure 9-17. Deploying a package in staging

Your screen should now look like Figure 9-18. To start your virtual machine, click Run under Staging. This operation may take a few minutes.

When the startup operation is completed, you see the status of your service as Ready. At this point, you can test your ASP.NET application in the cloud by clicking the Web Site URL link in Staging. Notice that this isn't the URL you originally requested—the public URL previously registered is reserved for production. Instead, staging is given a deployment GUID that's also part of the web site's URL. In this case, the URL for the staging environment is

http://de2d988c570d4c36b43a72686391d4b5.cloudapp.net/

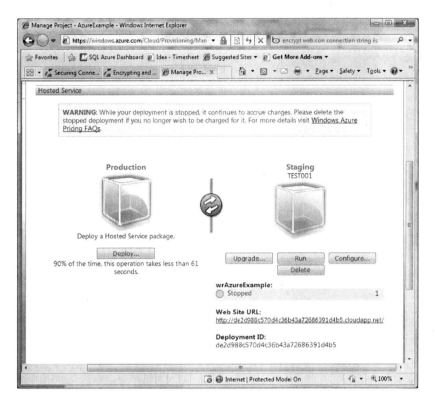

Figure 9-18. Completed deployment of your service

Clicking the link opens another browser and runs your service in the cloud (see Figure 9-19).

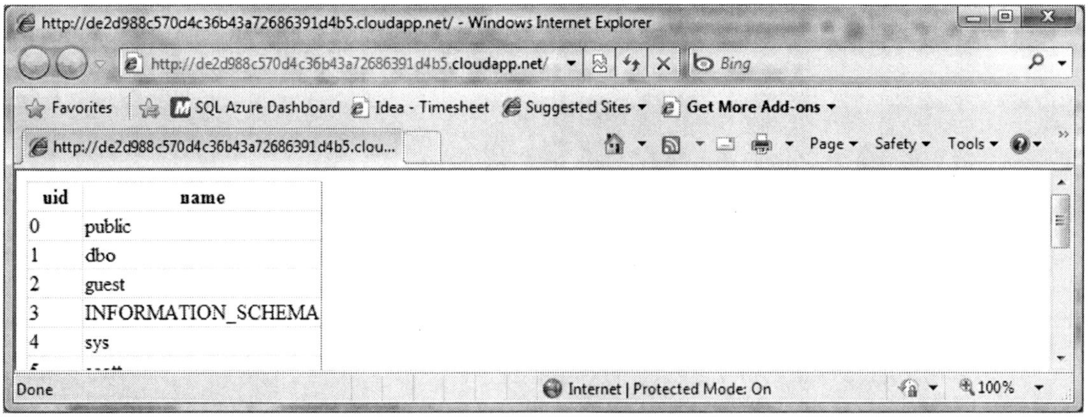

Figure 9-19. Running the service in the cloud

> ■ **Note** As mentioned previously, you're now paying for this Windows Azure service. You must first suspend your service (by clicking Suspend) if it's running; however, that alone doesn't stop you from accruing charges. You must also click the Delete button under both your staging and production environments. On the same page is a Delete Service button; it releases your service altogether and doesn't affect how you're billed.

Now that the code has been tested in staging, go back to the service management page (shown earlier in Figure 9-18) and click the center icon (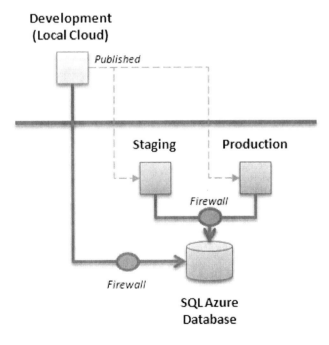) to promote your code to production. A confirmation message comes up. This operation swaps both environments (production and staging); you can expect to wait a few minutes while the swapping takes place. Once in production, the URL you registered previously works.

You may have noticed that you haven't changed any database settings between staging and production. Staging and production environments refer only to Windows Azure services, not the SQL Azure database running behind the scenes.

As a result all versions of your ASP.NET application (when run locally, in staging or in production) point to the same SQL Azure database by default, unless you specifically change your configuration settings in each environment (see Figure 9-20). You also need to make sure your firewall configuration is correctly set, or you may have a surprise when publishing your web application in the cloud.

Figure 9-20. Summary of deployment scenarios

Conclusion

This chapter showed you how to create a simple ASP.NET application that connects to a SQL Azure database. This requires a few configuration steps, including the creation of a Windows Azure service in the cloud and the installation of a Visual Studio extension called the Windows Azure Tools.

While this chapter focused primarily on deploying an ASP.NET application in the cloud, you can very easily deploy ASP.NET projects on your enterprise IIS servers and configure the connection string to connect to a SQL Azure database. This gives you multiple deployment options to consider, although you must keep in mind that each deployment option has a different cost structure. Data transfer between Windows Azure and SQL Azure is free within the same region, but you pay for compute time in Windows Azure.

■ ■ ■

CHAPTER 10

Designing for High Performance

This chapter focuses on a few key topics that can help you design high-performance applications that consume data in SQL Azure and SQL Server databases. The approach used in this chapter builds a simple but effective WinForms application that consumes data from both on-premises and cloud data. You first explore a few general concepts and then quickly go into the design and development of a shard library that reads data from multiple databases. Finally you see how to add multithreading to the shard library using the Task Parallel Library (TPL) and caching using the Enterprise Library (formally known as application blocks).

General Performance Concepts

Before diving into the details, let's discuss a few concepts related to performance. The first thing you should know is that achieving high performance is difficult. Although making sure applications perform to acceptable levels is important, advanced performance tuning requires careful planning and should be included as a design goal only if requirements drive you to believe that high performance is necessary. For example, if you expect your application to be used by thousands of concurrent users, then you may need to use caching and even multithreading. On the other hand, certain high-performance techniques can make code difficult to read and maintain, and in such cases knowledge transfer may be difficult.

Chatty vs. Chunky

The encrypted network connection to SQL Azure yields slower applications and may impact your application design significantly. An application that opens a database connection for every database call and performs a roundtrip for every update (that is, a *chatty* application) performs slower than an application that loads data for multiple objects in a single call and sends changes in bulk (a *chunky* application). LINQ to SQL and the Entity Framework are data access layers that provide good control over the use of bulk operations (the SaveChanges method on the object context).

For example, if you design a data access layer that contains a lot of business rules, your code may perform many roundtrips to the database to load the data needed to execute the business rules. If this is the case, you can implement certain data-intensive business rules in stored procedures (close to the data) and/or use caching to avoid unnecessary roundtrips.

Lazy Loading

On the other hand, although it's good to have fewer roundtrips from a performance standpoint, you should load only the data you need, for two reasons: the more data you load, the more you pay for the SQL Azure service; and loading more data than necessary can slow down your applications. So, you may want to consider using a *lazy loading* mechanism by which certain properties of your objects are loaded only when necessary. LINQ to SQL and the Entity Framework 4.0 support lazy loading (through the use of the DeferredLoadingEnabled property).

Although lazy loading minimizes the amount of data loaded, it also creates a chattier application by design. It's important to strike the right balance between using bulk data transfers and minimizing the amount of data needed to run an application function.

Caching

Another important technique used to minimize roundtrips is *caching*. Your application (or service) may use caching to avoid unnecessary roundtrips if some of your data doesn't change often. This may also impact your database design choices. For example, if you have a table that stores a list of states, the table will probably remain unchanged for a long time, which makes it a great candidate for caching.

Caching can be performed in memory or on disk (in a local database, for example). You have a few options:

- **ASP.NET caching**. ASP.NET offers a cache object that provides good caching capabilities. However, ASP.NET caching is tied to IIS. Restarting IIS clears the ASP.NET cache unless you've taken the necessary steps to persist the cache.

- **Windows Server AppFabric**. The AppFabric offers a next-generation distributed cache (previously known as Velocity). This cache can run on multiple computers and is made available through a .NET API.

- **Enterprise Library**. The Enterprise Library offers a collection of application blocks that Microsoft makes available under public license. The Enterprise Library contains a cache mechanism that doesn't depend on ASP.NET. This caching mechanism is provided natively in .NET 4.0 and can be found under the System.Runtime.Caching namespace.

Asynchronous User Interface

Ultimately, performance is a measure that impacts the user experience and can be controlled to a certain degree by offering highly responsive user interfaces. A Windows application that becomes unresponsive while loading data, or a web page that doesn't load until all the data has been retrieved, is perceived as slow. As a result, developing with multithreading techniques may become more important to provide a better experience to your users.

For web development, you should consider using asynchronous controls (such as AJAX) that give you more control over partial page loading. For Windows development, you may need to use a multithreaded user interface development approach.

To implement a highly responsive application in WinForms, use the Invoke method, shown on line 3 of the following example, to refresh your user interface on the UI thread:

```
1)  void OnPassCompleted()
2)  {
3)      this.Invoke(new EventHandler(UpdateProgressBar), null);
4)  }
5)
6)  private void UpdateProgressBar(object o, System.EventArgs e)
7)  {
8)      if (progressBarTest.Value < progressBarTest.Maximum)
```

```
9)    {
10)       progressBarTest.Value++;
11)    }
12) }
```

In this example, `OnPassCompleted` is a custom event received by the main form, which then calls the `Invoke` method to refresh a progress bar. The call to `Invoke` forces the execution of the progress bar refresh on the UI thread, which is different than the thread on which the `OnPassCompleted` event was raised.

Parallel Processing

In addition to asynchronous user interfaces, your code may need to execute on multiple processors. Two primary scenarios can lead you to choose parallel processing for your application:

- **Many calculations**. Your application is CPU intensive, especially if computations can be independent from each other. Advanced graphics or complex mathematical computations are examples of CPU-intensive operations.

- **Many waits**. Your application needs to wait between each call, and the cost of creating parallel threads and aggregating results is insignificant. Database shards are an example: calling five databases in parallel is roughly five times faster than calling five databases serially.

Two choices are available to write parallel processes. If you can, you should use the Task Parallel Library (TPL), because it's easier:

- **Task Parallel Library**. The TPL is a newer library that Microsoft is providing as part of .NET 4.0. It allows you to take advantage of multiple CPUs quickly and easily. You can find the TPL under `System.Threading.Tasks`.

- **Threads**. Managing threads the old-fashioned way using the `System.Threading` namespace gives you the most flexibility.

Shards

Shards offer another mechanism by which your code can read and write data against any number of databases almost transparently. Later in this chapter, you create a horizontal partition shard (HPS) using the read-write shard (RWS) design pattern as described in Chapter 2, with the round-robin access method. A horizontal partition implies that all the databases have identical schema and that a given record can written in any database that belongs to the shard. From a performance standpoint, reading from multiple databases in parallel to search for records yields greater performance; however, your code must keep breadcrumbs if you need to perform updates back to the correct database. Finally, using a shard requires parallel processing for optimum performance.

Coding Strategies Summary

Table 2-1 provides a summary of the concepts discussed so far regarding some of the coding strategies available to you when you develop against a SQL Azure database with performance in mind.

Table 2-1. Coding Strategies to Design for Performance

Technique	Comments
Bulk data loading/changing	Minimizes roundtrips by using a data access library that supports loading data in bulk, such as the Entity Framework.
Lazy loading	Allows you to create objects for which certain properties are loaded only when first called, to minimize loading unnecessary data (and improve performance). The Entity Framework 4.0 supports this.
Caching	Lets you to keep in memory certain objects that don't change frequently. The caching application blocks provided by Microsoft offer this capability as well as expiration and scavenging configuration settings.
Asynchronous user interface	Not technically a performance-improvement technique, but allows users to use the application while your code is performing a long-running transaction and thus provides a better user experience.
Parallel processing	Allows you to run code on multiple processors for optimum performance. Although complex, this technique can provide significant performance advantages.
Shards	Lets you to store data in multiple databases to optimize reads and spread the load of queries over multiple database servers.

Because shards are considered a newer technology, the remainder of this chapter focuses on building a HPS using caching and parallel processing in order to improve performance and scalability.

Building a Shard

Let's build a shard library that can be used by applications that need to load and update data against multiple SQL Azure databases as quickly and transparently as possible. For the purpose of building an efficient shard library, you stipulate the following requirements for the shard:

1. Adding new databases should be simple and transparent to the client code.

2. Adding new databases shouldn't affect performance negatively.

3. The library should function with SQL Server, SQL Azure, or both.

4. The library should optionally cache results for fast retrieval.

5. The library should support mass or selective reads and writes.

6. Data returned by the library should be accepted as a data source for controls.

These requirements have very specific implications from a technology standpoint. Table 2-2 outlines which requirements are met by which technology.

Table 2-2. *Technologies Used to Build the Shard*

Technology	Requirement	Comment
Configuration file	1	The configuration file stores the list of databases that make up the shard.
Multithreading	2	Using the TPL lets the library to spawn multiple threads to use computers with multiple CPUs, allowing parallel execution of SQL statements.
SqlClient	3	Using SqlCommand objects allows the shard to connect to both SQL Azure and SQL Server databases.
Caching	4	Caching lets the library store results temporarily to avoid unnecessary roundtrips.
Breadcrumbs	5	The library creates a virtual column for each record returned that stores a breadcrumb identifying the database a record it came from.
DataTable	6	The library returns a DataTable object that can be bound to objects easily.

Designing the Shard Library Object

The library accepts requests directly from client applications and can be viewed as an API. Note that you're using extension methods to make this API blend in with the existing SqlCommand class; this in turn minimizes the amount of code on the client and makes the application easier to read.

Figure 10-1 shows where the library fits in a typical application design. It also shows how the library hides the complexity of parallel processing and caching from the client application. Finally, the shard library abstracts the client code from dealing directly with multiple databases.

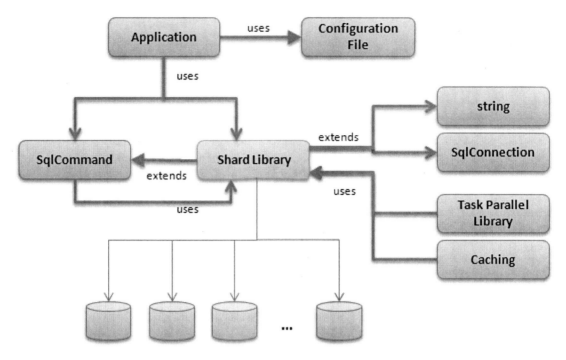

Figure 10-1. Shard library object diagram

A sample application is provided to demonstrate how to use the shard library. Although the application is very simple, it uses all the features of the shard for reference.

■ **Note** Check `http://EnzoSqlShard.Codeplex.com` for the latest shard library. This shard library is made available as an open source project.

Managing Database Connections

This section walks through a few coding decisions that are necessary when creating this shard. Because the shard library needs to be able to connect to multiple databases, the client has two options to provide this list: it can provide the list of connections to use whenever it makes a call to the library, or it can preload the library with a list of connection objects that are then kept in memory for all future calls.

The shard library declares the following property to hold the list of preloaded connection objects. The `ShardConnections` property is declared as static so it can be used across multiple calls easily; the client application only needs to set this property once:

```
public static List<SqlConnection> ShardConnections {get;set;}
```

In addition, an extension method is added to `SqlConnection` to provide a GUID value that uniquely identifies a connection string. The connection GUID is critical for the shard; it provides a breadcrumb for every record returned by the shard. This breadcrumb is later used by the shard to determine, for example, which database to use when performing an update statement.

The following code shows how a connection GUID is calculated. It uses the SqlConnectionStringBuilder helper class and another extension method on strings called GetHash() (on line 8). This extension method returns a SHA-256 hash value. Note that if the connection string doesn't specify a default database (Initial Catalog), you assume the user is connected to the master database. This assumption is correct for SQL Azure, but it may not hold true for SQL Server:

```
1)  public static string ConnectionGuid(this SqlConnection connection)
2)  {
3)      SqlConnectionStringBuilder cb = new
    SqlConnectionStringBuilder(connection.ConnectionString);
4)      string connUID =
5)      ((cb.UserID != null) ? cb.UserID : "SSPI") + "#" +
6)      cb.DataSource + "#" +
7)       ((cb.InitialCatalog != null) ? cb.InitialCatalog : "master");
8)      string connHash = connUID.GetHash().ToString();
9)      return connHash;
10) }
```

For reference, here is the extension method that returns a hash value for a string. Technically, you could use the string's native GetHashCode() method. However, the built-in GetHashCode method varies based on the operating system used (32-bit versus 64-bit) and the version of .NET. In this case, you create a simple GetHash() method that consistently return sthe same value for a given input. The string value is first turned into an array of bytes using UTF-8 (on line 3). The hash value is then computed on line 4. Line 5 returns the hash as a string value:

```
1)  public static string GetHash(this string val)
2)  {
3)      byte[] buf = System.Text.UTF8Encoding.UTF8.GetBytes(val);
4)      byte[] res =
    System.Security.Cryptography.SHA256.Create().ComputeHash(buf);
5)      return BitConverter.ToString(res).Replace("-", "");
6)  }
```

By default, the application code loads the initial set of connections using the application configuration file. In the current design, it's the application's responsibility to load the connections. This sample application reads the configuration file on startup and adds every entry in the ConfigurationStrings of the configuration file that contains the word *SHARD*:

```
1)  foreach (System.Configuration.ConnectionStringSettings connStr in
    System.Configuration.ConfigurationManager.ConnectionStrings)
2)  if (connStr.Name.ToUpper().StartsWith("SHARD"))
3)      Shard.ShardConnections.Add(
    new SqlConnection(connStr.ConnectionString));
```

The application can also add connections based on user input. The following code shows how the application adds a new connection to the shard:

```
Shard.ShardConnections.Add(new SqlConnection("connection string here"));
```

When running the test application, you can add a connection to the shard by clicking Add Connection on the Shard Connections tab. The GUID value for this connection is calculated automatically and displayed. Figure 10-2 shows the screen that allows you to add a connection manually, and Figure 10-3 displays all the connections defined in the shard.

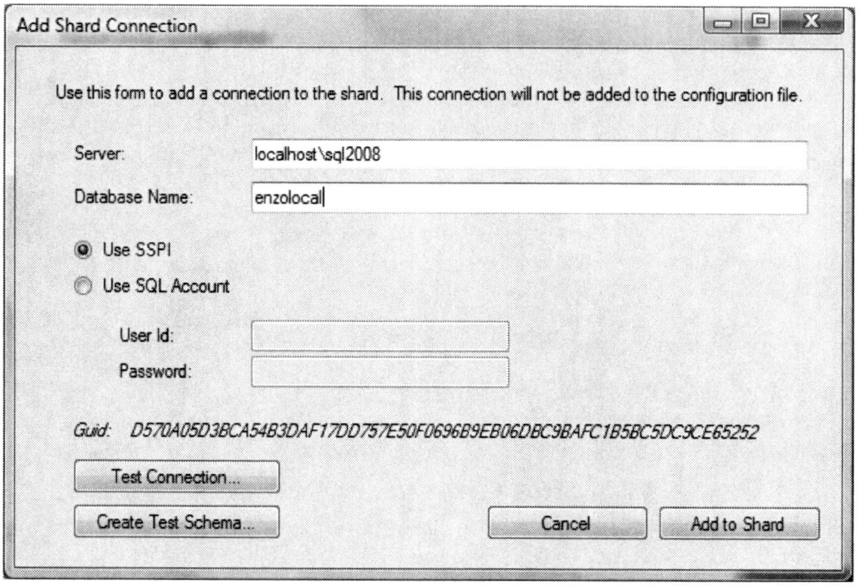

Figure 10-2. Adding a custom connection to the shard

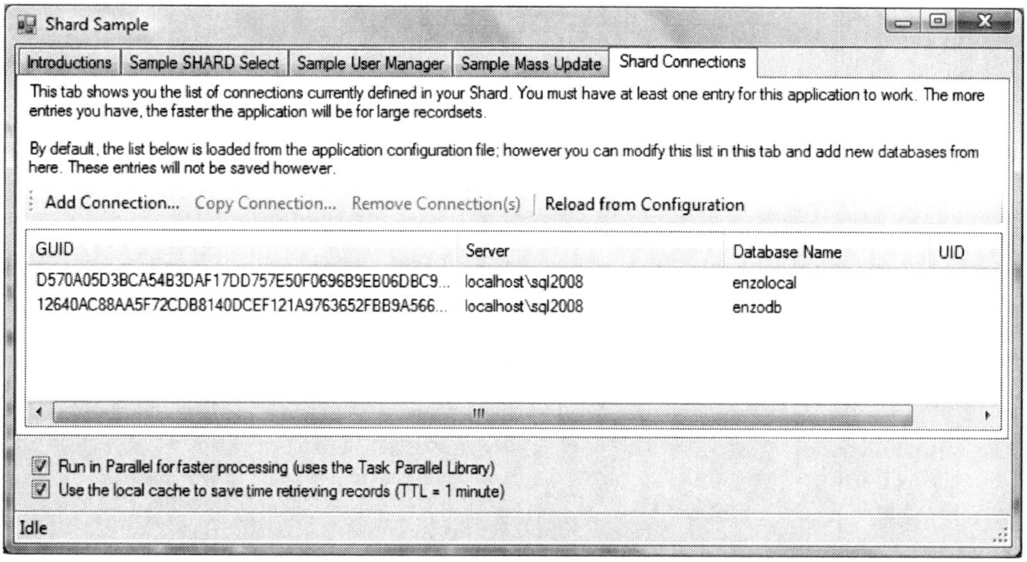

Figure 10-3. Viewing shard connections

Reading Using the Shard

Now that you've reviewed how connections strings are handled in the application and the library, you need to know how the shard handles a SELECT operation against multiple databases. In its simplest form, the library executes the SELECT operation against the list of connections defined previously.

The client application calls ExecuteShardQuery, which in turn loops over the list of SqlConnection objects (see Figure 10-4). If you look at the code, you see that a copy of each connection object is made first; this is to avoid any potential collisions if the client code makes a call to this method multiple times (a connection can only make one call at a time). Then, for each connection, the code calls ExecuteSingleQuery, which is the method in the shard library that makes the call to the database.

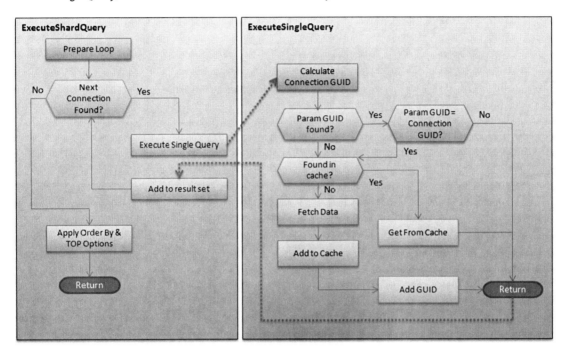

Figure 10-4. Reading from the shard

The ExecuteShardQuery method is designed to call the ExecuteSingleQuery method multiple times in parallel using the TPL. The TPL provides many useful methods to easily handle parallel processing without having to manage threads. The shard library uses Parallel.ForEach, which is a construct that allows the code to execute an inline method concurrently, and automatically adjusts the number of threads depending on your computer's hardware configuration. So, the more CPUs you have, the faster the following code executes, if you have enough connections to loop through. Note, however, that you need to lock the data object (line 5), which is a DataTable, because it could be accessed by other executing threads. Finally, the Merge method on the DataTable object concatenates resultsets from the various connections. After the loop has executed, the resulting data object has the list of records retrieved from the shard, in no guaranteed order:

```
1)  Parallel.ForEach(connections,
2)      delegate(SqlConnection c)
```

```
3)        {
4)          DataTable dt = ExecuteSingleQuery(command, c, exceptions);
5)          lock (data)
6)              data.Merge(dt, true, MissingSchemaAction.Add);
7)        }
8)  );
```

The following code is a simplified version of the actual sample application. (For clarity, some code that calculates execution time and performs exception handling has been removed.) Line 4 sets the command text to be executed, such as a SELECT statement, and line 5 executes it against the shard. Instead of calling ExecuteReader, the code calls ExecuteShardQuery to use the shard. Line 7 binds the resulting DataTable and displays the records returned by the shard:

```
1)  SqlCommand cmd = new SqlCommand();
2)  DataTable dataRes = new DataTable();
3)
4)  cmd.CommandText = this.textBox1.Text;
5)  dataRes = cmd.ExecuteShardQuery();
6)
7)  dataGridView2.DataSource = dataRes;
```

Figure 10-5 shows the outcome of this code. The SELECT statement is designed to return database object names and types. Executing the statement against the shard performs as expected. However, notice that an extra column has been added to the display: __guidDB__. This is the name of the GUID column introduced previously. This column doesn't help much for reading, but it enables updates and deletes, as you see later.

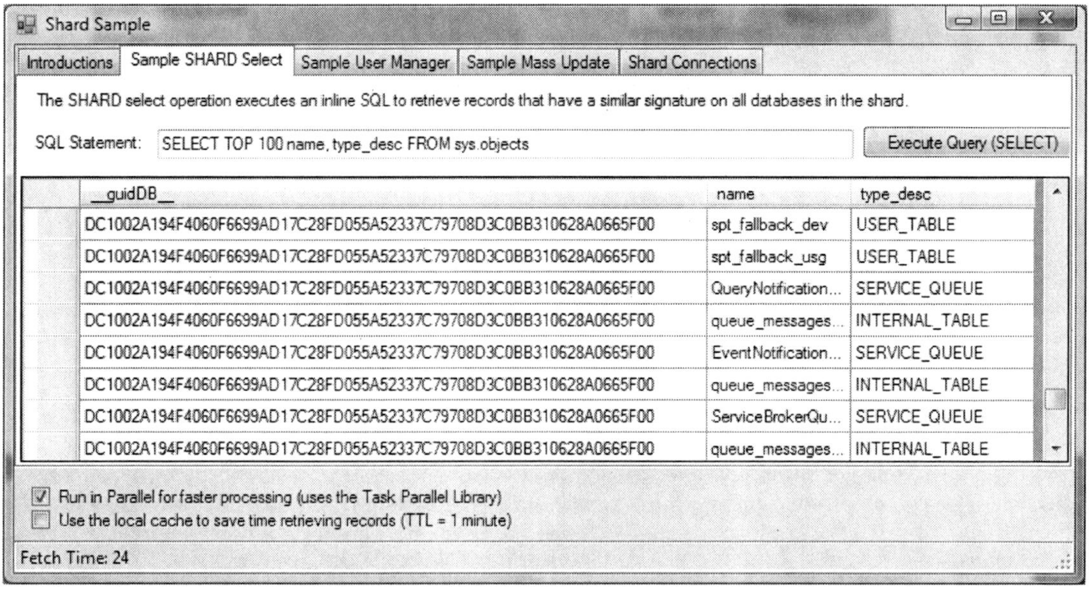

Figure 10-5. Showing records returned by the shard

The GUID provided is unique for each database connection, as long as one of the key parameters is different in the connection string of each connection. It's added by the ExecuteSingleQuery method described previously. Within this method, a column is added in front of all the others, which carries the GUID. In the following code extract, line 3 creates the data column of type string, and line 4 sets its default value to the connection's GUID. Line 7 fills the data table with the query's result, along with the added GUID column. The following is the logic used to add this GUID:

```
1)  // Add the connection GUID to this set of records
2)  // This helps us identify which row came from which connection
3)  DataColumn col = dt.Columns.Add(_GUID_, typeof(string));
4)  col.DefaultValue = connection.ConnectionGuid();
5)
6)  // Get the data
7)  da.Fill(dt);
```

Caching

To minimize roundtrips to the source databases, the shard library provides an optional caching mechanism. The caching technique used in this library offers basic capabilities and can be extended to address more complex scenarios. The objective of this library is to cache the entire DataTable of each database backend whenever requested. Figure 10-6 shows the logical decision tree of the caching approach. It's important to note that this library calculates a cache key based on each parameter, the parameter value, each SQL statement, and the database's GUID.

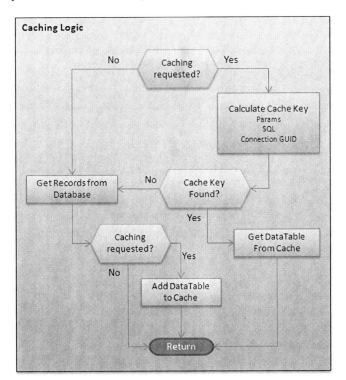

Figure 10-6. Caching logic

The effect of the cache is visible when you connect to SQL Azure. Considering that connecting to a SQL Azure database takes up to 250 milliseconds the first time, memory access is significantly faster. The importance of the cache increases as the number of records increases and the number of databases increases in the shard.

The cache provided by this library also provides a time to live (TTL) mechanism that implements an absolute expiration or a sliding expiration scheme. An absolute expiration resets the cache automatically at a specific time in the future, whereas the sliding setting moves the expiration time if the cache items are used before expiring. The following code shows how the caching is implemented. Line 1 creates a CacheItemPolicy used to define the behavior of the cache. Line 3 implements the sliding window cache, and line 5 implements the absolute approach:

```
1)  CacheItemPolicy cip = new CacheItemPolicy();
2)  if (UseSlidingWindow)
3)      cip.SlidingExpiration = defaultTTL;
4)  else
5)      cip.AbsoluteExpiration =
    new DateTimeOffset(System.DateTime.Now.Add(defaultTTL));
6)  MemoryCache.Default.Add(cacheKey, dt, cip);
```

You can enhance this caching technique in multiple ways. For example, the DataTable object stored in the cache can be compressed when it contains many rows. Compression algorithms tend to increase latency, but the overall performance benefits may be worth a slight delay.

Another way to enhance this caching storage is to create different cache containers, so you can control at a more granular level which container holds which kind of data. Doing so lets you control a different setting per container, for example; or you may decide to always compress one cache container but not another.

Finally, the cache provided in this library isn't distributed; it's local to the machine running the library. If you need to develop a more robust cache, consider looking into the Windows Server AppFabric; its caching technology provides enterprise-level capabilities.

■ **Note** For more information about the Windows Server AppFabric, visit
`http://msdn.microsoft.com/appfabric`.

Updating and Deleting Records in the Shard

At this point, you're ready to see how updates and deletes take place through the shard. Updates and deletes against the databases in the shard can either be performed for records in a given database or against all databases. At a high level, here are some guidelines you can use to decide on an approach:

- **Update or delete records in a single database.** You update or delete one or more records in a database when you already know the database GUID to use. This is the case when you use the shard to retrieve records, because the database GUID is provided for all records returned.

- **Update or delete records across databases.** Generally speaking, you update or delete records across databases in the shard whenever you don't know which database a record is in, or when all records need to be evaluated.

To update or delete records in a single database, you must provide a command parameter that contains the database GUID to use. Here's the code that updates a single record in the shard. On lines 1 through 7, the code creates a command object that calls a stored procedure that requires two parameters. On line 9, the code adds the database GUID to use. This extra parameter is removed by the shard library before making the call to the requested database:

```
1)  cmd.CommandText = "sproc_update_user";
2)  cmd.CommandType = CommandType.StoredProcedure;
3)
4)  cmd.Parameters.Add(new SqlParameter("@id", SqlDbType.Int));
5)  cmd.Parameters["@id"].Value = int.Parse(labelIDVal.Text);
6)  cmd.Parameters.Add(new SqlParameter("@name", SqlDbType.NVarChar, 20));
7)  cmd.Parameters["@name"].Value = textBoxUser.Text;
8)
9)  cmd.Parameters.Add(new SqlParameter(
    PYN.EnzoAzureLib.Shard._GUID_, labelGUID.Text));
10)
11) ExecuteShardNonQuery (cmd);
```

Note that calling a stored procedure isn't required for this code to run. All that is required is that a SqlCommand object be used; the SQL code may very well be inline SQL.

Deleting a record from the shard is virtually identical. The command object is created with the required stored procedure parameters from lines 1 through 5. On line 7, the code adds the database GUID to use:

```
1)  cmd.CommandText = "sproc_delete_user";
2)  cmd.CommandType = CommandType.StoredProcedure;
3)
4)  cmd.Parameters.Add(new SqlParameter("@id", SqlDbType.Int));
5)  cmd.Parameters["@id"].Value = int.Parse(labelIDVal.Text);
6)
7)  cmd.Parameters.Add(new SqlParameter(
    PYN.EnzoAzureLib.Shard._GUID_, labelGUID.Text));
8)
9)  ExecuteShardNonQuery (cmd);
```

▓ **Note** The ExecuteShardNonQuery method behaves differently if it has no database GUID parameter (it executes the query against all databases), if it has a database GUID parameter with a value (it executes the query against the specified database), or if it contains a database GUID parameter with a NULL value (it executes the query against the next database in the shard using round-robin). You see how to use round-robin calls when adding records in the shard shortly.

Figure 10-7 shows the sample application updating a record from the shard. When you click Reload Grid, a SELECT statement is issued against the shard, which returns the database GUID for each record. Then, when you select a specific record, the record details are loaded in the right section of the screen, along with the record's database GUID. At this point, the record can be updated or deleted.

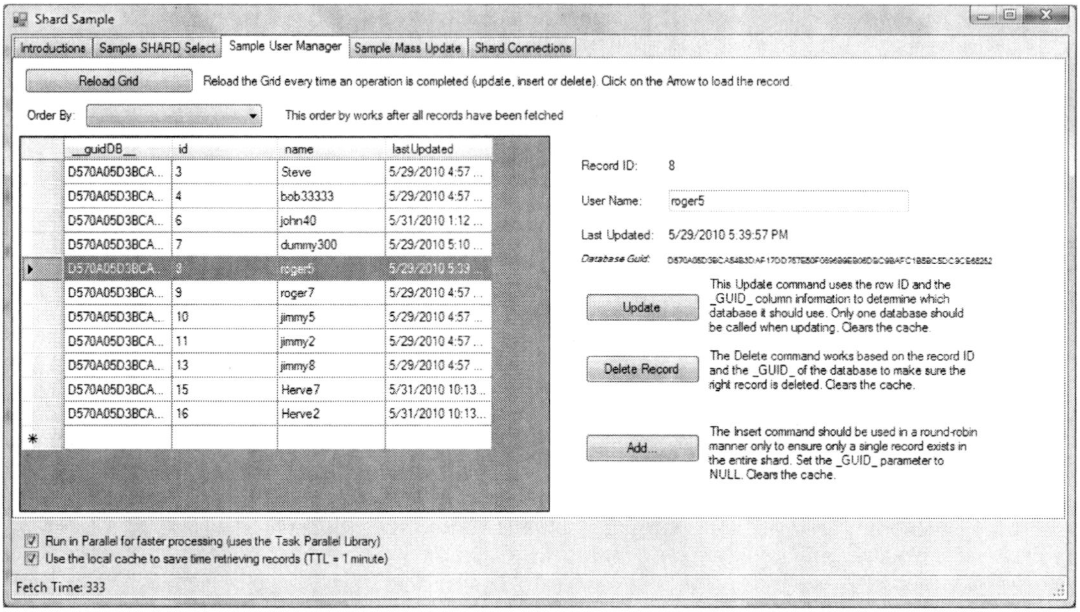

Figure 10-7. Sample application updating a record in the shard

Because records are being updated or deleted, the client code clears the cache to force future SELECT statements to fetch records from the databases in the shard. The shard library exposes a ResetCache method that does just that. You can improve this logic by also performing the same update or delete operation of records in the cache.

Updating or deleting records across databases in the shard is even simpler. The following code executes an inline SQL statement using a SqlCommand object. Because no database GUID is provided, this statement executes the statement across all databases in the shard. When you perform updates or deletes across databases, it's important to set the parallel flag correctly, as shown on line 1:

```
1)  PYN.EnzoAzureLib.Shard.UseParallel = checkBoxParallel.Checked;
2)  cmd.CommandText = "UPDATE TestUsers2 SET LastUpdated = GETDATE()";
3)  cmd.CommandType = CommandType.Text;
4)  ExecuteShardNonQuery (cmd);
```

Adding Records to the Shard

You see how easy it is to add records to the shard databases. This shard works best from a performance standpoint when all databases in the shard have a roughly equal number of records; this is because parallel processing is performed without any deterministic logic. As a result, the more spread out your records are in the shard, the faster it is. You can add records in the shard in two ways:

- **In a single database.** If you're loading the shard for the first time, you may decide to load certain records in specific databases. Or you may decide to load one database with more records than others, if the hardware is superior.

- **Across databases.** Usually, you load records in the shard without specifying a database. The shard library uses a round-robin mechanism to load records.

Adding a record in a specific database is no different than updating or deleting a record in a database; all you need to do is create a SqlCommand object, set the INSERT statement, and add a SqlParameter indicating the database GUID to use.

Adding one or more records across databases requires a slightly different approach. The round-robin logic stores the last database used to insert records in the shard. The shard library exposes two methods to perform inserts:

- ExecuteShardNonQuery. As you've seen previously, this method extends the SqlCommand object and executes statements against the next database in the shard (round-robin) if the GUID parameter is NULL. This convention is used to let the shard library know that it should move its internal database pointer to the next database in the shard for the next round-robin call.

- ExecuteParallelRoundRobinLoad. This method extends List<SqlCommand> and provides a mechanism to create a collection of SqlCommand objects. Each SqlCommand object contains an INSERT statement to execute. This method adds a NULL database GUID and calls ExecuteShardNonQuery to execute all the statements with round-robin support. This construct simplifies loading a shard quickly by spreading INSERT statements evenly across all databases.

The following code shows how the client prepares the call to ExecuteParallelRoundRobinLoad. Line 1 creates a collection of SqlCommand objects. Then, on line 3, an outer loop executes for each value found in the userName array (this is a list of names to add to the shard). From lines 5 to 16, a SqlCommand object is created for each name to INSERT and is added to the collection. Line 22 makes the actual call to ExecuteParallelRoundRobinLoad. Finally, on line 23, if all goes well, the library's cache is cleared:

```
1)  List<SqlCommand> commands = new List<SqlCommand>();
2)
3)  foreach (string name in userName)
4)  {
5)      if (name != null && name.Trim().Length > 0)
6)      {
7)          SqlCommand cmdToAdd = new SqlCommand();
8)          cmdToAdd.CommandText = "sproc_add_user";
9)          cmdToAdd.CommandType = CommandType.StoredProcedure;
10)
11)         cmdToAdd.Parameters.Add(
12)         new SqlParameter("name", SqlDbType.NVarChar, 20));
13)         cmdToAdd.Parameters["name"].Value = name;
14)
15)         commands.Add(cmdToAdd);
16)     }
17) }
18)
19) // Make the call!
20) if (commands.Count > 0)
21) {
22)     commands.ExecuteParallelRoundRobinLoad();
23)     Shard.ResetCache();
24) }
```

> ■ **Note** The call to `ExecuteParallelRoundRobinLoad` is different in two ways from all the other methods you've seen so far. First, there is no need to add the database GUID parameter; it creates this parameter automatically with a `NULL` value. Second, this method executes on a `List<SqlCommand>` object instead of `SqlCommand`.

Figure 10-8 shows the sample application screen that creates the array of names to load in the shard. Six names are added in the shard using round-robin, as previously described.

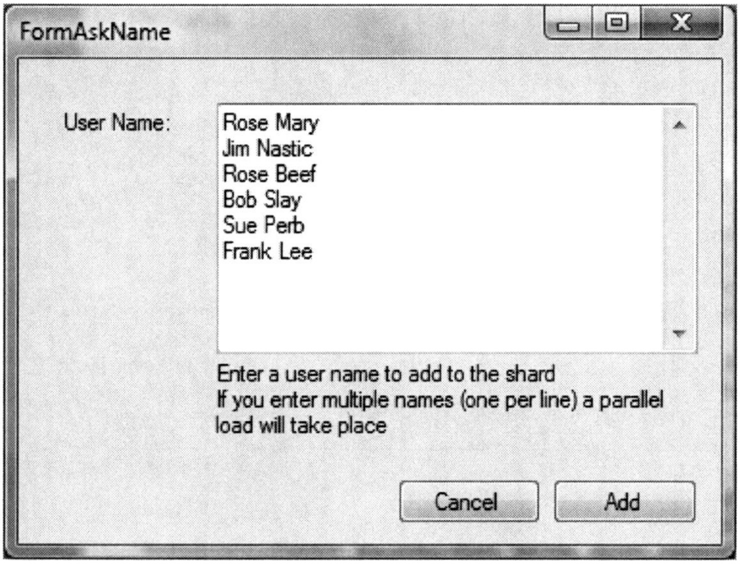

Figure 10-8. Sample application adding records using round-robin

Managing a Shard

Having created a shard and reached the point of being able to run queries and add data, you can begin to think about higher-level issues: how to handle exceptions, manage performance, control transactions, and more.

Managing Exceptions

So far, you've learned the basic principles of the sample shard library. You saw how to select, insert, update, and delete records in various ways through the methods provided by the library. Let's discuss how you can manage exceptions that the shard may throw at you.

The current library doesn't handle rollbacks, but it may throw exceptions that your code needs to capture. In the previous example (Figure 10-8), all the records were inserted except Jim Nastic: that name was too long for the SqlParameter object (hence it threw a "Value Would Be Truncated" exception).

The library handles exceptions through the AggregateException class provided by the TPL; this class holds a collection of exceptions. This is necessary because the library executes database calls in parallel. As a result, more than one exception may be taking place at the same time. You need to aggregate these exceptions and return them to the client for further processing.

For example, the shard library's ExecuteSingleNonQuery method takes a ConcurrentQueue<Exception> parameter, which represents an object that stores exceptions. This object is thread-safe, meaning that all running threads can add new exceptions to it safely without running into concurrency issues. The following code shows that if an exception is detected in the ExecuteSingleNonQuery method, the code adds the exception to the queue on line 14. Also, as a convention, the exception is rethrown if the queue isn't provided (line 16):

```
1)   private static long ExecuteSingleNonQuery(
2)    SqlCommand command,
3)    SqlConnection connectionToUse,
4)    System.Collections.Concurrent.ConcurrentQueue<Exception> exceptions
5)   )
6)   {
7)         try
8)         {
9)         // ...
10)        }
11)        catch (Exception ex)
12)        {
13)         if (exceptions != null)
14)               exceptions.Enqueue(ex);
15)         else
16)               throw;
17)        }
18)   }
```

The following code shows the ExecuteShardNonQuery method, which calls the ExecuteSingleNonQuery method just described. Line 1 creates the exception queue (ConcurrentQueue), which is passed as a variable to ExecuteSingleNonQuery. After the parallel execution of the database calls is complete, the code checks whether the exception queue is empty. If it isn't empty, an AggregateException is thrown, which contains the collection of exceptions stored in the exception queue (lines 13 and 14):

```
1)   var exceptions = new System.Collections.Concurrent.ConcurrentQueue<Exception>();
2)
3)   Parallel.ForEach(connections, delegate(SqlConnection c)
4)   {
5)       long rowsAffected = ExecuteSingleNonQuery(command, c, exceptions);
6)
7)       lock (alock)
8)           res += rowsAffected;
9)
10)    }
11) );
12)
13) if (!exceptions.IsEmpty)
14)     throw new AggregateException(exceptions);
```

As you can see, managing exceptions can be a bit tricky. However, these exception helper classes provide a good mechanism to store exceptions and return a collection of exceptions that the client code can consume.

Managing Performance

So far, you've seen how the shard library works and how you can use it in your code. But it's important to keep in mind why you go through all this trouble—after all, there is nothing trivial in creating a shard library. This shard library does something important: it allows a client application to grow parts (or all) of a database horizontally, with the intention of improving performance, scalability, or both.

What does this mean? It means the shard library can help an application keep its performance characteristics in a somewhat consistent manner as more users use the application (scalability), or it can help an application perform faster under a given load (performance). If you're lucky, the shard library may be able to achieve both. However, this won't happen without proper planning. The shard library by itself is only a splitter, in the sense that it spreads calls to multiple databases.

Shards don't necessarily help performance; in certain cases, a shard hurts both performance and scalability. The reason is that a shard imposes an overhead that wouldn't otherwise exist. Figure 10-9 shows the difference between a standard ADO.NET call selecting records and best case and worst case scenarios when fetching the same records from a shard. In the best case scenario, all records are assumed to be split in three distinct databases; the shard is able to concurrently access all three databases, aggregate the three resultsets, and filter and/or sort the data. The shard must then manage all of the following, which consumes processing time:

- Loops for connecting to the underlying databases

- Loops for fetching the data

- Data aggregation, sorting and filtering

In the worst case scenario, all these operations can't be executed in parallel and require serial execution. This may be the case if the TPL detects that only a single processor is available. Finally, you may end up in a situation that mixes worst and best case scenarios, where some of the calls can be made in parallel, but not all.

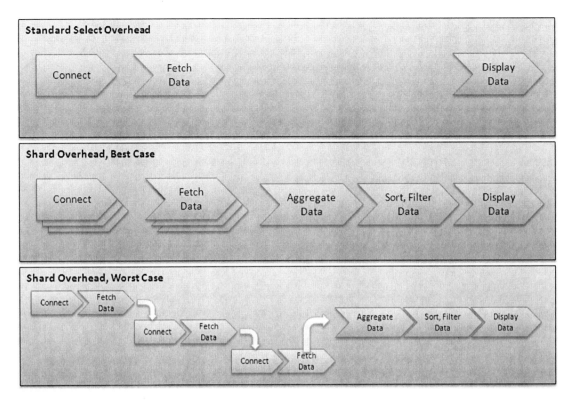

Figure 10-9. Data access overhead comparison

Now that all the warnings are laid out, let's look at a scenario for which a shard makes sense and probably improves both performance and scalability. Imagine a DOC table that contains only two records. The table contains a few fields that represent document metadata, such as Title and Author ID. However, this table also contains a large field: a varbinary column called Document that holds a PDF file. Each PDF file is a few megabytes in size. Figure 10-10 shows the output of the table. Because this database is loaded in SQL Azure, the SELECT * FROM DOCS statement returns a few megabytes of data on an SSL encrypted link. The execution of this statement takes about 2.5 seconds on average, or roughly 1.25 seconds per record.

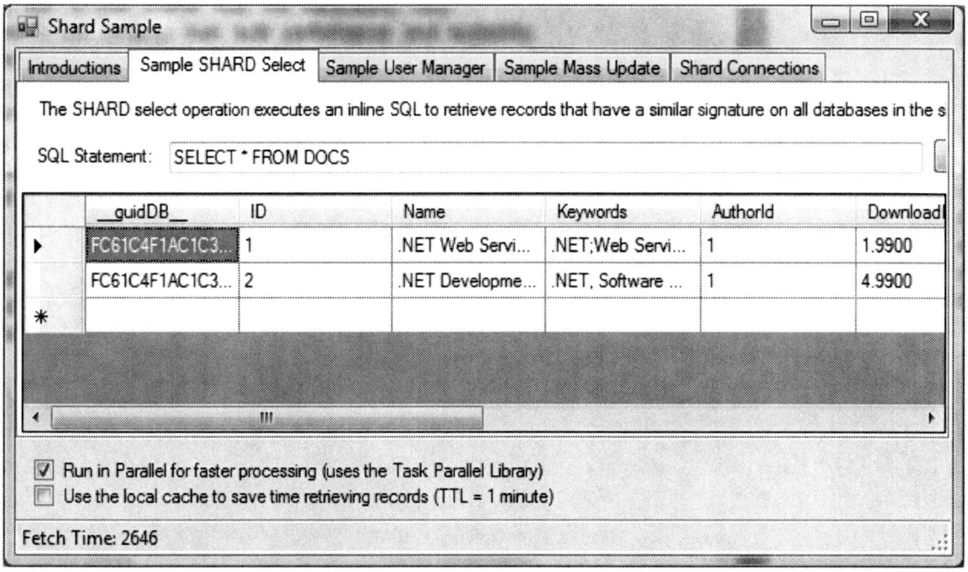

Figure 10-10. Sample table containing documents in one database

Both records come from the database; you can see this by looking at the database GUID, which is similar for both records. However, if you move the second record to another SQL Azure database, the average execution time drops to about 1.8 seconds. Figure 10-11 shows the result of the same statement that executed in 1.4 seconds (you can see that the database GUIDs are now different). This is half the execution time of the first result.

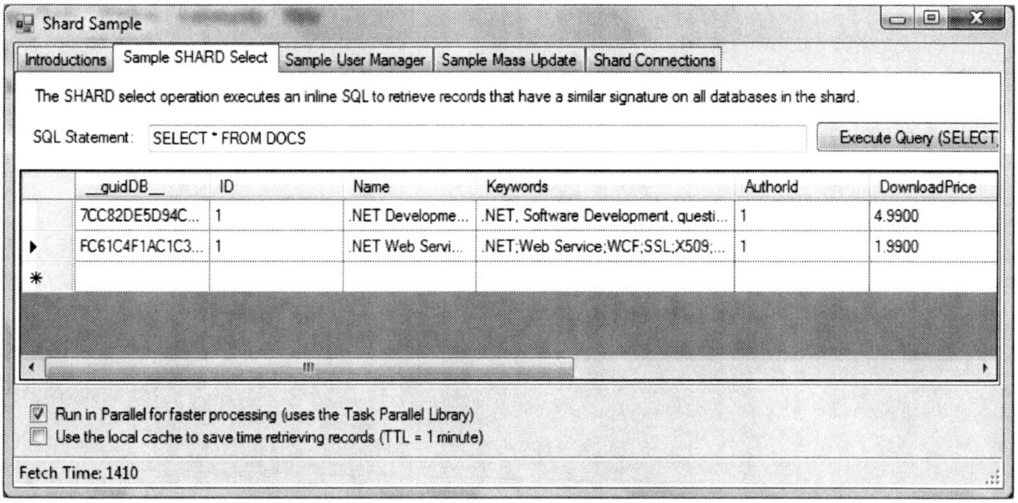

Figure 10-11. Sample table containing documents in two databases

You can execute this statement much more quickly because almost the entire time is spent returning the Document field. Figure 10-12 tells you that returning all the fields against both databases without the Document field takes only 103 milliseconds. This shows that using a shard can provide performance benefits even if there is a processing overhead; however, this may not always be the case. Be sure to carefully evaluate your database design to determine which tables, if any, can take advantage of parallel execution.

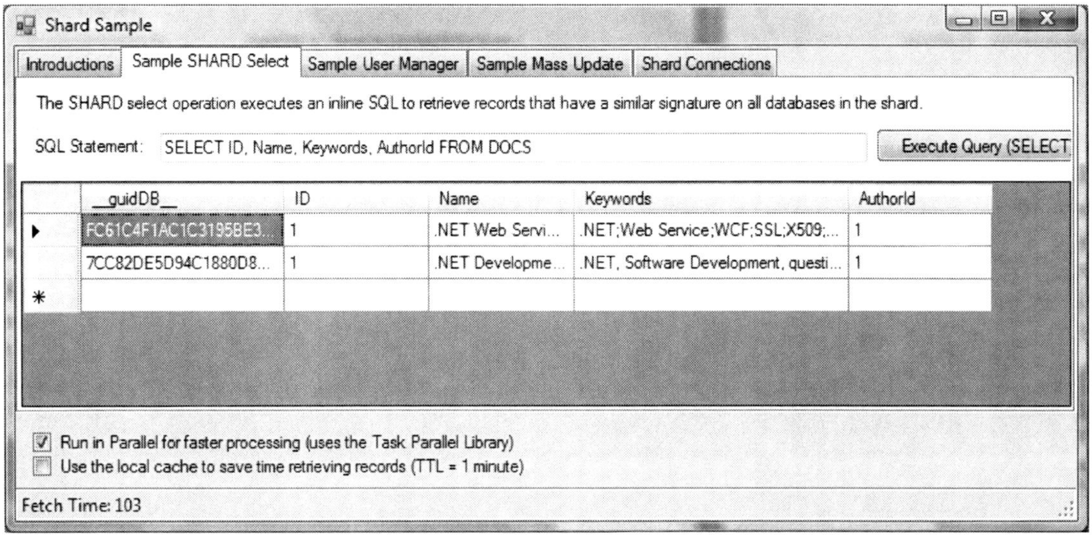

Figure 10-12. Excluding the Document field from the SELECT

Working with Partial Shards

Note that building a shard isn't an all-or-nothing approach. You can easily create a partial shard for a set of tables. Depending on how your code is structured, you may or may not need to build logic that uses the shard library, depending on which tables you need to access. This logic is best built in a data access layer (DAL), where the physical organization of tables is separated from the organization of business objects.

For example, you can design an application that consumes business objects directly. These business objects in turn consume command objects, which are specialized routines smart enough to load data in memory structures by calling execution objects. Figure 10-13 shows the Authors object calling two command objects that load data from two separate libraries: the standard ADO.NET library and the shard library. The complexity of determining which library to call is deferred to the lowest level possible, protecting the application and business objects from database structural changes.

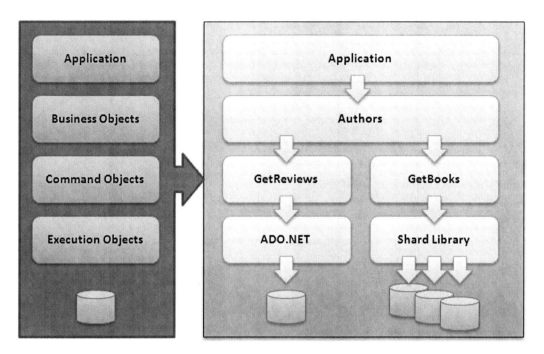

Figure 10-13. Example application design implementing a partial shard

Managing Transaction Consistency

Because this library is meant for SQL Azure, and distributed transactions aren't supported in SQL Azure, the shard library doesn't offer transactional consistency by default. But you should look carefully at your transactional needs and what this means to your application design.

You can add transactional capabilities in the shard library fairly easily by changing the ExecuteShardNonQuery and ExecuteParallelRoundRobinLoad methods. To do so, you need to add a separate transaction context to all connection objects and commit them in a loop at the end of the last execution. If any exception occurs, you must roll back all the changes.

■ **Note** As mentioned earlier, the shard library is an open-source project and is likely to evolve over time. Check for the latest release to see which features are supported.

Managing Foreign Key Constraints

Another interesting issue to consider in shard databases is related to foreign key constraints. Because the shard library proposed in this book splits tables horizontally, you may quickly realize that maintaining referential integrity can be challenging.

To maintain relational integrity, the following concerns apply:

- **Data duplication.** Because you don't know which records are where in the shard, the parent tables needs to be duplicated in every database. For example, a table that contains the list of states (Florida, Illinois, and so on) may need to be replicated across all databases.

- **Identity values.** Adding records in one database can't be easily replicated across to other databases. Thus, using an identity value as the primary key may be difficult because you aren't guaranteed to have the same value in all databases in the shard. For example, the StateID value for Florida may be 10 in one database and 11 in another.

When it comes to data duplication, you can either treat the parent tables as overhead and duplicate them across databases, allowing you to maintain strong referential integrity (RI), or sacrifice RI in the database by sharding the parent tables as well. If you decide to shard parent tables, you can no longer enforce RI in the database; but you may still be able to enforce RI in your code by adding RI constraints to your DataTable objects. You can do so by creating a DataRelation object in the DataTable's ParentRelations collection. For example, the following code adds RI to the DOCS and AUTHORS DataTable objects:

```
1)  SqlCommand cmd1 = new SqlCommand("SELECT * FROM Authors");
2)  SqlCommand cmd2 = new SqlCommand("SELECT * FROM Docs");
3)  DataTable authors = ExecuteShardQuery(cmd1);
4)  DataTable docs = ExecuteShardQuery(cmd2);
5)  DataRelation dr = new DataRelation("RI",
6)  authors.Columns["authorId"],
7)  docs.Columns["authorId"]);
8)  docs.ParentRelations.Add(dr);
```

The issue with identity values lies in the fact that an automatic identity is created for each record. But because the tables are split across databases, you aren't guaranteed to have the same values over time. To solve this issue, you need to create RI rules that depend not on identity values, but on codes. In the case of the table that stores states, you create a StateCode column (that stores FL for Florida) and use that column as your primary key and in your RI rules. This ensures that all databases in the shard use the same values to maintain integrity.

Creating Vertical Partition Shards

The majority of this chapter discussed the HPS, but it's important to also be familiar with vertical partition shards (VPSs). A VPS stores an application database schema across multiple databases; in essence, the application database is split in such a way that no database in the shard holds the complete schema.

Let's consider a simple application database that is made of two tables: Users and Sales. The Users table contains a few thousand records, and the Sales table contains a few million records. You can design a VPS with two databases: the first contains the Users table, and the second contains the Sales table.

This type of shard makes it easy to isolate the processing power needs of certain tasks without affecting the other database. For example, you can use the Users table to process login requests from users while at the same time using the Sales table for a CPU-intensive calculation process or to run long reports.

You can also build a VPS by splitting a table across multiple databases. For example, the Sales table may store large binary fields (such as documents). In this case, you can split the Sales table such that common fields are stored in one database and the field containing documents is stored in another database.

A VPS does bring it own set of challenges, such as the difficulty of keeping strong RI between databases and, in the case of SQL Azure, ensuring transaction consistency. These considerations are only meant to bring certain design issues to the surface when you're thinking about a VPS. Depending on your database design, a VPS may work very well and may be simpler to implement than an HPS.

Conclusion

As you've seen, building databases with SQL Azure can be complex if you need to scale your database design or if you're looking to develop a high-performance system. This chapter introduced you to the design and implementation of a shard library that gives you the necessary building blocks to experiment with a flexible and scalable architecture.

You saw how to use caching in a data access layer and how parallel processing of SQL statements can increase performance of your applications. You also explored more advanced topics, such as referential integrity and exception management. This chapter provides you with the necessary background to create your own shard and create high-performing applications against SQL Azure databases.

CHAPTER 11

■■■

SQL Azure Data Sync Services

In November 2009, at the Microsoft PDC in Los Angeles, Microsoft announced Project Huron, a project that allows database synchronization capabilities in the cloud. If you've been following the hype and reading keeping up with the blog posts regarding Huron, Microsoft has been billing it and associated database sync functionality as "friction free," meaning easy to set up and maintain. Microsoft's goal with Huron was to eliminate many of the emblematic complexities and idiosyncrasies that are associated with data sharing between databases, such as scalability and configuration. Along with these goals, Microsoft also wanted to include user-friendly tools that allow administrators to easily configure and synchronize their data.

In June 2010, at the start of Tech-Ed in New Orleans, Microsoft announced the public preview availability of the Data Sync Service for SQL Azure, part of the Huron project. This is Microsoft's solution to allow users to easily and efficiently share data between databases without regard to database locations and connectivity. Sharing data is only the beginning: Microsoft also has visions of including data collaboration, providing users and developers the ability to use and work on data regardless of the data's location.

This chapter focuses entirely on the capabilities and features of the SQL Azure Data Sync Service. It begins with a brief overview and then shows you how to get started by setting up and configuring the Data Sync Service. You then work through several examples of using the SQL Azure Data Sync Service in different scenarios and situations. You also see some patterns and best practices along the way to help ensure a solid understanding of the Data Sync Service.

Understanding the Data Sync Service

The SQL Azure Data Sync Service is a bidirectional synchronization between two or more databases. On the surface, it's as simple as that; but even behind the scenes, it doesn't get much more complicated. With zero lines of code, you can quickly and easily configure your SQL Azure database to be synchronized with other SQL Azure databases in any of the Microsoft Azure data centers.

Why the Need?

Why is the ability to sync data between SQL Azure databases important? That's a fair question to ask. Let's explore a couple of answers.

First, you may be a fan of SQL Server replication, but it isn't the easiest to set up and configure. Granted, transactional replication gives you real-time updates, but setting up and maintaining transactional replication isn't a cake walk.

Second, although the SQL Azure Data Sync Service doesn't give you real-time updates, it does allow you to extend your data to the location closest to your users *without* a lot of headaches. The Data Sync Service lets you move data changes between databases seamlessly, ensuring that the appropriate changes are proliferated to all the other databases in the current data center as well as other databases in other data centers that you've defined in your configuration to be part of your synchronization.

The SQL Azure Data Sync Service is part of Windows Azure and runs in Windows Azure, so it can take advantage of the web and worker roles. A key component of the SQL Azure Data Sync Service is its use of the Microsoft Sync Framework, a synchronization platform provided in the .NET Framework. The great thing is that all this synchronization functionality is provided for you, hosted in the South Central US data center; there is no application you need to run or installation you need to perform.

The Basic Scenario

Every SQL Azure synchronization environment includes a single database *hub* and has one or more database *members*, as shown in Figure 11-1. Setting up synchronization includes creating and defining a synchronization group in which you specify the hub database and then assign the database members to that hub.

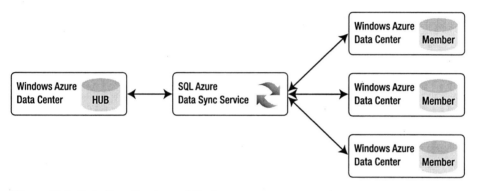

Figure 11-1. Data Sync Service architecture

Let's talk about the initial synchronization for a minute, because it's helpful to understand the process and changes that take place. When the initial sync takes place, it's a two-step process:

1. The hub database schema is copied to the member database(s).

2. The data is copied from the hub database to the member database(s).

This may seem simple, but let's discuss what happens during these two steps. First, you don't have to generate the target (member) database schemas yourself. During the first step, the Data Sync Service does that for you (for the tables you specify to sync). As part of this process, foreign key constraints are *not* copied. This is because a full schema synchronization capability hasn't been built into the Data Sync Service as of yet.

Because foreign keys aren't copied, you may be wondering what happens in the scenario where data is entered at the member that could potentially break synchronization back to the hub. The answer is that you can control the order in which data is applied, and this helps make certain the changes that are applied don't affect any foreign key constraints. During the initial sync, changes are made to both the hub and member databases to effectively track data changes. You see this behavior in the example later in this chapter.

The next step in the process is the data synchronization that takes place after all the member databases are provisioned. Provisioning of the members takes place during the initial sync. Data synchronization is as simple as copying the data from hub to member in the order specified in the configuration. Because there are no foreign keys on the member databases, there is no particular order in which the tables need to be synchronized. However, it's a good practice to add the tables in an order that indicates the order in which the changes will be applied when a data sync occurs. This helps you ensure that the changes are applied in a way that doesn't affect any foreign key constraints.

Configuring Synchronization

Now that you're familiar with the foundation of how the Data Sync Service works, let's dive in and configure a new sync for the SQL Azure Data Sync Service to sync two databases. This example synchs the TechBio database (the hub database). For this, you need to create a member database, which you do by going into the SQL Azure portal and creating a second database called TechBio2 (see Figure 11-2).

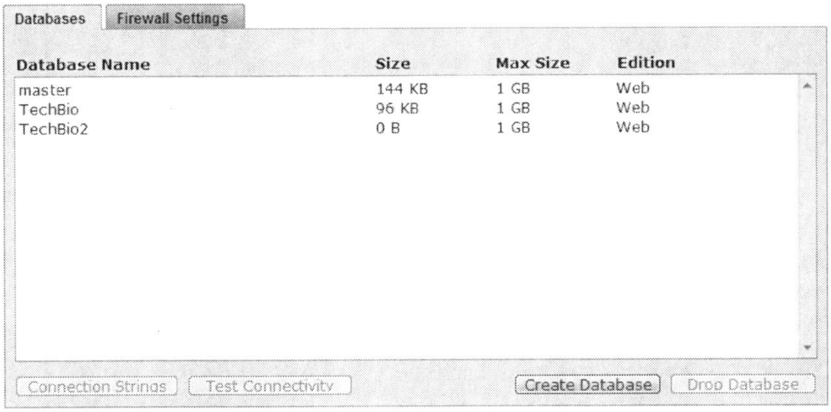

Databases	Firewall Settings			
Database Name		**Size**	**Max Size**	**Edition**
master		144 KB	1 GB	Web
TechBio		96 KB	1 GB	Web
TechBio2		0 B	1 GB	Web

[Connection Strings] [Test Connectivity]   [Create Database] [Drop Database]

Figure 11-2. Databases

You can now begin configuring your SQL Azure data synch, which you walk though over the next few pages.

Agreeing to the Terms of Service

SQL Azure Data Sync is part of the SQL Azure Labs, which is currently in developer review. To begin, open your browser and go to the following URL: `https://datasync.sqlazurelabs.com/SADataSync.aspx`. You're taken to a Terms of Service page, and your first step is to agree to the terms. Like other Azure portals, the SQL Azure Data Labs is based on your Live ID, so you will need to sign in with your Live ID if you have one or create one if you do not have a Live ID. Any time you access the SQL Azure Data Labs, you will be asked to sign in if you are not already signed in.

Creating a Sync Group

After you agree to the terms of service, you're taken to the Windows Azure Platform SQL Azure Labs home page. On this page, select the SQL Azure Data Sync link at left, to display the Sync Group

Management page shown in Figure 11-3.

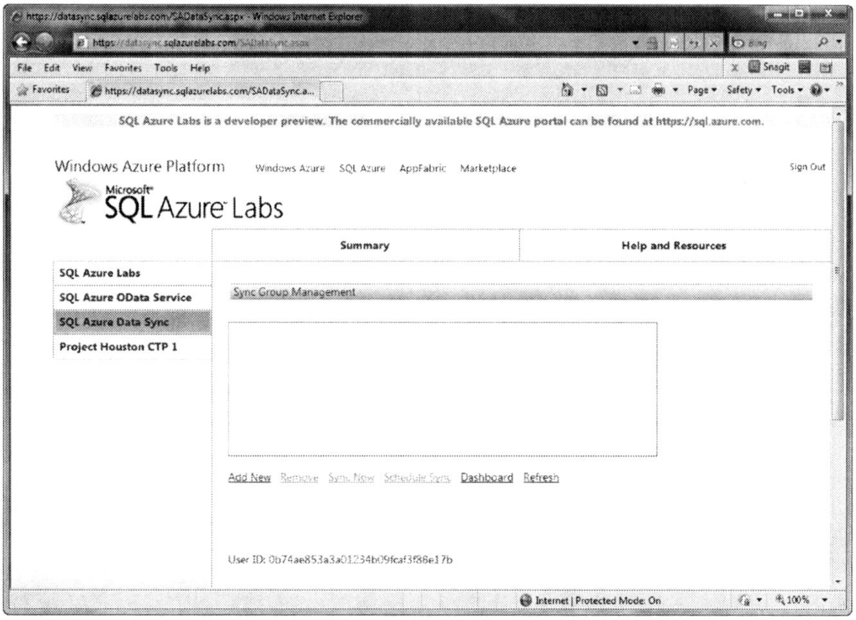

Figure 11-3. *SQL Azure Labs home page*

The SQL Azure Data Sync page is where you create and configure data synchronization by first creating a *sync group*. A sync group is where you define the databases (hub and associated members) that you want to synchronize and the data to be shared between these databases. You can have multiple sync groups, with each sync group having a single hub and multiple members.

To create a new sync group, follow these steps:

1. Click the Add New link below the Sync Group list. Doing so starts a simple multistep wizard to walk you through defining your sync group.

2. The first step of the wizard asks you to provide a name for the sync group you're creating. Sync group names must be unique and should be informative enough that you can look at the name and know what you're syncing. The text box appears to accept an endless number of characters; but the text box shown in Figure 11-4 displays only around 70, so keep the name short but descriptive. For this example, enter the name TechBioSync, as shown in Figure 11-4, and click the Next link.

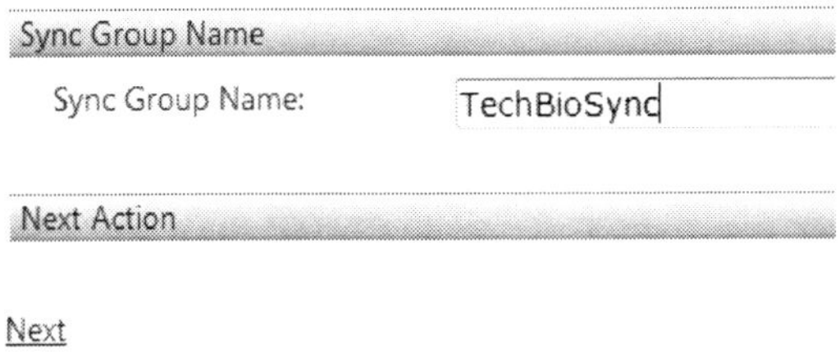

Sync Group Name

Sync Group Name: TechBioSync

Next Action

Next

Figure 11-4. Sync Group Name

3. The next step of the wizard asks you to provide Member Information, which means the server name and database(s) that will be your hub and members. You see a Server Name drop-down and a Database drop-down, as well as an Add HUB link and a Register New Server link. Initially, both drop-downs have no values, because you haven't defined any servers. Click the Register New Server link; doing so displays the three text boxes shown in Figure 11-5. Enter your server name, username, and password for your SQL Azure server, and click Next.

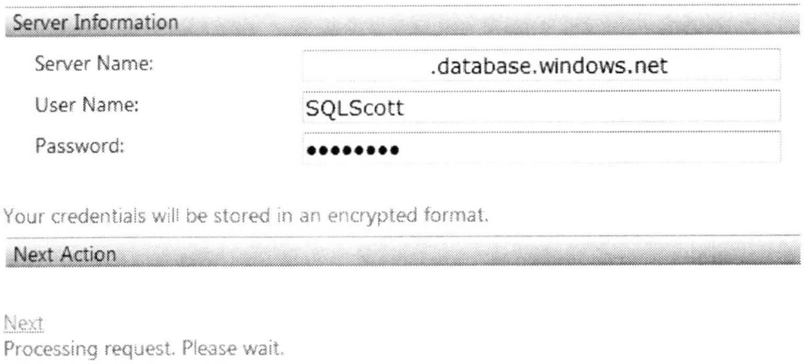

Server Information

Server Name: .database.windows.net

User Name: SQLScott

Password: ••••••••

Your credentials will be stored in an encrypted format.

Next Action

Next
Processing request. Please wait.

Figure 11-5. Sync Group Server Information section

It's important to notice that the Server Information section informs you that your credentials will be stored in an encrypted format. This is because the information is kept and stored for the next time you run this wizard. Subsequent runs through the wizard will automatically display the server name and associated databases, as shown in a moment in Figure 11-6.

The credentials are also stored to support the scheduled sync. The SQL Azure Data Sync Service launches the sync process and as such needs access to the SQL Azure databases to complete the sync.

Clicking Next in the Server Information section of the wizard takes you back to the Member Information section with the server selected and the associated databases listed in the Database drop-down.

Defining the Hub and Member Databases

Your next action is to select which database will be the hub. In this example, it's the TechBio database. Select TechBio from the Database drop-down, as shown in Figure 11-6, and click the Add HUB link.

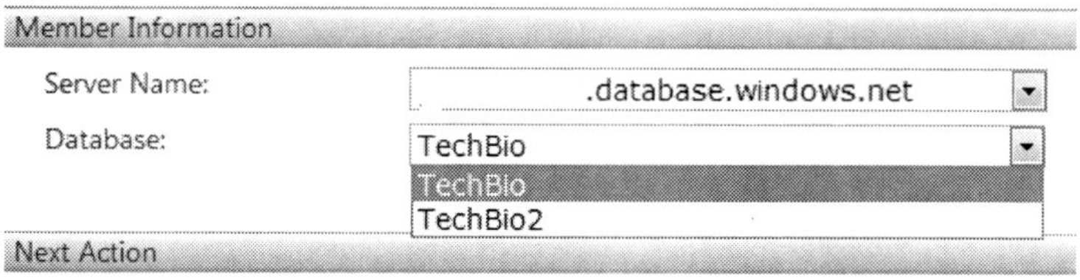

Figure 11-6. Selecting the hub

As you add hub and member databases, they're displayed in the Member List section along with their role in the sync group. For example, Figure 11-7 shows the TechBio database listed as the hub.

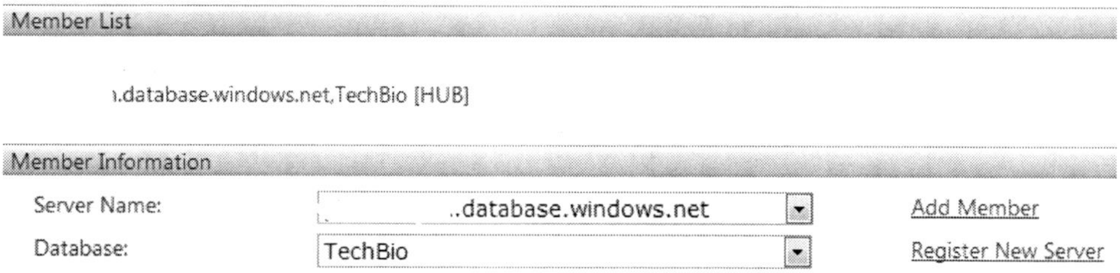

Figure 11-7. Member List section with hub

You next need to add one or more member databases. Notice that because you've added the hub, the Add HUB link has changed to Add Member. Select the TechBio2 database from the Database drop-down, and click Add Member. The Member List section now displays the hub and associated member database, as shown in Figure 11-8.

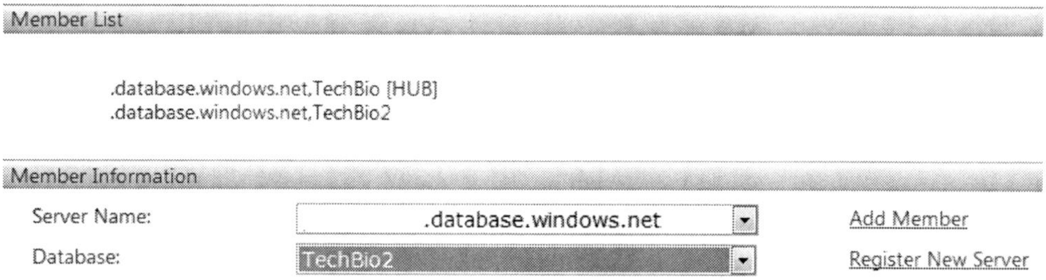

Figure 11-8. Member List section with hub and member

Selecting Tables to be Synchronized

After you've selected your hub and member databases, click Next. You're shown a list of available tables from the hub database. Select the tables that you want to synchronize with the selected member databases, and click the right-pointing green arrow to move them to the "Selected tables" list. For this example, select the Users table and move it to the "Selected tables" list, as shown in Figure 11-9. Then, click the Finish link.

■ **Note** The order in which you add the tables indicates the order in which changes are applied, thus affecting how foreign key constraints are evaluated.

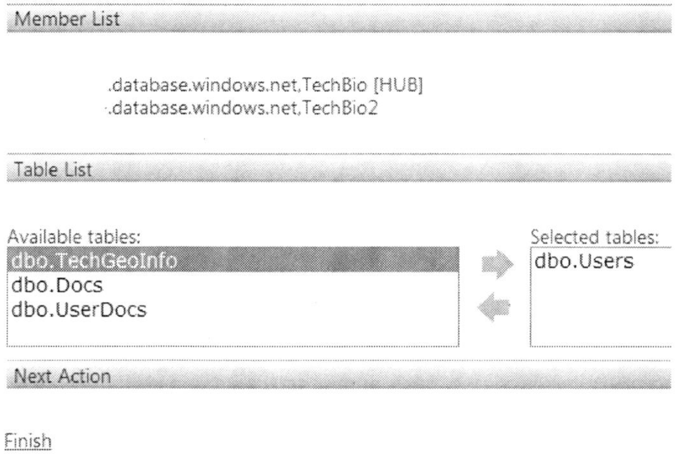

Member List

.database.windows.net,TechBio [HUB]
.database.windows.net,TechBio2

Table List

Available tables: Selected tables:
dbo.TechGeoInfo   dbo.Users
dbo.Docs
dbo.UserDocs

Next Action

Finish

Figure 11-9. Selected tables

Be aware that the SQL Azure Data Sync Service doesn't sync schema changes, except for the initial synchronization. For example, if you add a column to or remove a column from a table, that information isn't synchronized. The question then becomes, how do you sync schema changes? Right now, there is no way to sync schema changes unless you reprovision the database for sync, which basically means dropping the member database tables and re-creating them.

Congratulations—you've successfully created and configured your first SQL Azure data synch! You should see a Sync Group Management window similar to that in Figure 11-10.

■ **Note** You've configured the sync group, but the initial synchronization hasn't yet taken place. You see how to initiate that first synchronization shortly, in the section "Manually Synchronizing."

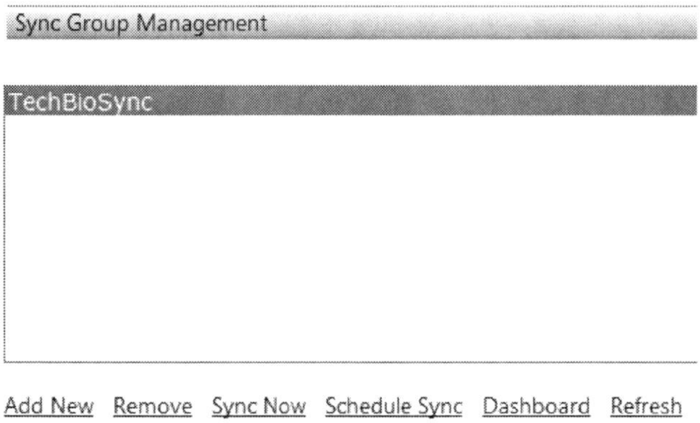

Sync Group Management

TechBioSync

Add New   Remove   Sync Now   Schedule Sync   Dashboard   Refresh

Figure 11-10. TechBioSync sync group

Modifying a Sync Group

Currently, Microsoft doesn't support editing or modifying a sync group. After a group is created, that's it. However, Microsoft is planning to provide editing capabilities for sync groups in the next service update.

Manually Synchronizing

The SQL Azure Data Sync Service gives you the ability to manually sync at any time as well as schedule data synchronizations. Let's first run your sync manually so you can see the fruits of your labors. (Not that you're impatient, but developers hate waiting.)

Before you sync manually, let's look at the member database you created earlier. Open SQL Server Management Studio, and connect to your SQL Azure instance (be sure to connect to the master database so you see all the databases in Object Explorer). Expand the Tables node for the TechBio2 database. It should have no tables, as shown in Figure 11-11.

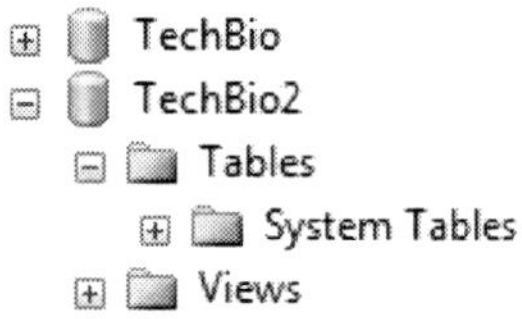

Figure 11-11. Empty TechBio2 database

Back on the Sync Group Management page, select your newly created sync group, and click Sync Now. The SQL Azure Data Sync page (see Figure 11-12) displays the time the sync is scheduled, the sync group, the status of the sync, and a link to the sync job log. Notice that the scheduled time is the second you clicked the Sync Now link (displayed in UTC time). Also notice that the status is Scheduled—the synchronization is currently running, but it hasn't completed yet.

Scheduled Sync Jobs:

Scheduled Time (*)	Sync Group	Status	Sync Job Log
8/3/2010 12:30:28 AM	TechBioSync	Scheduled	ViewLog

Figure 11-12. Scheduled Sync Jobs list

In this example the synchronization is simple, so by the time you're finished reading this, you can press F5 to read the page. The Status changes to Completed, as shown in Figure 11-13. If you refresh quickly enough, you see the status with a value of Processing.

Scheduled Time (*)	Sync Group	Status	Sync Job Log
8/3/2010 12:30:28 AM	TechBioSync	Completed	ViewLog

Figure 11-13. A completed synchronization

One of the great things about the Data Sync page in Figure 11-13 is that below the list of scheduled sync jobs is the Sync Job Log. By clicking the ViewLog link for a given sync job, you can view the log information for the selected sync job in the Sync Job Log section. Information from the log provides great detail pertaining to the synchronization process, including the total changes and how long those changes took. For example, the following log shows a sync like the one you just executed. It shows that there were no sync changes from member to hub, that there were a total of 105 total changes from hub to member, and that the sync took a mere 2 seconds:

```
Retrieving DbSyncScopeDescription from Hub

Checking to see if Scope 71793881-3437-4861-870a-af5eaebe7197 exists in endpoint↵
 plqfubbqom.database.windows.net,TechBio2

        Scope doesnt exist. Provisioning server.

Synchronizing Endpoint plqfubbqom.database.windows.net,TechBio2 ==> HUB.
Conflict Endpointwins
        Total Changes Transferred = 0, Total Changes Failed = 0.
        Sync time (in seconds): 2.4.

Synchronizing HUB ==> Endpoint plqfubbqom.database.windows.net,TechBio2.
Conflict HUB wins
        Total Changes Transfered = 105, Total Changes Failed = 0.
        Sync time (in seconds): 2.0.
```

Looking at the Database Changes

Earlier, this chapter mentioned that the SQL Azure Data Sync Service makes changes to the databases, so let's look at those. Back in SQL Server Management Studio, expand the Tables nodes of both the TechBio database and the TechBio2 database. Notice that the SQL Azure Data Sync created four new tables in both databases, and it also created the Users table in the TechBio2 database, shown in Figure 11-14.

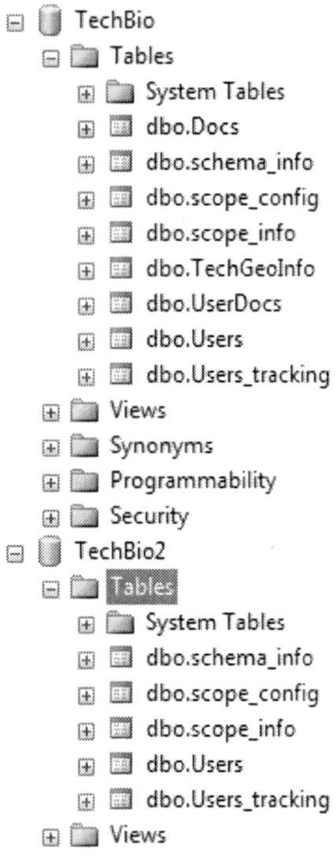

```
⊟ 🗄 TechBio
  ⊟ 📁 Tables
    ⊞ 📁 System Tables
    ⊞ 🖽 dbo.Docs
    ⊞ 🖽 dbo.schema_info
    ⊞ 🖽 dbo.scope_config
    ⊞ 🖽 dbo.scope_info
    ⊞ 🖽 dbo.TechGeoInfo
    ⊞ 🖽 dbo.UserDocs
    ⊞ 🖽 dbo.Users
    ⊞ 🖽 dbo.Users_tracking
  ⊞ 📁 Views
  ⊞ 📁 Synonyms
  ⊞ 📁 Programmability
  ⊞ 📁 Security
⊟ 🗄 TechBio2
  ⊟ 📁 Tables
    ⊞ 📁 System Tables
    ⊞ 🖽 dbo.schema_info
    ⊞ 🖽 dbo.scope_config
    ⊞ 🖽 dbo.scope_info
    ⊞ 🖽 dbo.Users
    ⊞ 🖽 dbo.Users_tracking
  ⊞ 📁 Views
```

Figure 11-14. Database changes

Let's take a quick look at the four system synchronization tables the SQL Azure Data Sync created:

- **schema_info.** Tracks member schema information.

- **scope_config / scope_info.** Used by the Sync Framework to determine what tables, filters, and so on are being synchronized. Each database that is participating in a sync includes these tables and includes at least one scope (if they're being synchronized).

- **Users_tracking.** Tracks changes to the Users table.

Each relationship has its own scope—thus the need for the scope tables. For example, the hub-to-Member1 relationship has a scope, and the hub-to-Member2 relationship has its own, different scope. Just like sync groups, these scopes define the data to be shared among members; multiple scopes make up a sync group. Scopes aren't exposed in order to simplify management of the Data Sync Service.

In this example, four tables were created, but keep in mind that a tracking table is created for each table included in the sync. For example, had you included the Docs and UserDocs tables in the sync, you would also see Docs_tracking and UserDocs_tracking tables. Each tracking table is responsible for storing the changes for its respective table.

Also added, but not shown in Figure 11-14, are *triggers.* A trigger is added to each base table that updates the tracking table when a change occurs. Some stored procedures are also added to each database; the Data Sync Service uses them to efficiently get and apply changes.

Looking at the Synchronized Data

Let's move on. Just for validation, query the Users table in the TechBio2 database, and look at the data. Yep, it's all there. You should see data similar to that shown in Figure 11-15.

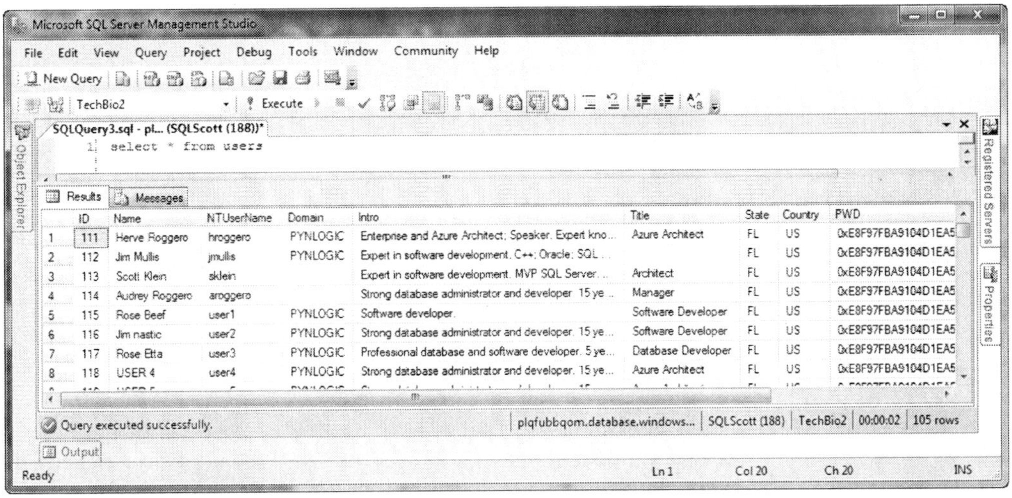

Figure 11-15. Users data

Let's go back the other way and make a change to the Users table in TechBio2 (the member database) and resync. In Figure 11-16, you can see a query that updates the Title column.

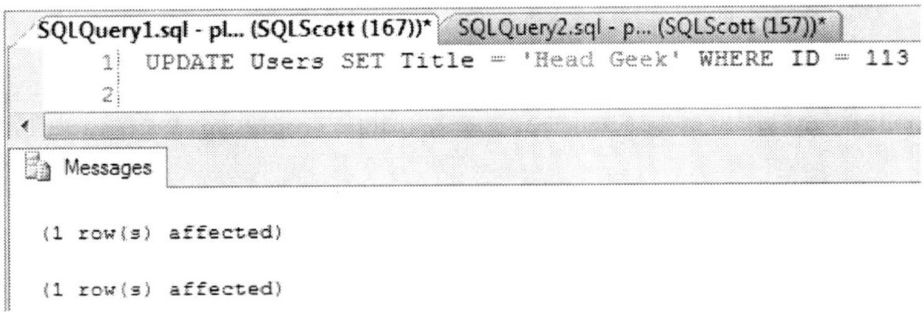

Figure 11-16. Updating member data

Go back to the Sync Group Management page, and click the Sync Now link. When the sync finishes, click the job log for the latest sync and view the details. You can see in the log that there was no sync from hub to member, but a single change was transferred from member to hub. Here are the detailed log entries:

```
Retrieving DbSyncScopeDescription from Hub

Checking to see if Scope 7e2d9af0-aea3-48db-96a9-deed2c0c2c14 exists in endpoint⏎
plqfubbqom.database.windows.net,TechBio2
```

```
Synchronizing Endpoint plqfubbqom.database.windows.net,TechBio2 ==> HUB. Conflict↵
  Endpoint wins
        Total Changes Transferred = 1, Total Changes Failed = 0.
        Sync time (in seconds): 1.8.

Synchronizing HUB ==> Endpoint plqfubbqom.database.windows.net,
TechBio2. Conflict HUB wins
        Total Changes Transfered = 0, Total Changes Failed = 0.
        Sync time (in seconds): 1.7.
```
Looking back at Figure 11-16, you see that the UPDATE statement generated two "1 row(s) affected" updates. Where did the second update come from? It came from the trigger on the base table. When you updated the Users table, the Users_tracking table was also updated such that when a data sync takes place, the data sync knows there is a change on the member side.

Scheduling Data Synchronization

Let's talk about scheduling a data sync. Go to the SQL Azure Data Sync home page, select your sync group, and then click the Schedule Sync link. A schedule recurrence pattern is displayed, giving you the option to choose the frequency of the sync recurrence: None, Hourly, Daily, Weekly, and Monthly. If None is selected, data synchronization occurs manually. Select any of the other options to display additional options for running the data sync. For example, in Figure 11-17, the Weekly option is selected, and additional options are displayed that let you select days of the week and what time to run the data synchronization.

Recurrence Pattern:

○ None   ○ Daily   ○ Monthly

○ Hourly   ● Weekly

(*) Times are relative to:
GMT Standard Time

(*) Time: 12:00 AM ▾

☐ Sunday   ☐ Monday   ☐ Tuesday   ☐ Wednesday

☐ Thursday   ☐ Friday   ☐ Saturday

Figure 11-17. Scheduling a data sync

Defining a schedule for a data sync doesn't display the schedule on the Sync Group list page, but rest assured that the scheduled is indeed saved and runs when scheduled. Let's wrap up this chapter with a discussion of synching on-premises and SQL Azure databases.

Synching an On-Premises Database with SQL Azure

You read earlier that the SQL Azure Data Sync Service only works between SQL Azure databases. However, Microsoft has released a Community Technology Preview (CTP) of a tool called Microsoft Sync Framework Power Pack for SQL Azure. This tool lets you synchronize your local database with an Azure database.

You can download the Power Pack by going to www.microsoft.com/downloads and searching for "Sync Framework Power Pack". The download page includes a Microsoft Word document that walks you through the Power Pack's features, functionality, and components. Download the Power Pack and also that Word file with the documentation. Be sure to read the documentation!

After the tool is downloaded, you can install it by double-clicking the `.msi` setup file. The install is simple and takes only a few minutes. When it's finished, a new SQL Azure Data Sync item appears on your Start menu. Click it to open the SQL Azure Data Sync wizard, shown in Figure 11-18.

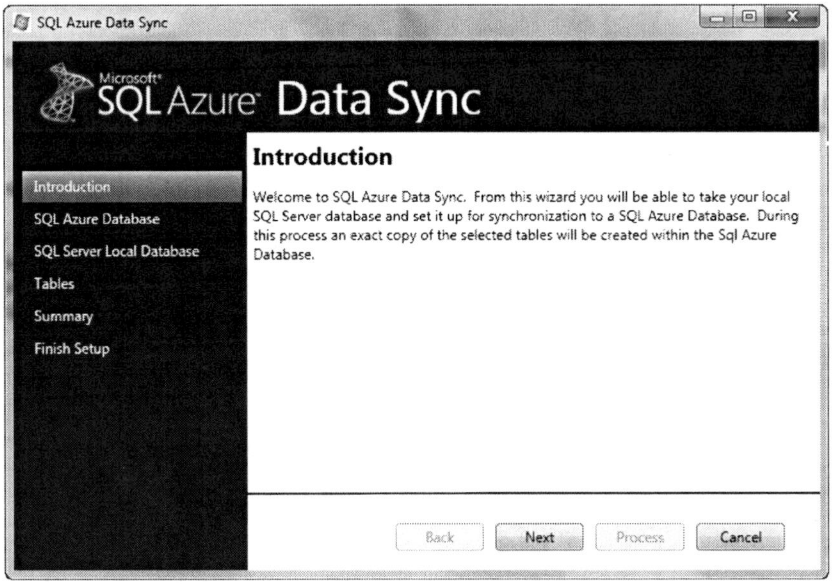

Figure 11-18. SQL Azure Data Sync Wizard

■ **Note** This tool requires the Microsoft Sync Framework 2.0 SDK. Even though you may be able to start the tool and walk though the wizard, synchronization will fail if you don't have the Microsoft Sync Framework 2.0 SDK installed.

The SQL Azure Data Sync Wizard walks you through several steps to connect to your SQL Azure database and a local SQL Server instance, and select the local tables you want to synchronize. Your progress through the wizard is displayed at left.

This tool is smart. First, the destination database doesn't need to exist in SQL Azure—the tool creates it for you. Second, if any of your local tables don't have a primary key, the sync doesn't happen.

One of the components included in the Power Pack is a Visual Studio plug-in that adds a new template called SqlAzureDataSyncClient. This template allows developers to write applications that provide offline synchronization. If you're using VS 2010, the template doesn't appear in the list of available templates until you copy the `AddSqlAzureDataSyncCacheTemplate.zip` file found on your C drive at
`Users\[Username]\My Documents\Visual Studio 2008\Templates\ItemTemplates\Visual C#\`
to the following, new destination:
`Users\[Username]\My Documents\Visual Studio 2010\Templates\ItemTemplates\Visual C#\`

Restart Visual Studio, and the template shows up in the list of templates when you add a new item to your Visual Studio project, as shown in Figure 11-19.

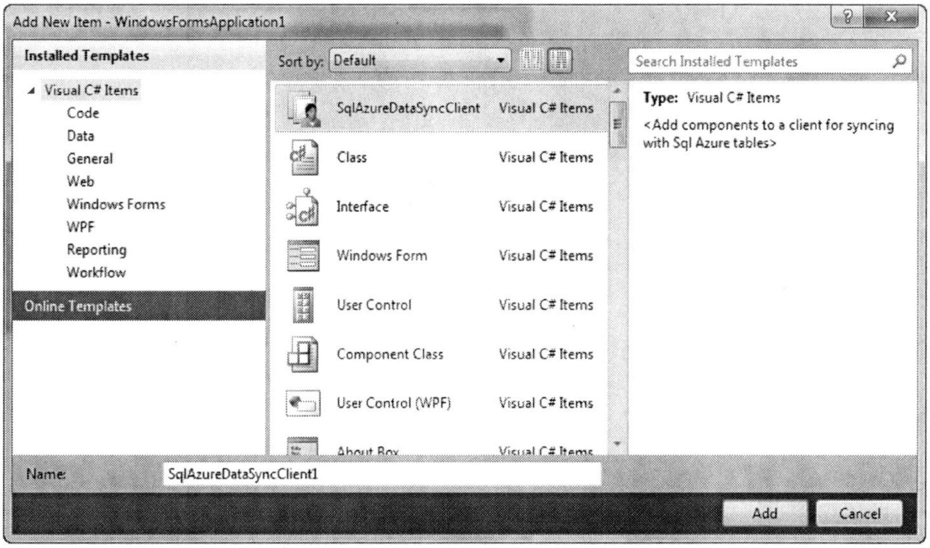

Figure 11-19. SQL Azure Data Sync template

Selecting the SQLAzureDataSyncClient template starts a wizard similar to the one shown in Figure 11-18, which walks you through creating an offline data cache in SQL Compact. When the wizard is completed, a SQL Compact database is created, and code is generated that allows for offline synchronization to sync changes on demand. The code generated is a set of classes that provides the synchronization capability.

Data Sync Best Practices

One of the things we see when training and consulting is that many companies use the SQL Azure Data Sync Service as a solution for database backup and restore functionality. This may seem like a viable solution, but it isn't the right solution, especially in light of the topics discussed in Chapter 6 regarding new backup capabilities. The Data Sync Service wasn't meant as a backup solution—it's meant to share data with one or more databases in or outside of a data center. It's designed to synchronize data between multiple data sources (the hub and one or more members).

With the SQL Azure Data Sync and the Sync Framework Power Pack still in CTP as of this writing, best practices are still being defined. However, when you approach your design of synchronization, ask yourself the following questions:

- When will you use the .NET Sync Framework or SQL Server Integration Services (SSIS) over the SQL Azure Data Sync?

- What design options do you need to consider, such as scheduling a sync, or the type of data to sync?

- What type of design will create more or fewer issues? For example, should you use GUIDs versus INTs for record identifiers?

- How can you use data synchronization in a data warehouse environment? For example, with geographically placed data centers, it may be beneficial to sync region-specific data.

The answers to these questions will certainly change between now and release to public, and even past release as SQL Azure Data Sync is put to use. They will also differ depending on the environment. These questions are meant to give you some guidance about what to consider when you're looking at using SQL Azure Data Sync in your environment.

Conclusion

Although the SQL Azure Data Sync Service is yet to be officially released, this chapter provided a detailed walkthrough of the functionality you can expect to see when it's released. You learned how to set up a sync, and the different options you have for syncing your data. You also now have several items to think about as you plan your synchronization.

In Chapter 12 we discuss SQL Azure performance tuning, discussing topics such as Sharding which are aimed at ensuring that your Azure experience is a successful.

■ ■ ■

Performance Tuning

Designing for high performance is becoming more important when using a database running in the cloud because development objectives tend to minimize roundtrips and the amount of data being returned. This chapter provides an overview of some of the most common tuning and troubleshooting techniques available in SQL Azure. Keep in mind that performance tuning is a very complex topic; as a result, this chapter can introduce only selected techniques.

The techniques presented are similar to the ones available in SQL Server, although some of the tools aren't supported in SQL Azure. Along the way, you walk through a few examples of how to improve the performance of a SQL statement and the steps required to tune it.

What's Different with SQL Azure

Before diving into the specifics, let's review some of the things you need to remember when tuning your SQL Azure databases. Some of the techniques you may be using today are available, but others may not be.

Methods and Tools

Because SQL Azure is a hosted and shared infrastructure, it's important to understand which tuning methods are available and which aren't. Table 12-1 outlines some of the key methods traditionally used by developers and DBAs in tuning a database system. The term *system* is appropriate here because at times you need to tune the database server, and in other instances you need to tune the actual database code or even address database design issues.

The table lists some tuning methods and tools that you may be familiar with. It also indicates which are available for use with SQL Azure. The unsupported tools listed in the table (such as SQL Profiler and Perfmon) are typically those that are—say, in a SQL Server environment—used by DBAs and system administrators.

Table 12-1. Typical tuning methods and tools

Method or Tool	Available?	Comments
SQL Profiler	No	Tools using server-side traces, such as most auditing tools, SQL Profiler, and the Index Tuning Wizard, aren't supported.
Execution plan	Yes	SQL Server Management Studio can display actual execution plans against a SQL Azure database. You review this later in the chapter.

Method or Tool	Available?	Comments
Perfmon	No	Any Windows monitoring tool that is typically used for performance tuning is unavailable.
DMVs	Limited	A few dynamic management views (DMVs) are available and provide insightful information about running sessions and statements previously executed.
Library metrics	Yes	ADO.NET provides library-level statistics that offer additional insight to developers, such as the total processing time from the consumer standpoint and bytes transferred.

Coding Implications

Because you have no access to the server-side configuration settings of SQL Azure, such as disk configuration, memory allocation, CPU affinitization, and so forth, you need to place more emphasis on the quality of your SQL statements—and, now more than ever, your network traffic. Indeed, the number of network roundtrips your code generates and the number of packets returned have an impact on performance because the connection to SQL Azure is a far link and the communication is encrypted.

Your performance-tuning exercise should include the following areas:

- **Connection pooling**. Because establishing a new connection requires multiple network roundtrips by itself and can affect your application's performance, you should ensure that your connections are pooled properly. In addition, SQL Azure will throttle you if you establish too many connections. This behavior is controlled by the denial of service (DoS) feature briefly discussed in Chapter 4.

- **Packet count**. Because the time spent to return data is greater than you may be used to, you need to pay attention to SQL code that generates too many packets. For example, Print statements generate more network traffic than necessary and should be removed from your T-SQL if at all possible.

- **Indexing**. You may remember from chapter 2 that SQL Azure may throttle your connection if it detects that your statement is consuming too many resources. As a result, proper indexing becomes critical when tuning for performance.

- **Database design**. Of course, certain database designs are better than others for performance. A heavily normalized design improves data quality, but a loosely normalized database typically improves performance. Understanding this tradeoff is also important when you're developing in SQL Azure.

Tuning Techniques

Let's dive into the specifics of performance tuning, keeping in mind what you've learned so far. You start by looking at database tuning capabilities and then move up the stack, all the way to the client library making the actual SQL call.

Dynamic Management Views

SQL Azure provides a few handy system views called dynamic management views (DMVs) that are also available in SQL Server. SQL Azure exposes a subset of the DMVs, but all those related to query execution are available. SQL Azure supports the DMVs listed in Table 12-2.

Table 12-2. Dynamic management views used for performance tuning

DMV	Comments
sys.dm_exec_connections	Returns the list of connections established in SQL Azure. Note that some of the interesting columns, such as client_net_address (returning the client machine's MAC address), aren't available.
sys.dm_exec_query_plan	Fully supported. Returns the XML execution plan of a SQL query or a batch.
sys.dm_exec_query_stats	Fully supported. Returns aggregate performance information for cached query plans.
sys.dm_exec_requests	Fully supported. Returns information about the statements being executed by SQL Azure.
sys.dm_exec_sessions	Partially supported. Returns the current session opened along with performance information about that session. However, it doesn't return last-login information, such as the last_successful_logon column.
sys.dm_exec_sql_text	Returns the text of a SQL batch.
sys.dm_exec_text_query_plan	Returns the execution plan in text format for a SQL query or batch.

■ **Note** Although queries against some of these views can run when you're connected to the master database, they don't return the information you're looking for unless you connect to the database that your application is running against. Also, a user must have VIEW DATABASE STATE permission to see all executing sessions on the database; otherwise, the user sees only the current session.

If you're looking for performance metrics for a SQL statement and you can isolate the statement to a unique database connection, or the statement is no longer executing, the dm_exec_sessions DMV is for you. This is one of the system views that provides performance metrics such as CPU time and duration. However, this DMV accumulates the performance metrics over all the statements executed through the same connection. So, in order to test a database query and retrieve performance metrics of that query alone, you need to establish two connections: one to execute the query, and another to read the performance metrics so as not to interfere with the performance data that SQL Azure has collected.

■ **Note** You need to establish two connections using the same login name, or you can't retrieve the performance metrics of the SQL statement you're trying to tune.

For example, establish a connection to SQL Azure, and run the following SQL query:

```
SELECT TOP 50 * FROM sys.indexes
```

Note your session id; it's found on the status bar in Microsoft SQL Server Management Studio. You can also find it on the query tab, in parentheses. For example, in Figure 12-1, the session id is 144: you can see it both on the selected tab and in the status bar at the bottom.

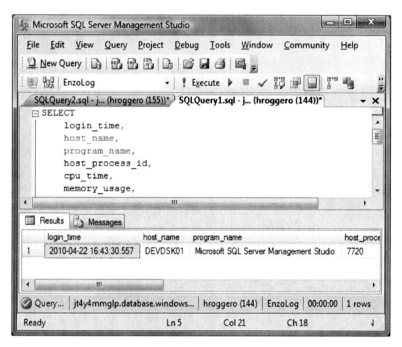

Figure 12-1. Capturing a statement's performance metrics

Next, open another query window, which opens a new connection in SQL Azure. Run the following query (see Figure 12-1), and make sure to specify the session id being investigated:

```
SELECT
    login_time,
    host_name,
    program_name,
    host_process_id,
    cpu_time,
    memory_usage,
    total_elapsed_time,
    reads,
    writes,
```

```
    logical_reads,
    row_count,
    original_login_name
FROM sys.dm_exec_sessions
WHERE session_id = 176              // replace with your session_id
```
This statement returns important performance metrics for your previous SQL statement, as explained in Table 12-3.

Table 12-3. *Selected columns from sys.dm_exec_sessions*

Metric	Value	Comment
login_time	2010-04-22 16:43:30.557	The login time of the session. Note that sessions can be reused over time, through connection pooling. This time represents the last successful login.
host_name	DEVDSK01	The machine name that made the connection to the SQL Azure database.
program_name	SSMS	The application name that is executing the statement on the client workstation.
host_process_id	7720	The Windows Process ID (PID) that is executing the statement on the client workstation. You can view the PID of your applications in Task Manager in Windows.
cpu_time	15	The CPU time, in milliseconds, consumed by the SQL statements since the connection was established.
memory_usage	2	Number of 8KB bytes consumed by the connection so far.
total_elapsed_time	32	The duration of the statement in milliseconds. This includes the time to execute the statement and the time it takes to return the data to the client machine.
reads	1	Number of physical reads.
writes	1	Number of physical writes.
logical_reads	322	Number of logical reads.
row_count	50	Number of rows returned.
original_login_name	MyTestLogin	The login name of the user who successfully connected.

At this point, you need to be aware of a point that is very important for performance tuning. The cpu_time is perhaps the best metric you can use to determine how long a statement takes to execute in SQL Azure. The total_elapsed_time can be misleading. Elapsed time represents the time it takes for SQL Azure (or SQL Server) to fetch the data and return all the data to the client. So, if your client is slow at displaying data, SQL Azure slows down to match the speed of the client; the slowdown is a function of TCP (Transmission Control Protocol) programming and has nothing to do with SQL Azure. As a result, total_elapsed_time shows the entire time it takes to execute the statement and the client time necessary to finish fetching the data. The total_elapsed_time is the same than the Duration measure returned by SQL Profiler.

Connection Pooling

Earlier, this chapter mentioned that connection pooling is an important consideration for performance. Although this statement is generally accurate in the world of database programming, it becomes critical for SQL Azure. A poorly designed application may create too many connection requests, which can end up flooding SQL Azure. If too many connection requests are established, your connections will be *throttled*, meaning that you can no longer connect for a period of time.

■ **Note** Tests confirm that a SQL Azure database becomes unavailable for more than a minute if you quickly issue in excess of 50 distinct database connections. After the same test was run multiple times, the database became unavailable for a few hours.

As you can see, you need to minimize the creation of database connections, which you can achieve through proper connection pooling. First, you should know that connection pooling is affected if any part of the connection string is changed (even slightly), such as the application name or the login id (UID). A new connection pool is created even if you change the order of the parameters of a connection string. For example, if you have an application that performs three database operations, and the operations use the following connection strings, respectively, three pools are created, and hence three distinct database connections in SQL Azure on the same database:
```
Server=XYZ;Initial Catalog=DB1;UID=hroggero;PWD=123456
Server=XYZ;Initial Catalog=DB1;PWD=123456;UID=hroggero
Server=XYZ;Initial Catalog=DB1;UID=hroggero;PWD=123456;Application Name=MyApp
```
To ensure that the same database connection is used, you must ensure that the three operations use the exact same connection string:
```
Server=XYZ;Initial Catalog=DB1;UID=hroggero;PWD=123456
Server=XYZ;Initial Catalog=DB1;UID=hroggero;PWD=123456
Server=XYZ;Initial Catalog=DB1;UID=hroggero;PWD=123456
```
To measure the number of database connections open on a given database, you can use the sys.dm_exec_connections management view. A row is returned for each distinct database connection; the fewer rows, the better!

Execution Plans

Sometimes you need to dig deeper and understand how SQL Azure fetches data, and then use that information to improve performance. In SQL Server, you can also use execution plans to observe the impact of changes to the underlying hardware, such as changing memory configuration. Although you have no control over configuration settings with SQL Azure, execution plans can still be very useful to see the impact of your indexes and to view which physical operators are being used.

Whereas logical operators are used in a SQL statement, such as LEFT JOIN, *physical operators* tell you which technique SQL Azure is using to solve a given logical operation or to fetch additional data. The most common physical operators SQL Azure uses to represent JOIN operations are listed in Table 12-4.

Table 12-4. Physical JOIN operators

Operator	Symbol	Comment
Nested loop		A loop is performed in SQL Azure to retrieve data. For each record in Table 1 matching the WHERE clause, find the matching records in Table 2. On large recordsets, loops can be costly.
Hash match		A hash is calculated for each record in each table participating in a JOIN, and the hashes are compared for equality.
Merge		Merge operators are usually the fastest operators because they perform a single pass of the tables involved by taking advantage of the order in which the data is stored or retrieved.

You can give SQL Azure certain hints to use a specific physical operator, but using them isn't generally recommended. You have three proper ways to influence SQL Azure to select an effective physical operator:

- **Review your WHERE clause**. This is perhaps the most overlooked aspect of performance tuning. When you have the choice, applying the WHERE clause on the tables that have the most rows gives you new opportunities for indexing.

- **Optimize your database design**. Highly normalized databases force you to create more JOIN statements. And of course, the more JOIN statements, the more tuning you need to do. You shouldn't plan to have a database design at first normal form; however, in certain cases, denormalizing has its benefits.

- **Create better indexes**. Having a good indexing strategy is important. The order of your columns and the number of columns can make a world of difference for SQL Azure. This chapter reviews indexing shortly.

▥ **Note** To run the following examples, you need to execute the Tuning.sql script. It creates a few sample tables with test data. Make sure to select a user database when running this script.

To show which physical JOIN operators have been selected, execution plans provide insights into the volume of data being worked on and the relative cost of certain operations. For example, execute the following SQL statement (after running the tuning.sql script):

```
SELECT T.Name, T.UserType
FROM TestUsers T INNER JOIN TestUserType UT
   ON T.UserType = UT.UserType
WHERE T.AgeGroup > 0 AND UT.UserTypeKey = 'Manager'
```

This statement returns 25 rows. To view the execution plan, you need to request it before running the statement. Either press Ctrl + M or choose Query → Include Actual Execution Plan from the menu in SQL Server Management Studio, and re-run the SQL statement. You should now see an Execution Plan tab. Click the tab to see output similar to that shown in Figure 12-2.

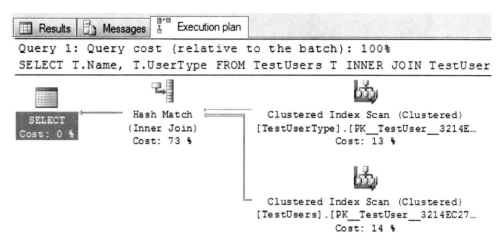

Figure 12-2. Sample execution plan, not tuned

In order to fully understand the previous execution plan, let's review additional symbols often seen in execution plans. Table 12-5 shows a few symbols that have clear performance implications.

Table 12-5. Lookup, index scan, and index seek operators

Operator	Symbols	Comment
Lookup		Lookups can be costly when the statement returns thousands of rows and a lookup is needed for every row. If you determine that the lookup is costly, consider creating a covering index.
Index scan		An index or clustered index scan may or may not be a bad thing. *Scanning* means that SQL Azure reads all the records sequentially in the index. Scanning isn't good for performance if you return a fraction of the records being scanned, in which case an index is needed. But if you want to return all the records from a table, a scan is necessary.
Index seek		An index or clustered index *seek* means the first record matching the query is found quickly, without scanning.

Execution plans can show many other symbols that have very specific meanings, including hints that a query is using multiple processors, and so on.

Because no indexes are defined on the underlying tables and the execution plan in Figure 12-2 shows two index scans, you have a potential performance problem. The INNER JOIN logical operator is executed with a hash match physical operator. You can see a thicker line coming into the hash match;

hovering your cursor on this line shows you that 50 records are being consumed by the JOIN operation (see Figure 12-3). Also, you can see that a clustered index scan is being used to fetch data for both tables. Finally, note that the hash match operation consumes 73% of resources of the entire statement; this means it takes more time to JOIN the records than to read the data from disk.

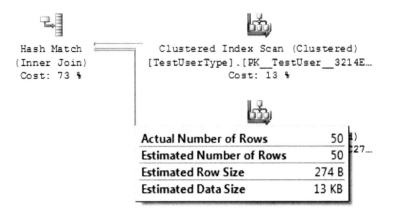

Figure 12-3. Verifying how many records are being consumed by a JOIN operator

In summary, the statement you've been working with has three potential issues:

- **Index scans**. An index scan is performed on both tables, causing more reads than necessary.

- **Heavy operator processing**. The hash match operation is consuming most of the processing time.

- **More reads than records returned**. As you can see from Figure 12-3, the statement is processing 50 records but returning only 25. This may be a hint that you're reading more records than necessary. However, this isn't always a problem in itself—just something to keep an eye on.

■ **Note** For those familiar with heap tables, SQL Azure doesn't allow them. If you intend to insert records into a table, a primary key must be defined on the table.

You see shortly how indexing can help you tune this statement. But before leaving the topic of execution plans, it's important to be familiar with a few more points:

- **Relative query cost**. Notice in Figure 12-2, shown earlier, that near the top of the window, a query cost is displayed. This is a relative measure compared to all the other statements being executed as a batch. In this example, the value is 100% because it's the only statement. You should know, however, that this value can be misleading. It's calculated dynamically by SQL Server Management Studio based on estimated costs, not actual costs. As a result, this value is rarely accurate.

- **Advanced calls**. Certain operations, such as XML calls and using functions in your SQL statements, are usually misrepresented in an execution plan; as such, SQL Azure (and even SQL Server) may return 1% as a cost for those operations. This may lead you down the wrong path when tuning your SQL statements.

- **Discarding output**. As discussed previously, the duration (as measured by sys.dm_exec_sessions) includes display time, and that applies to SQL Server Management Studio. To minimize the time it takes to display the data, you can disable the output by checking the necessary settings in Query → Query Options. The same option appears in two places: in the Grid and Text Results. Figure 12-4 shows how to disable the output from the Grid display.

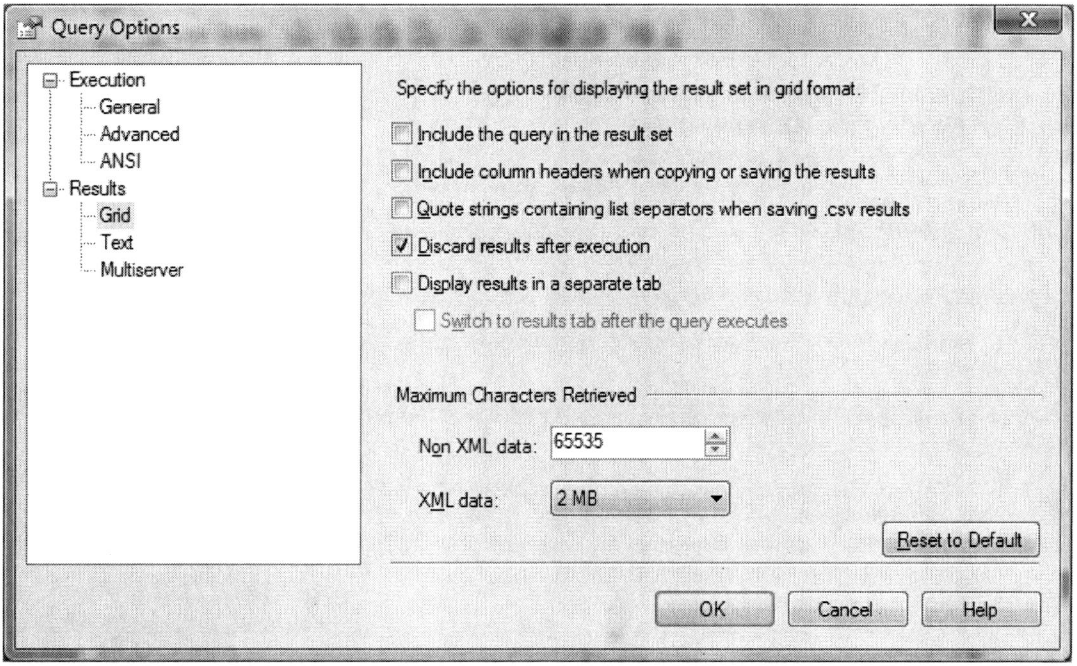

Figure 12-4. Disabling output in SQL Server Management Studio

Indexing

Creating the right indexes can be complex; it can take a long time to fully understand indexing and fine-tune database queries. One of the most important things to remember with indexing is that its primary purpose is to help SQL Azure find the data it needs quickly.

Indexes are like smaller tables that contain a subset of the primary table. The tradeoff is that indexes consume space and must be maintained by the SQL Azure engine as the primary data changes, which can impact performance under certain scenarios.

Let's quickly review a simplified syntax to create an index:

```
CREATE INDEX [index_name] ON [table_name]
```

```
(col1, col2...)
INCLUDE (col3, col4...)
```
Although creating an index is simple, it's important to verify that it's being used by SQL Azure and that it has the desired effect. To continue the previous example (from Figure 12-2), you can create an index on the TestUsers table. But first, let's back up and review a few things about the table and the statement you wish to optimize.

It's important to realize that the columns included in the first part of the index are used as a key when searching for data in the index and when joining tables. And because it's acceptable to have multiple columns as part of the key, their order is absolutely critical! At times, you pick the columns that are included in the WHERE clause first and then those that are part of the JOIN. You may find, however, that sometimes it's best to start with the JOIN columns; this depends on your statement. Next come the columns in the INCLUDE section of the CREATE INDEX command; these columns are here for only one reason: they help avoid a lookup into the primary table for data that is needed by the SELECT clause. Performing lookups isn't always a performance issue, but it can become an issue if you have a lookup operation in a large batch of records.

■ **Note** An index that contains all the columns needed to serve a query is called a *covering index*.

If you dissect the previous SELECT query, you obtain the columns in the following list (in order of placement in the index) that belong to the TestUsers table:

- WHERE. Contains the AgeGroup field from TestUsers.

- JOIN. Contains the UserType field from TestUsers.

- SELECT. Contains the Name and UserType fields. The UserType column is already part of the JOIN clause; there is no need to count it twice.

Let's begin by creating an index that looks like this:
```
CREATE INDEX idx_testusers_001 ON TestUsers
    (AgeGroup, UserType)
INCLUDE (Name)
```
Running the statement now yields the execution plan shown in Figure 12-5. This is a better plan than the one in Figure 12-2 because SQL Azure is performing an index seek instead of an index scan. Using an index seek means SQL Azure is able to locate the first record needed by the statement very quickly. However, you still have an index scan on the TestUserType table. Let's fix that.

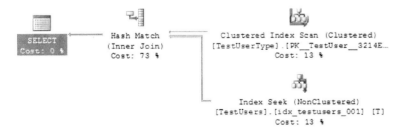

Figure 12-5. Effect of adding an index on the TestUsers table

To remove the index scan on TestUserType, you add another index following the previous guidelines. Because no columns are needed in the SELECT clause, you can leave the INCLUDE section alone. Here's the index:

```
CREATE INDEX idx_testusertype_001 ON TestUserType
(UserTypeKey, UserType)
```

■ **Note** Although it's minimal, there is a risk associated with adding new indexes in production systems. Certain routines, especially batch programs, typically depend on data being properly ordered to calculate running sums or carry out specific tasks. If an index is favored over another to run a query, it's possible for the new index to be used, which has the potential to change the order in which the data is returned. If all your statements include an ORDER BY clause, this problem won't affect you. But if some of your programs rely on the natural order of records, beware!

Your execution plan should now look like that in Figure 12-6. Notice that the physical operator has been changed to a loop. Also notice that the cost of the query has shifted away from the JOIN operator: the highest relative cost (76%) of the plan is spent reading the data from the TestUserType index.

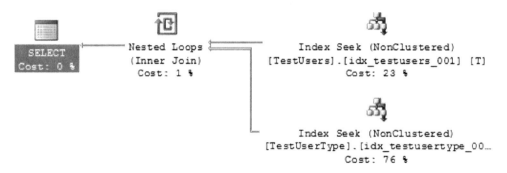

Figure 12-6. *Effect of indexing on the physical operators*

But the tuning exercise isn't over just yet. If you hover your cursor on the TestUserType_001 index, you see that the loop performed a lookup (index seek) on that index 50 times (look for Number of Executions in Figure 12-7)! This isn't great, but it's probably better than without the index, because SQL Azure picked this new execution plan.

To reduce the number of lookups, you can change the order of the fields by creating a new index. Let's run this statement:

```
CREATE INDEX idx_testusers_002 ON TestUsers
    (UserType, AgeGroup) INCLUDE (Name)
```

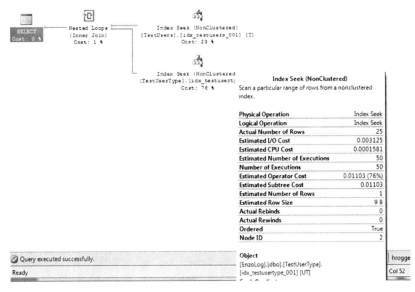

Figure 12-7. *Number of executions of an operation*

■ **Note** Instead of creating a new index, you could change the one previously created. However, when troubleshooting database performance issues, it's important to see how the SQL Azure query engine behaves; SQL Azure chooses the index it deems the most effective. So go ahead—create as many indexes as you want until you have a good execution plan, and then clean up the unnecessary indexes when you're finished.

If you run the statement again, you see a result close to Figure 12-8. The execution plan is now well balanced. The data search is virtually equal on both tables (49%), with seek operations on both; the number of executions is 1 for both; and the cost of the loop operation is minimal (2%) because there is no real looping taking place.

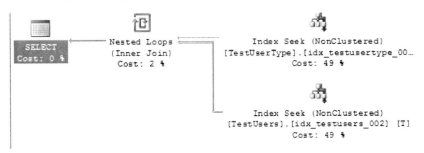

Figure 12-8. *Well-balanced execution plan*

If you pay attention to the Actual Number of Rows value, you see that this statement fetches only 25 records from the underlying table, instead of 50; this reduces disk reads.

Last but not least, if you were to look at the SELECT statement from a design standpoint, you could ask whether the UserTypeKey value should be unique. The table schema doesn't carry a unique index on that field, but should it? Can there be only one Manager user type? If the answer is yes, then you know the TestUserType table will always return a single record for a Manager user type, in which case you may be able to remove the JOIN entirely and apply the WHERE clause on the TestUsers table directly:

```
SELECT T.Name, T.UserType
   FROM TestUsers T
   WHERE T.AgeGroup > 0 AND T.UserType = 1
```

Not only is this statement much simpler, but the execution plan becomes trivial, meaning that SQL Azure can serve this request without spending much time optimizing it. This change means you're moving the filter from a table with few records (only 3 in TestUserType) to a table with many records (100 in TestUsers). And whenever you have the option to make such a move, you should. SQL Azure spends far fewer resources this way. Of course, such a move isn't always possible, but you need to know the importance of having a proper database design before you begin tuning.

Note Performance tuning can be fun. However, you may end up tuning forever if you don't set yourself performance objectives.

Indexed Views

Indexed views are an excellent alternative when you absolutely need to JOIN data, and traditional indexing doesn't yield the performance you're looking for. Indexed views behave like tables; the data covered is materialized to disk so it can be retrieved quickly. Before jumping on indexed views, understand that they have certain limitations and that due to their nature, you may incur a performance hit through the usual Insert, Delete, and Update statements. Taking the previous statement as an example, let's see how to create an indexed view to support the JOIN operation.

First, create a view that contains the statement you want to tune. Make sure you include all the columns you need in the SELECT clause:

```
CREATE VIEW vTestUsersType WITH SCHEMABINDING AS
    SELECT T.Name, T.UserType, T.AgeGroup, UT.UserTypeKey
    FROM dbo.TestUsers T INNER JOIN dbo.TestUserType UT ON       T.UserType = UT.UserType
```

Next, create a unique clustered index on the view:

```
CREATE UNIQUE CLUSTERED INDEX IDX_VIEW_TestUsers
ON vTestUsersType
(UserTypeKey, AgeGroup, Name, UserType)
```

Et voilà. When you run the statement again, you see a beautiful execution plan like the one in Figure 12-9. Because the view contains all the necessary columns, and the clustered index contains all the columns of the view, you obtain the fastest possible data-retrieval technique, next to caching.

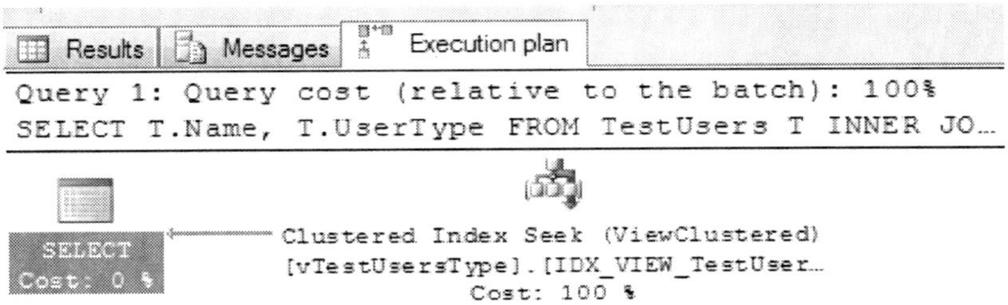

Figure 12-9. Indexed view example

Stored Procedures

You've seen various ways to tune your statements and improve execution plans. However, keep in mind that you also have stored procedures at your disposal.

Stored procedures can give you an edge if you need to execute logic that requires a large volume of data. Because you know that returning lots of data turns into a performance problem in SQL Azure, you can place the business logic that needs the data in a stored procedure, and have the procedure return a status code. Because you aren't charged for CPU time, this becomes an affordable option.

Stored procedures can also be an interesting security tool, allowing you proxy the calls to underlying tables through a procedure and never allowing direct access to the tables.

Imagine that you need to calculate the cost of an item; however, in order to calculate the cost, you must loop to obtain certain values and perform advanced operations. You can make a call from your application and calculate the cost in the application code as follows:

```
float cost = 0.0;        // the total cost
int id = 15; // the product category

string sql = "SELECT * FROM category WHERE catergoryId = " + id.ToString();
SqlConnection conn = new SqlConnection(connString);
SqlCommand cmd = new SqlCommand(sql, conn);
cmd.CommandType = CommandType.Text;
conn.Open();
SqlDataReader dr = cmd.ExecuteReader();

try
{
    while (dr.Read())
    {
        cost += 0.25 * ...; // calculation logic goes here
    }
}
finally
{
    dr.Close();
    conn.Close();
}
```

Or you can calculate the cost in a stored procedure and change the previous code to call the stored procedure instead:

```
float cost = 0.0;        // the total cost
```

```
int id = 15;        // the product category

string sql = "proc_CalculateCost";
SqlConnection conn = new SqlConnection(connString);
SqlCommand cmd = new SqlCommand(sql, conn);
cmd.Parameters.Add(new SqlParameter("categoryId", SqlDbType.Float);
cmd.Parameters[0].Value = id;
cmd.CommandType = CommandType.StoredProcedure;
conn.Open();
SqlDataReader dr = cmd.ExecuteReader();

try
{
   if (dr.Read())
      cost = (float)dr[0];
}
finally
{
   dr.Close();
   conn.Close();
}
```

The code for the stored procedure looks something like this:

```
CREATE PROC proc_CalculateCost
 @categoryId int
AS

DECLARE @i intDECLARE @cost float
SET @cost = 0.0

SET @i = (SELECT count(*) FROM category WHERE ID = @categoryId)
WHILE (@i > 0)
BEGIN
   SET @cost = @cost + 0.25*(SELECT Min(dollars) FROM ...)
   SET @i = @i - 1
END

SELECT @cost
```

The advantage of calling a stored procedure is that you don't need to fetch the necessary records across the Internet to calculate the cost figure. The stored procedure runs where the data is located and returns only a single value in this case.

Provider Statistics

Last but not least, let's look at the ADO.NET library's performance metrics to obtain the library's point of view from a performance standpoint. The library doesn't return CPU metrics or any other SQL Azure metric; however, it can provide additional insights when you're tuning applications, such as giving you the number of roundtrips performed to the database and the number of packets transferred.

As previously mentioned, the number of packets returned by a database call is becoming more important because it can affect the overall response time of your application. If you compare the number of packets returned by a SQL statement against a regular SQL Server installation to the number of packets returned when running the same statement against SQL Azure, chances are that you see more packets returned against SQL Azure because the data is encrypted using SSL. This may not be a big deal most of the time, but it can seriously affect your application's performance if you're returning large recordsets, or if each record contains large columns (such as a varbinary column storing a PDF document).

Taking the performance metrics of an ADO.NET library is fairly simple, but it requires coding. The methods to use on the SqlConnection object are ResetStatistics() and RetrieveStatistics(). Also, keep in mind that the EnableStatistics property needs to be set to true. Some of the most interesting metrics to look for are BuffersReceived and BytesReceived; they indicate how much network traffic has been generated.

You can also download from CodePlex an open source project called Enzo SQL Baseline that provides both SQL Azure and provider statistics metrics (http://EnzoSQLBaseline.CodePlex.Com). This tool allows you to compare multiple executions side by side and review which run was the most efficient. Figure 12-10 shows that the latest execution returned 624 bytes over the network.

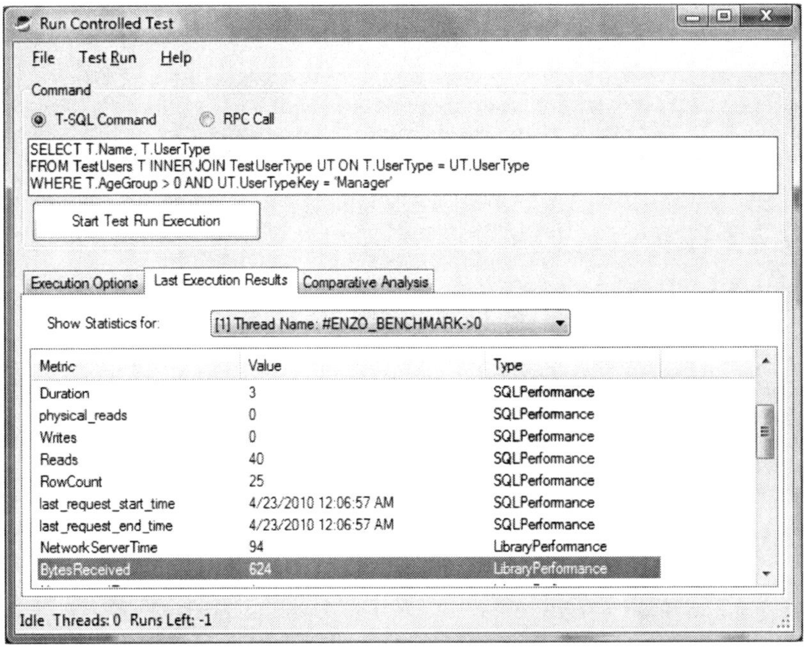

Figure 12-10. *Viewing performance metrics in Enzo SQL Baseline*

■ **Note** If you'd like to see a code sample using the ADO.NET provider statistics, go to
http://msdn.microsoft.com/en-us/library/7h2ahss8.aspx.

Application Design

Last, but certainly not least, design choices can have a significant impact on application response time. Certain coding techniques can negatively affect performance, such as excessive roundtrips. Although this may not be noticeable when you're running the application against a local database, it may turn out to be unacceptable when you're running against SQL Azure.

The following coding choices may impact your application's performance:

- **Chatty design**. As previously mentioned, a chatty application uses excessive roundtrips to the database and creates a significant slowdown. An example of a chatty design includes creating a programmatic loop that makes a call to a database to execute a SQL statement over and over again.

- **Normalization**. It's widely accepted that although a highly normalized database reduces data duplication, it also generally decreases performance due to the number of JOINs that must be included. As a result, excessive normalization can become a performance issue.

- **Connection release**. Generally speaking, you should open a database connection as late as possible and close it explicitly as soon as possible. Doing so improves your chances of reusing a database connection from the pool.

- **Shared database account**. Because SQL Azure requires a database login, you need to use a shared database account to retrieve data instead of using a per-user login. Using a per-user login prohibits the use of connection pooling and can degrade performance significantly, or even render your database unusable due to throttling.

There are many other application design considerations, but the ones listed here apply the most to programming against SQL Azure. For more information, read the following chapter from Microsoft's Patterns and Practices: http://msdn.microsoft.com/en-us/library/ff647768.aspx.

Conclusion

This chapter provided an overview of some of the most important tuning techniques that are available to help you address SQL Azure performance issues. As you've seen, troubleshooting and tuning statements can be complex and require various tools and methods to obtain the desired outcome. You saw a few dynamic management views and execution plans, took a quick tour of indexing, and briefly touched on the statistics provided by the ADO.NET library. You also learned about some design considerations that can affect application performance.

Many more tuning options are available in SQL Azure that couldn't fit in this chapter. You can discover additional techniques and concepts on Microsoft's web site at http://msdn.microsoft.com/en-us/library/ms190610(v=SQL.90).aspx.

APPENDIX A

■ ■ ■

Houston

This appendix introduces you to the online SQL Azure database-management application built by Microsoft, code-named Houston. It's a web-based application built atop Silverlight.

The ability to manage SQL Azure databases from a cloud-based management interface is necessary for many developers because it allows them to manage a SQL Azure database without having to use SQL Server Management Studio. At the time of this writing, Houston is available as a Customer Technical Preview (CTP), which means that not all features are completed and you can expect certain issues with the use of the product.

Launching Houston

To easily access Houston, you can go to the SQL Azure Labs website at www.sqlazurelabs.com. Click Project Houston CTP 1, and you see a short description of Houston. When you're ready to start, click Launch Houston at the bottom of the page. There, you're asked to select the data-center location where your SQL Azure database was created, as shown in Figure A-1. Click the appropriate location.

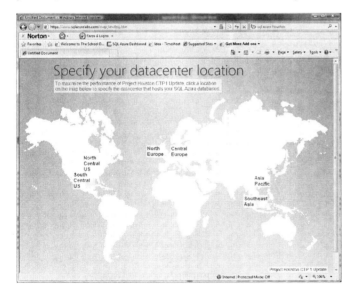

Figure A-1. Select a location.

You're then prompted to accept the Terms of Use by clicking OK. Figure A-2 shows the login screen that comes up after you do so. You need to provide the following information before clicking Connect:

- **Server**. The full name of the database server

- **Database**. The database name

- **Login**. The login name to use

- **Password**. The database password to use

Figure A-2. Login screen for Houston

After you're logged in, you finally see the Houston web application, from which you can manage your database. If you want to connect to another database, you need to log out and log in again by specifying another database name.

Using Houston

The Houston home page contains a menu system at upper left, a list of objects on the left, and one or more tabs in the middle, which you can use to change the central view where you perform various database-management tasks. Figure A-3 shows the main screen.

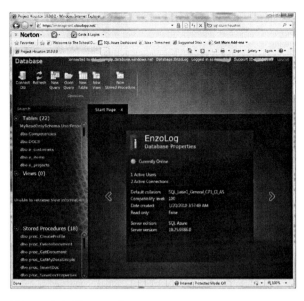

Figure A-3. Houston home page

For example, to edit a table definition, click a table at left on the page. Figure A-4 shows what a table definition looks like. A new tab is created, and the central part of the page now shows a list of the selected table's columns, including data types, default values, and more. Changing a table definition is as simple as making a change and clicking the Save button at upper left.

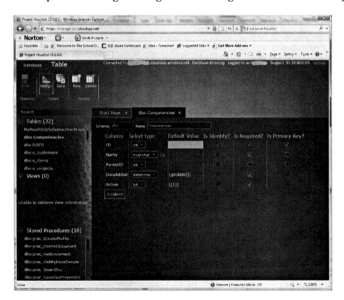

Figure A-4. Table definition

265

Note that the upper-left area of the page has changed. You now have two menu items—Database and Table—and the list of icons available is different. You can see in Figure A-4 that the Design icon is selected. Clicking Data shows the table's actual records, as shown in Figure A-5.

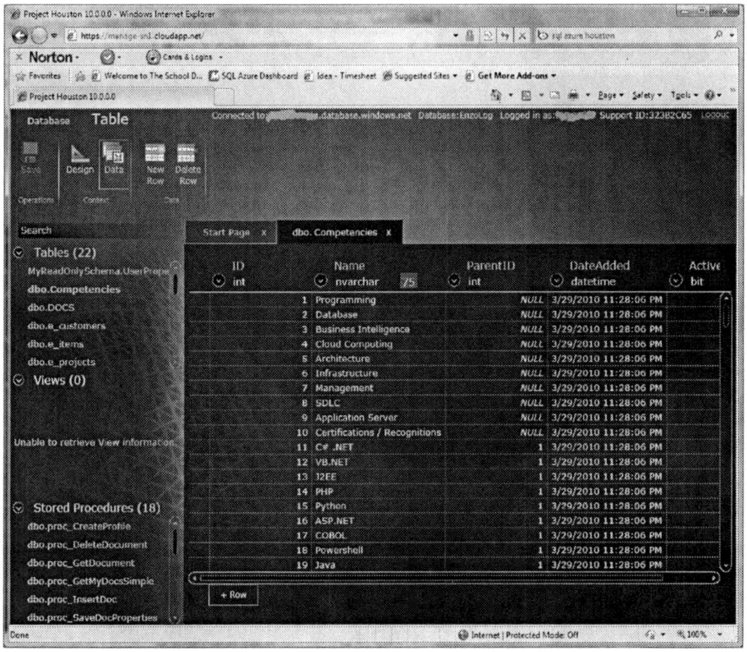

Figure A-5. Table content

You can also perform other tasks in Houston, such as running SQL statements against the database and managing views and stored procedures. Similar to editing a table, you can manage a view or a stored procedure by clicking the desired object name at left. A new tab opens, and you can manage the selected object.

As you can see from the figures, Houston is a simplified management interface that allows you to perform basic tasks against a SQL Azure database. Although Houston is created as a web application, none of the links open new pages; this makes navigation faster and simpler because all the management options are available on the same page.

■■■

SQL Azure Quick Reference

SQL Azure supports T-SQL. Chances are, you're already familiar with SQL Server T-SQL syntax if you're reading this book. However, the book includes this appendix because not everything you know and love about SQL Server is supported yet in SQL Azure. This appendix provides a quick reference to the syntax that is currently supported in SQL Azure as of Service Update 4.

■ **Note** You can find a complete list and reference that describes T-SQL supported in SQL Azure at
`http://msdn.microsoft.com/en-us/library/ee336281.aspx`.

Supported T-SQL

Table B-1 lists the supported T-SQL statements that you can use in SQL Azure. These statements can be used as exactly as you currently know them without any limitations.

Table B-1. Fully Supported T-SQL Statements

ALTER ROLE	DECLARE CURSOR	OPEN
ALTER SCHEMA	DELETE	OPTION Clause
ALTER VIEW	DENY Object Permissions	ORDER BY Clause
APPLOCK_MODE	DENY Schema Permissions	OUTPUT Clause
APPLOCK_TEST	DROP LOGIN	OVER Clause
BEGIN_TRANSACTION	DROP PROCEDURE	PRINT
BEGIN...END	DROP ROLE`	RAISERROR
BINARY_CHECKSUM	DROP SCHEMA	RETURN
BREAK	DROP STATISTICS	REVERT

CAST and CONVERT	DROP SYNONYM	REVOKE Object Permissions
CATCH (TRY…CATCH)	DROP TYPE	REVOKE Schema Permissions
CEILING	DROP USER	ROLLBACK TRANSACTION
CHECKSUM	DROP VIEW	ROLLBACK WORK
CLOSE	END (BEGIN…END)	SAVE TRANSACTION
COALESCE	EXCEPT and INTERSECT	SELECT @local_variable
COLLATE	FETCH	SELECT Clause
COLUMNPROPERTY	FOR Clause (XML and BROWSE)	SET @local_variable
COMMIT TRANSACTION	FROM	SWITCHOFFSET
COMMIT WORK	GO	TERTIARY_WEIGHTS
COMPUTE	GOTO	TODATETIMEOFFSET
CONTEXT_INFO	GRANT Object Permissions	TOP
CONTINUE	GRANT Schema Permissions	TRIGGER_NESTLEVEL
CONVERT	GROUP BY	TRUNCATE TABLE
CREATE ROLE	GROUPING_ID	TRY…CATCH
CREATE SCHEMA	HashBytes	UNION
CREATE STATISTICS	HAVING	UPDATE
CREATE VIEW	Hints (Query, Table, Join, etc)	UPDATE STATISTICS
CRYPT_GEN_RANDOM	IDENTITY (Property)	USER
CURRENT_REQUEST_ID	IF…ELSE	SWITCHOFFSET
CURSOR_STATUS	INSERT BULK	WAITFOR
DBCC SHOW_STATISTICS	IS [NOT] NULL	WHERE
DEALLOCATE	MERGE	WHILE

DECLARE @local_variable	MIN_ACTIVE_ROWVERSION	WITH (Common Table Exp.)

Partially Supported T-SQL

Table B-2 lists the partially supported T-SQL statements that you can use in SQL Azure. "Partially supported" means you can use these statements, but with some variations (or limitations) to the syntax. Examples are provided following the table.

Table B-2. *Partially Supported T-SQL Statements*

ALTER AUTHORIZATION	CREATE PROCEDURE	DROP TRIGGER
ALTER DATABASE	CREATE SPATIAL INDEX	DISABLE TRIGGER
ALTER FUNCTION	CREATE SYNONYM	ENABLE TRIGGER
ALTER INDEX	CREATE TABLE	EXECUTE
ALTER LOGIN	CREATE TRIGGER	EXECUTE AS
ALTER PROCEDURE	CREATE TYPE	EXECUTE AS Clause
ALTER TABLE	CREATE USER	GRANT Database Permissions
ALTER TRIGGER	CREATE VIEW	GRANT Database Principle Perm.
ALTER USER	DENY Database Permissions	GRANT Type Permissions
ALTER VIEW	DENY Database Principle Perm.	INSERT
CREATE DATABASE	DENY Type Permissions	REVOKE Database Permissions
CREATE FUNCTION	DROP DATABASE	REVOKE Database Principle Perm.
CREATE INDEX	DROP INDEX	REVOKE Type Permissions
CREATE LOGIN	DROP TABLE	USE

For example, when you're creating or altering a stored procedure in SQL Azure, the FOR REPLICATION and ENCRYPTION options aren't supported. Thus, the following isn't valid:

```
CREATE PROCEDURE GetUsers
WITH ENCRYPTION
FOR REPLICATION
AS
```

```
        SET NOCOUNT ON;
        SELECT Title, Name, Intro
        FROM Users
GO
```

However, the following is valid:

```
CREATE PROCEDURE GetUsers
WITH RECOMPILE, EXECUTE AS CALLER
AS
        SET NOCOUNT ON;
        SELECT Title, Name, Intro
        FROM Users
GO
```

The CREATE/ALTER table syntax for SQL Azure is a bit trickier, because there are several unsupported options:

- ON keyword {*partition_schema* | *filegroup*} (such as ON PRIMARY)
- TEXTIMAGE_ON
- FILESTREAM_ON
- <column_definition>
  - FILESTREAM
  - NOT FOR REPLICATION
  - ROWGUIDCOL
  - SPARSE
- <data type>
  - CONTENT
  - DOCUMENT
  - xml_schema_collection
- <column_constraint>
  - FILLFACTOR
  - ON
  - NOT FOR REPLICATION
- <column_set_definition>
- <table_constraint>
  - FILLFACTOR
  - ON

- NOT FOR REPLICATION
- <index_option>
    - PAD_INDEX
    - FILLFACTOR
    - ON PARTITIONS
    - DATA_COMPRESSION
    - ALLOW_ROW_LOCKS
    - ALLOW_PAGE_LOCKS
- <table_option>

Although this list may give the impression of much missing functionality, keep in mind that most of the items in the list are there due to the fact that they're operating-system or hardware related. As an example, the following CREATE TABLE statement is invalid:

```
CREATE TABLE [dbo].[Users](
        [ID] [int] IDENTITY(1,1) NOT FOR REPLICATION NOT NULL,
        [Name] [nvarchar](50) NULL,
        [NTUserName] [nvarchar](128) NULL,
        [Domain] [nvarchar](50) NOT NULL,
        [Intro] [nvarchar](100) NULL,
        [Title] [nvarchar](50) NOT NULL,
        [State] [nvarchar](10) NOT NULL,
        [Country] [nvarchar](100) NULL,
        [PWD] [varbinary](100) NULL,
        [rowguid] [uniqueidentifier] NULL,
PRIMARY KEY CLUSTERED
(
        [ID] ASC
)WITH (PAD_INDEX  = OFF, STATISTICS_NORECOMPUTE  = OFF,
IGNORE_DUP_KEY = OFF, ALLOW_ROW_LOCKS  = ON, ALLOW_PAGE_LOCKS  = ON)
ON [PRIMARY]
) ON [PRIMARY]
```

This syntax is invalid for several reasons. The NOT FOR REPLICATION clause on the IDENTITY column isn't supported. Nor are the two ON PRIMARY clauses, the ALLOW_ROW_LOCKS clause, and the ALLOW_PAGE_LOCKS clause. However, the following syntax *is* valid:

```
CREATE TABLE [dbo].[Users](
    [ID] [int] IDENTITY(1,1) NOT NULL,
    [Name] [nvarchar](50) NULL,
    [NTUserName] [nvarchar](128) NULL,
    [Domain] [nvarchar](50) NOT NULL,
    [Intro] [nvarchar](100) NULL,
    [Title] [nvarchar](50) NOT NULL,
    [State] [nvarchar](10) NOT NULL,
    [Country] [nvarchar](100) NULL,
```

```
      [PWD] [varbinary](100) NULL,
      [rowguid] [uniqueidentifier] NULL,
PRIMARY KEY CLUSTERED
(
      [ID] ASC
)WITH (STATISTICS_NORECOMPUTE  = OFF, IGNORE_DUP_KEY = OFF))
```

For detailed information about exactly what is supported and what isn't, visit
http://msdn.microsoft.com/en-us/library/ee336267.aspx.

Unsupported T-SQL

The list of unsupported T-SQL statements is long, but that isn't as negative a thing as it may appear. In most cases, unsupported statements are operating-system or hardware related, and they don't apply in the SQL Azure environment.

Because there are so many unsupported statements, this appendix doesn't list them all. You can find a complete list at http://msdn.microsoft.com/en-us/library/ee336253.aspx. Table B-3 provides a shorter list, highlighting some unsupported statements that you should particularly be aware of.

Table B-3. *Unsupported T-SQL Statements*

BACKUP CERTIFICATE	DBCC CHECKTABLE
BACKUP MASTER KEY	DBCC DBREINDEX
BACKUP SERVICE MASTER KEY	DBCC DROPCLEANBUFFERS
CHECKPOINT	DBCC FREEPROCCACHE
CONTAINS	DBCC HELP
CREATE/DROP AGGREGATE	DBCC PROCCACHE
CREATE/DROP RULE	DBCC SHOWCONTIG
CREATE/DROP XML INDEX	DBCC SQLPERF
CREATE/DROP/ALTER APPLICATION ROLE	DBCC USEROPTIONS
CREATE/DROP/ALTER ASSEMBLY	KILL
CREATE/DROP/ALTER CERTIFICATE	NEWSEQUENTIALID
CREATE/DROP/ALTER DEFAULT	OPENQUERY
CREATE/DROP/ALTER FULLTEXT (CATALOG, INDEX, STOPLIST)	OPENXML

CREATE/DROP/ALTER PARTITION FUNCTION	RECONFIGURE
CREATE/DROP/ALTER QUEUE	RESTORE
CREATE/DROP/ALTER RESOURCE POOL	SELECT INTO Clause
CREATE/DROP/ALTER SERVICE	SET ANSI_DEFAULTS
CREATE/DROP/ALTER XML SCHEMA COLLECTION	SET ANSI_NULLS
DBCC CHECKALLOC	SET ANSI PADDING_OFF
DBCC CHECKDB	SET OFFSETS
DBCC CHECKIDENT	WITH XML NAMESPACES

Supported Data Types

If you've been following SQL Azure since its initial release to the public, you realize that Microsoft has come a long way in supporting much of the functionality and many of the data types found in your local, on-premises instance of SQL Server. Table B-4 lists those data types currently supported in SQL Azure as of Service Update 4.

Table B-4. SQL Azure Supported Data Types

Numerics	bigint
	bit
	decimal
	int
	money
	numeric
	smallint
	smallmoney
	tinyint
	float

	real
Date and time	date
	datetime2
	datetime
	datetimeoffset
	smalldatetime
	time
Character strings	char
	varchar
	text
Unicode character strings	nchar
	nvarchar
	ntext
Binary strings	binary
	varbinary
	image
Spatial	geography
	geometry
Other	cursor
	hierarchyid
	sql_variant
	table
	timestamp

uniqueidentifier

xml

For a complete list of supported methods for the geography, geometry, hierarchyid, and xml data types, go to http://msdn.microsoft.com/en-us/library/ee336233.aspx.

Index

■ Symbols and Numerics

3DES (Triple Data Encryption Standard), 69

■ A

■ B

■ P

■ Q

■ X, Y, Z

Breinigsville, PA USA
03 November 2010
248550BV00003B/3/P